SHAKESPEARE'S
PROFESSIONAL SKILLS

SHAKESPEARE'S
PROFESSIONAL
SKILLS

BY

NEVILL COGHILL

*Merton Professor of English Literature in the
University of Oxford*

CAMBRIDGE
AT THE UNIVERSITY PRESS
1965

PUBLISHED BY
THE SYNDICS OF THE CAMBRIDGE UNIVERSITY PRESS

Bentley House, 200 Euston Road, London, N.W.1
American Branch: 32 East 57th Street, New York, N.Y. 10022
West African Office: P.O. Box 33, Ibadan, Nigeria

©

CAMBRIDGE UNIVERSITY PRESS

1964

First Edition 1964
Reprinted 1965

Printed in Great Britain by The Broadwater Press Ltd, Welwyn Garden City, Hertfordshire

FOR
HUGO DYSON
AND
PATRICK COGHILL

CONTENTS

He that hath not the craft, let him shut up shop.

GEORGE HERBERT, *Outlandish Proverbs*

PREFACE

De Stogumber. If you only saw what you think about you would think quite differently about it. It would give you a great shock.

(G. B. Shaw, *Epilogue to St Joan*)

These essays are based on the Clark Lectures for 1959, and I would first like to express my gratitude to the Master and Council of Trinity College for the honour they did me in asking me to deliver them.

They were addressed to an audience of scholars and students and so, mainly, is this book. At the same time I hope it may not be without appeal for less highly specialised lovers of Shakespeare, particularly for those interested in the ways in which his art as a poet is conditioned by his art as a writer for the theatre, and who enjoy studies in the use of a medium.

Shakespeare is known to have worked at extreme speed and, evidently, under an inconceivable pressure of spontaneous imagination. This is so richly evident in the dialogue of all his plays that the study of his imagery, after a generation of specialised scrutiny, still reaps harvest upon harvest of poetic discovery. I have not here attempted to discuss this aspect of his genius, knowing that it is already in many better hands than mine, and has been so for a long time, at least since the publication of Miss Spurgeon's remarkable book, *Shakespeare's Imagery*, that has influenced all study of Shakespeare since its first appearance in 1935.

Nor have I directly attempted the study of his sense of character, another aspect of supreme interest and importance in his dramaturgy, because an even longer line of striking critics, that began with Samuel Johnson and Maurice Morgann, and broke the new ground of introspection with S. T. Coleridge, has continued to illuminate it; this line of study may be thought to culminate in the work of A. C. Bradley, who shows a true understanding of the importance of character in the medium of theatre in his masterly *Shakespearean Tragedy* (1904).

ix

These two aspects—of verbal imagery and human character—may be thought of as wholly poetic, as if stemming from some instant, unargued, creative vision or impulse in Shakespeare; we find them both importantly in many great poets other than poets of the theatre; the aspect these essays attempt to discuss is less that which can be attributed to imagination, than that which we feel as the effect of a surpassing *intelligence* in him. What I am seeking to show, dispersedly among his plays, is the continual exercise of craftsmanlike understanding in his art, such as I think cannot be matched (save for flashes here and there) in the work of his contemporaries. He always seemed to know how to use, or to extend (by a kind of dramatic strategy) the resources at the disposal of a playwright.

To show this, I have attempted a series of analytical approaches, from the same starting-point, to the gulf between analysis and synthesis, to throw, with as much brinkmanship as I may have, some light across it.

My starting-point is how to tell a story on a stage, and this was also Shakespeare's primal starting-point, so far as one can tell; for he ransacked history and fiction for stories that could be made significant and told, or re-told, upon a stage. He was a supreme stage-story-teller and perceived that the basic source of all meaning that can be presented through this medium was the image of a human action.

Some actions are meaningful and others not, and some can be made meaningful, or more meaningful, by alterations in them, or by adding a second or a third to the first, in such a way that a complex of actions infiltrate into one another, to multiply the effects of meaning, whether by contrast or parallelism, or in other ways.

For an action—that is, the shape of a story—is in itself a declaration of the moral judgments it contains; it embodies and suggests them. I do not merely mean ethical judgments, but value judgments of all kinds, arising in, or put into question by the action itself. These values include (in the totality of the play) whatever the imagination and the intelligence can discover in its action.

An action is an outline and an analogy may be taken from other art. An outline drawing by a supreme draughtsman (a Watteau, a Picasso) contains and suggests modelling, texture, movement, even colour—many more things than are actually on the paper. The parables of Christ are outlines, worlds of imagination in a few sentences. There are no outlines in nature but there are plenty in art. The rightness of an outline is its pregnancy.

Stories have to be planned into plays. Shakespeare's plays are neither loose ramblers, disguising their shapelessness under wild shows of blossom, nor are they tightly espaliered into 'Five-Act Form', the Unities and the *liaison des scènes*. Nevertheless they can be shown, in many places, to exhibit subtle calculations in structure, a seemingly magical care in the disposition of theatrical effect, for the sake of intensified significance.

I do not deny that there are puzzles, greater and smaller, here and there, in Shakespeare's dramaturgy, moments of seeming carelessness, signs of haste, evidences of faulty corrections, and even of failures in invention. But for all that I have been convinced, by the experience of trying to direct his plays, that they are often more subtly planned than is generally thought: that the scenes are designed, both internally and in relation to the play as a whole, with an intellectual power for which I can hardly find a parallel in other drama; to use Bottom's phrase, they 'grow to a point'. Their endless originality and variation is not haphazard but experimental. Like other great artists, Shakespeare was continually exploring and extending his medium.

That medium is no more than a stage with actors on it and a touch or two of scenery; yet it is the most convincing of all media for presenting our human situation. The medium of a painter (paint and canvas) allows him many things that are beyond the scope of theatre, landscape particularly, still-life, abstraction; but when he attempts a picture of human action or character, his battle-scenes and portraits cannot but be mute and static. So too the medium of the novelist has its special superiorities over that of the playwright: but print is only print, as paint is paint. Neither can have the immediacy of the stage in regard to human beings, for print and paint are not the thing itself, as actors are. In the theatre men and women present men and women. It is an anthropomorphic art.

The questions with which I have armed myself have mostly been in terms of *function*, of bare dramatic analysis. Why is the story turned this way and not that? What is the use or point of this act, scene, speech, movement, gesture and so forth? Where are the climaxes and how are they approached and achieved? Why is this scene placed next to that? Why is there a soliloquy here and not there? To whom are soliloquies allowed? Is there an audience-craft as well as a stage-craft in Shakespeare?

These and others like them are questions that pour into the mind the moment one attempts a production. If there is any value in the answers I have tried to formulate, it is the result of this kind of work in the main, and I am deeply indebted to every company, amateur or professional, that I have worked with; and especially to the Oxford University Dramatic Society and to other university and college societies here and in America, whose contribution to the study of Shakespeare is of great consequence. No university can afford to be without this kind of work in continual progress. It can illuminate or call in question what is said in lectures or written in books, restore neglected plays to currency, and keep alive the simple but important idea that plays are written to be acted. How important that is we shall see.

Nevertheless, reading him privately will perhaps always be the main road to a knowledge of Shakespeare. In either approach (stage or study) desolating distortions can occur. I am not speaking of simple blunders (incompetent acting, ignorance of words) but, in the case of the stage, of distortions imposed by those directors whose pitiable ambition is to be 'different' (to use their phrase) whereas the true virtue and fountain of all originality in production is to be finely perceptive. The distortions of the study are mainly due to that lawlessness that can overtake an imagination that has forgotten the nature of the medium in which it is trying to imagine. To imagine continuously in three dimensions and in colour, in terms of human voices and bodies, is a considerable strain.

I say it is extremely difficult and tiring, when reading a play, to hold it in the mind's eye, and in the mind's ear, with any constancy, as it moves from moment to moment. It asks more concentration than most of us have to remember (for instance) while we are reading, what characters are on the stage, in what costumes and attitudes. The less we can do this, the more we are likely to lose important inflections of meaning. In a small scene, such as that between the Old Countess and Helena in the first act of *All's Well that Ends Well*, we may be able to visualise the two figures, both in their mourning black, each with her special grace—the graces of age and nobility and the grace of youth in love—the Countess seated, perhaps, with Helena kneeling at her side, and see their gestures and expressions, hear the tones of their talk as they flow through the dialogue, packing it with live meaning. But with more complex scenes, who can hold all their detail for long in his imagination, as the moods and movements change, while he reads?

It is false to reply that such visual details cannot carry important significances, as we shall soon see. The Elizabethans were certainly alive to some of them; they had whole systems of colour-symbolism in dress for instance, and a lover would, by wearing the colours of his mistress, 'carry on a silent conversation or flirtation with her';[1] it was an elaborate language, highly expressive. The instinct survives; this afternoon I saw a young man whose hair was dyed and styled to match precisely the dye and style of the hair of his girlfriend; they were walking hand in hand. It gave an effect of meaning that the eye could not miss, but eludes a full expression in words.

But it is generally not from our incapacities to visualise, that our worst distortions of Shakespeare come; it is from the lawlessness of our imaginations that we are in real danger; ingenious fancies, that lack the discipline of theatre, lead us into every kind of licentious speculation, even to wresting anti-Shakespearean meanings from his texts. Those, however, who are seeking Shakespeare's own meanings—an activity that seems legitimate and not entirely hopeless—can teach themselves, at least in some cases, to distinguish between an interpretation that has genuine Shakespearean validity, and one that has it doubtfully, or not at all, by simply seeing if it could work on the stage; if not, it is a private fantasy.

Let us offer a swift example, taken from many years back, though it is still much quoted. In an essay on *Shakespeare and the Stoicism of Seneca*, by Mr T. S. Eliot, first published in 1927, he discusses Othello's last long speech, that begins:

> Soft you; a word or two before you goe: (v, ii, 341)

This he considers an example of what he calls *Bovarysme* in the Moor; *Bovarysme* he defines as 'the human will to see things as they are not', a thing exemplified (he thinks) in a high degree in these lines, though generations of readers and playgoers have mistakenly thought the speech to express 'the greatness in defeat of a noble but erring nature'.

But Mr Eliot will not allow this consoling view to be the true burden of Othello's speech, for he takes it as that of a man 'endeavouring to escape from reality': Othello has 'ceased to think about Desdemona' to indulge in self-pity; what he is really doing is '*cheering himself up*' for the frightful mess his folly has made.

What happens to this interpretation when we try it out in a theatre? What tones of voice, what move or gesture, can an actor use to suggest a Bovarist cheering himself up? Would he not choose precisely those that would seem to be 'expressing the greatness in defeat of a noble nature'? For a true Bovarist at such a moment would attempt to see himself as doing exactly that. Unless it be argued that there is no such thing in nature as greatness in defeat and that any attempt to show it must be instantly recognised by all as fraudulent, how is an audience to know whether Othello is cheering himself up for being so gross a fool and failure, or whether he is cheering his audience up by showing once again, and at the last moment, a true flash of that nobility for which they had first honoured him?

The gravamen of the charge against such criticism is not simply that it is foot-loose from the art it is attempting to criticise, but that it implies a shocking technical incompetence, or else a shocking moral irresponsibility, in Shakespeare as a playwright. For if

Shakespeare had wished to convey the 'terrible exposure of human weakness' that Mr Eliot sees in Othello's speech, he could very easily have made this simple purpose plain, unless he was a bungler, or quite indifferent to the effect he was creating. For if Mr Eliot is right, the better this speech is spoken and acted, the more it must deceive the audience; and this is, in effect, conceded by Mr Eliot, who says Othello 'takes in the spectator'. It follows then, that what begins as an attack on Othello's character turns out as undermining Shakespeare's craftsmanship. In the pleasures of self-abasement and the denigration of heroism, many have welcomed Mr Eliot's views without noticing where they were leading, all for want of thinking in terms of the medium Shakespeare used.

It is pardonable for a *reader*, under the spell of Othello's speech, to have forgotten that Iago is still on stage and in full possession of his faculties. His hatred of Othello is undiminished. Had it been Shakespeare's intention to suggest what Mr Eliot supposes, Iago was there to assist him. Shakespeare had endowed him with the capacity to puncture sentiment; we have heard him use it on Rodorigo:

Rodo. I cannot beleeue that in her, she's full of most bless'd condition.
Iago. Bless'd figges-end.   (II, i, 245–6)

What prevented Shakespeare, if he wished us to think ignobly of Othello's soul, from using Iago to guide our understanding to this crucial point? Iago had only to choose his moment in Othello's speech to ejaculate 'Thicklips!' or 'Buzze buzze!' (since, alas, the more sophisticated *'Bovarist!'* was not then available) to make his point. But the point was not made.

Under the discipline of theatre, then, the whole Bovarist conjecture collapses, like many other critical glosses on Shakespeare that have been offered without considering what can happen on a stage. An art moves in its own medium. Critics, like producers, must feel for the ways in which the plays they discuss were meant to *work*, both as a whole and in points of detail. These ways, or some of them, are the subject of this book.

It is customary and proper in a Preface to thank those who have helped the writer in studies of this kind, but I am under obligation to so many that I am unable to offer a manageable list. There is no idea here put forward that has not profited from the work of other people, over many years, in print, rehearsal, and conversation. It often happens that help of this kind becomes so much a part of one's own thinking that its true origin is forgotten. I have sought to record some of my indebtedness in the notes. I hope I have robbed no one by learning from him.

CHAPTER I

VISUAL MEANING

Your eares vnto your eyes Ile reconcile.

(*Pericles*, IV, iv, 22)

A chapter to show that Shakespeare had an acutely visual imagination which worked in terms of his theatre, and how this truism has subtle consequences in the detail, as well as in the larger effects of his stage-craft, in the conveying of meaning. Examples chiefly from Hamlet, Lear, Coriolanus, Titus Andronicus *and* Romeo and Juliet.

The art of theatre is unique in its power to convey meaning in two simultaneous and confluent streams, through eye and ear: and although the ear is the more important of the two (for a man stone-blind will generally receive more meaning from a play than a man stone-deaf), yet the eye has a great qualifying authority.

Hamlet, in his inky cloak, standing sadly aloof from the gaudy court of Claudius, brings something to our sense of his isolation that no dialogue can so finely disclose; the visual image offers a meaningfulness beyond what can be said. But so familiar has this image become that we no longer notice the stunning visual invention that first thought of it.

There are many passages in Shakespeare the significance of which is doubtful or ambiguous if we look only at the dialogue and ignore gesture, movement and other visual things; and what these things should be is by no means always a matter of subjective opinion. There is such a thing as objective stage-craft, which, if studied in detail, can often certify significance, as I shall show.

Unfortunately, even less is known about how Shakespeare's plays were staged than about how they were printed; yet, even so, touches of his incomparable stage-subtlety are almost everywhere apparent in his plays. Stage-craft is only a small part of dramaturgy, but it is perhaps the easiest part to study first, for it is practical, not theoretic. Our attention to it must first concern itself with the things of which we can be absolutely certain, such as necessary movements and gestures, dictated sometimes by explicit stage-directions, but more often by the dialogue itself.

A whole study of Shakespeare's stage-craft would, of course, include far more than this; such things, for instance, as the uses he made of the shape, structure and equipment of Elizabethan and Jacobean theatres and halls, public and private, their properties and costume. But unhappily there is as yet no agreement among scholars about most of these things; we do not know with any precision what scenery, machines, traverses, traps, props, painted cloths, variations in level or other devices were available to him. What was at the disposal of his Company at a Court performance may not always have been so readily obtainable in a public theatre, and *vice versa*. But when we turn to the smaller aspects of stage-craft, smaller yet crucial in significance, such as the stance, relative positions, movements, groupings, processions and gestures of actors and their facial expressions, of these visual effects we can often be certain, or at least reasonably well informed. It is here that we can watch Shakespeare's visual skill at work. Let us take a tiny example, unnoticed in the context of stage-craft.

In Act I Scene iii of *The Merchant of Venice*, Antonio enters up-stage just after Bassanio has explained to Shylock his need for a loan of three thousand ducats, for which Antonio is to be bound. Shylock notices Antonio's entry: 'Who is he comes here?' Bassanio replies 'This is signior *Anthonio*' and goes up-stage to greet his friend, leaving Shylock to his soliloquy:

> How like a fawning publican he lookes.
> I hate him for he is a Christian ...   (I, iii, 36–7)

How should the actor playing Antonio greet Bassanio as he joins him up-stage? With what expression on his face? Many may think this is a matter of no importance; it is Shylock's moment, after all, not Antonio's. But Shakespeare did not think like this; he specified exactly how the actor should play it, namely in a manner which to Shylock (a hostile witness) should seem a *fawning* manner.[1] This adjective was not put in just to scan: it is there to show the fond joy of Antonio's love at the very moment of its indulgence in a great gift. It is a stage-direction. It embodies visual meaning.

It is easy to show that Shakespeare saw the scene he was composing 'in the mind's eye' (a phrase he invented) with peculiar sharpness. Frequent phrases of the kind I have instanced are to be found, and some will show not only that he had all the visual details of the story vividly in his imagination as he wrote, but even that he saw them enacting themselves on a specifically Elizabethan stage. When Hermione laments her miseries at her trial, she reaches their climax with

> Lastly, hurried
> Here, to this place, i' th' open ayre, before
> I haue got strength of limit. (*Winter's Tale*, III, ii, 102–4)

'*i' th' open ayre*' shows that Shakespeare was, at that instant, thinking, not of the palace of Leontes, but of an Elizabethan stage, open to the sky. We shall see a richer example of this presently, but first it is necessary for our argument to re-describe a primary authority, well-known though it be, the famous drawing of the Swan Theatre, made by Johannes de Witt during his visit to London in 1596, and copied by his friend Arend van Buchell into his common-place book (see Plate I). The book is now in the Rijksuniversiteit at Utrecht.

The drawing occupies a page ($16\frac{1}{2} \times 11$ cm.) in this very elegant manuscript. No reproduction does justice to the neatness of the drawing and handwriting, which are both van Buchell's; for whoever did the drawing did the writing on it, and every feature of the writing is to be found in the passages of italic hand that occur in the rest of the book. This is the only drawing it contains.

The drawing, though accomplished, was not made in order to show accomplishment, but to offer information, to confirm and explain a traveller's tale: it is in a sense diagrammatic. Latin labels expound it: *planities siue arena: proscaenium: ingressus*, and so forth. This expository element is also seen in the figure blowing a trumpet at the door of the hut on top. He cannot be supposed to be a part of the play that seems to be in progress on the stage below, for 'when the vicar is preaching the organ does not play', as they say in

Mallorca.[1] The flag on his trumpet repeats the swan badge to be seen on the flagstaff banner above him; he is a theatre-servant, not a noise off, and his function in the drawing is simply diagrammatic —to show how the hut was used to announce the start of a performance.

The next point to notice is that the drawing is made, as a diagram should be, from the most advantageous viewing-point, that is, from the best seat in the house: everything can be seen from it and it is immediately opposite, and as close as a seat can be, to the actors: they face it and are as far down-stage as it is possible for them to be without falling off.

We can see the sturdy trestles upon which the stage is mounted. We can see, too, that the actors are in the open air, under the sky: the protecting roof does not begin until about half-way up-stage. At the back we see a wall pierced by two great doors with double valves: between them is written *mimorum aedes*. Above there is a pillared gallery in which eight persons are seated. There is no scenery visible on the stage, apart from the property bench, set far down-stage and occupied by what we know to be a boy in woman's dress, seated with some grace. Behind him stands another boy, a seeming lady too: below and to the left of them a bearded man in a hat is making an elaborate leg. He carries a staff in his left hand, which is helping him to balance. He might almost be Balthazar, addressing Portia, in the presence of Nerissa, in *Merchant of Venice*, III, iv, 56: 'Madam, I goe with all conuenient speed.' Apart from these three, the eight in the gallery, the trumpeter and, of course, the invisible de Witt himself, the theatre is empty.

Questions crowd in upon one. If this is a performance, why is there no audience? How did de Witt get the best seat in the house to do his drawing from? How could he have known (unless he came early or stayed late) that there were trestles to support the stage, for would not the groundlings, standing in the *planities siue arena*, have masked them? Why is there no scenery? Can the old-fashioned and romantic notion be true after all, that in the excess of their imaginative power, the Elizabethans preferred to dispense with scenery? And if old-fashioned notions may be true, what has happened to the 'Inner Stage' of which we have so often been told, and which—or something like it—seems at times so necessary to accommodate certain situations in many an Elizabethan play? Why is there no sign of it in the back wall, between those two great doors? If it had been there, how could de Witt have failed to notice it? Could he have forgotten it? Perhaps it was not in use in whatever play it was he saw? Perhaps, in his anxiety to label his diagram with *mimorum aedes*, he sacrificed a feature of the building the importance of which he did not perceive? Or perhaps there never was such a feature?

And where are the seats for the gallants on the stage? Where, indeed, are the gallants, of whom we have heard so much from Dekker?[1] Who are those people sitting in the gallery? What is there so special about them that they should be included and the gallants not? Are they diagrammatic too, like the trumpeter, or were they drawn from life?

A possible answer to some of these questions can be found if we suppose that the scene de Witt had drawn was one not in performance but in rehearsal. This conjecture was first advanced by Mr Martin Holmes[2] some years ago and has found endorsement from more recent scholars. I believe it to be true myself and must here elaborate it and, perhaps, carry it a little further.

It is easy to believe that a distinguished and admiring foreign visitor could have obtained permission to attend a rehearsal to make his sketch; he would then have had all the seats in the place to choose from, and none of the elbowings and distractions to be met with in a performance. There would have been no groundlings to interrupt his view of the trestles that support the stage, and no scenery, except for the indispensable property-bench; there would be neither gallants, nor stools for them on the stage. But there might well have been actors, awaiting their turn to rehearse, sitting listlessly in the gallery of their *mimorum aedes* as they watched their colleagues below, doing their routine.

If we look more closely at the eight figures in the gallery, their detail gives some support for this conjecture. As Mr Holmes has said, 'the artist, whether or not he knew anything about theatres, certainly knew about drawing': for the figures, both those on stage and those in the gallery, are very expressive (see Plate II).

In the gallery, on our extreme right, there are two, profoundly bored, with their backs to one another. One of them wears what seems to me a somewhat bumpkin hat: he is no lord or gallant. Next to this pair, moving leftwards, are two figures, one of which seems to be leaning against a pillar and looking towards the Balthazar-like figure below. The other figure is turned away from the stage and watches a bearded man, next to him in the gallery, who is glaring down at the actors and violently gesticulating. He is the central figure up there and the only one in movement: to the left again there are two men in hats rather more lordly than that worn by the man on the extreme right; they are seemingly engaged in casual converse, perhaps commenting upon the actors below. At the end of the row, to the left, the figure of what I take to be a young girl (or boy dressed up: could it be Jessica?) reclines on one elbow and looks expressionlessly on.

Surely these are actors waiting for their turn? May it not even be that the gesticulating figure is their director, their Peter Quince, concerned to ensure that his actors, when far down-stage, could still be heard from the expensive seats where the lords and gallants paid to sit and to be seen?

But why, if it is a rehearsal, are the boy-girls in full costume? This is a reasonable question and has a reasonable answer: they have to learn the manage of their skirts.

There is yet another point of interest in this drawing which I think no one has mentioned. The only entrances shown are the doors in the back-wall: consequently, on such a stage as this, all entrances and exits must be made up-stage, and all action (save that which concludes a scene) must tend to gravitate down-stage.

With this picture in mind, let us now turn to a passage in the second act of *Hamlet* which shows, in an extraordinary degree, how Shakespeare visualised the play he was composing in terms of just such a theatre; the very dialogue derives a sequence of ideas from it. The passage begins after the dismissal of Voltemand and Cornelius (II, ii, 85), when the King and Queen are left with Polonius '*here in the lobby*', as we learn later (II, ii, 160). Polonius suggests—and the King agrees—that Ophelia, whom Polonius has ordered to 'locke her selfe' from the resort of Hamlet, shall be 'loosed' (that is 'unlocked') to encounter the Prince: meanwhile the King and Polonius are to be placed behind a convenient arras, to overhear what goes on between the supposed lovers. 'We will try it,' says Claudius (II, ii, 166) and at that point we get the stage-direction in Folio:

Enter Hamlet reading on a Booke.

We know the conspirators see him coming, for the Queen points him out to them:

But looke where sadly the poore wretch comes reading.

He must enter from one or other of the great doors: let us suppose it is from the door on our right: if so, we may suppose the royal group to be on our left, and somewhat further down-stage (shielded a little from him by the pillar perhaps?): Hamlet comes down, passing without observing them, for he is reading. (He is, indeed, brought on *'reading'* in order that he may do so; though Shakespeare is economical enough to use the book again, later in the scene, when Hamlet quotes from it.)

Polonius takes command of the situation:

Away I do beseech you, both away,
Ile boord him presently.   *Exit King & Queen.*

The King and Queen slip up-stage and off, leaving Polonius to turn down-stage towards Hamlet, who is by now below the pillars, out on the apron: this is no conjecture, as the dialogue presently shows:

will you walke
Out of the ayre my Lord?

What Polonius is thinking is that the fresh air is no place for madmen: dark rooms were what really did them good, as we can see from Malvolio's case. Polonius is inviting Hamlet (whom he believes to be mad) to come back *out of the fresh air* (that is, *off the apron*) into the 'lobby' (that is, *above the pillars*). The remark could only have been written for such a stage; for how can one 'walk out of the

7

air' on the stage of an indoor theatre, bounded by a proscenium arch? But on a stage like that of the Swan Theatre, the meaning of Polonius's remark is instantly obvious, as obvious as that which I have just quoted from Hermione.

To Polonius's well-meant invitation, Hamlet strangely replies: 'Into my Graue?' Hamlet is certainly 'much possessed by death', and this surprising answer is one example of his possession. But to Shakespeare, thinking of Hamlet standing out on the apron, near or on the grave-trap into which the Prince would presently be leaping to grapple with Laertes over the corpse of Ophelia, it was a very natural, one might almost say an obvious, thought. That the grave-trap was far down-stage is certain from the Folio stage-direction in the last act:

Enter Hamlet and Horatio a farre off.   (v, i, 55)

Afar off can only mean up-stage, since all entries (at least in such a theatre as the Swan drawing shows us) must be up-stage. The trap must therefore have been far down.

The sequence continues; presently Polonius, routed, takes his leave. As he moves up towards the exit-doors he runs into Rosencrantz and Guildenstern who are making their entry: 'You goe to seeke my Lord *Hamlet*;' he asks, then, pointing down-stage with as much officious vanity as if he had himself laid the egg of their meeting—perhaps he had—'there hee is.'

The young spies join their Prince in the open air below the pillars, and presently we hear Hamlet saying to them:

... this goodly frame the Earth, seemes to me a sterrill Promontory; this most excellent Canopy the Ayre, look you, this braue ore-hanging, this Maiesticall Roofe, fretted with golden fire ...

Glendower speaks of the 'frame' of the earth (*1 Henry IV*, iii, i, 16), as Hamlet does; but in the context of thought I am attempting to uncover, it is relevant to note that *frame* was the technical name of the surrounding walls of a theatre, the walls at which Hamlet is pointing; it is the word used for them in the Fortune Theatre contract.[1] As for *sterrill Promontory*, what better description could he have found for the huge stage of bare boards on which he and his companions are standing? And then his eye turns upward to the sky to see the *excellent canopy of the air* above his head, with the thought added of *a majestical roof, fretted with golden fire*, which must have crowded into Shakespeare's head, as he wrote the passage, from the pent-house roof with its star-spangled ceiling called 'the heavens', that we see supported on the Swan pillars; thence his imagination comes back to Hamlet, standing out on the apron, and so down to his feet, below which stands the human concourse of his audience, their faces looking up at him: and a last thought comes to him from them:

What a piece of worke is a man!

The structure of the theatre suggested the structure of this speech.

Having shown reason for thinking that Shakespeare composed with sharp visual awareness of the theatre for which he was writing, I may steer my argument deeper into the same play, towards the unearthly scene of fugal hysteria when Hamlet, Horatio and Marcellus are sent, in startled rushes, across the huge stage, to and fro, by the ghostly voice from below. Hurriedly as they move, 'shifting their ground' so as to make a maximum of visual effect, they are followed by the pursuing voice that, wherever they are, seems to come up from immediately below, crying *'Swear!'*

In a modern theatre this scene goes for nothing; a stationary voice cries, not from below but from the wings; and this is meaningless. The voice does not even follow the fugitives. Modern Hamlets, on their smaller stages, usually are seen to take a few sedate and token steps, to 'shift their ground', not seeming to know why, or how to make them effective. But on a stage like that of the Swan they would know well enough and the astonished eyes of the audience would see the three swiftly-moving figures race in fear from side to side, and hear the voice always directly beneath them.

This is 'to amaze indeed the very faculties of eyes and ears'. But what sort of stage-craft have we here? Is it a sensational trick, or has it some real significance? Why should this sudden thing happen?

Sensational it is, but it is part of the play's deepest meaning too. It is safe to say that Shakespeare never uses violent stage-effects for

9

the sake of their violence; he draws on resources as wild as Webster's, but always in the service of theme. Let us look once again at the Swan drawing; there we see the penthouse supported by pillars, that was called 'the Heavens': below it, the great flat stage—our world: and below that again those lower regions that traditionally stood for Hell.[1] That Shakespeare was aware of this mediaeval significance in theatre-structure is evident from his use of it, if we look into the detail of this passage; a voice from this lowest region could suggest a voice from Hell by an illusion half visual and half auditory, especially if reinforced by hints in the surrounding dialogue.

Shakespeare prepares us for this suggestion by insinuating it into the language of the play long before giving us the full impact of it in sight and sound: on first seeing the Ghost, Hamlet says:

> Be thou a Spirit of health, or Goblin damn'd,
> Bring with thee ayres from Heauen, or blasts from Hell ...
> (I, iv, 40–1)

and later,

> Oh all you host of Heauen! Oh Earth; what els?
> And shall I couple Hell? (I, v, 92–3)

The idea, thus planted in the dialogue, alerts the audience for its flowering into the action, and when the hysterical fugue begins, it is recalled and confirmed by further touches. That the voice comes from *below* is stressed by Hamlet himself:

> you here this fellow in the selleredge (I, v, 151)

and the astonished group above it is seen to move, as if to avoid an infected place. But the voice moves too and Hamlet notes that it does:

> *Hic & ubique?* Then wee'l shift for grownd*... (I, v, 156)
> * [F; Qq *read* shift our ground]

Let us pause to consider the meaning of this Latin phrase; it is to be translated '*here and everywhere*' of course: but who in the Universe can be both here and everywhere? Only God and the Devil: certainly not a ghost. That this simple piece of theology was also known to Shakespeare and was, indeed, in his mind at the time when he was writing *Hamlet*, can be very easily shown: he had just used it in *Twelfth Night*, a play which is held to stand next to *Hamlet* in the chronology. When, at last, in Act V, Sebastian meets with his twin, Viola, the *hic et ubique* notion springs to his lips in his astonishment (my italics):

> *Seb.* Do I stand there? I neuer had a brother:
> Nor can there be *that Deity in my nature*
> *Of heere, and euery where.*　　　　　　　(v, i, 218–20)

A third time the voice of the Ghost cries '*Swear!*' and Hamlet retorts:

> Well said old Mole, can'st worke i' th' ground so fast?
> 　　　　　　　　　　　　　　　　　　(I, v, 162)

What can this '*old Mole*' mean? Dr Dover Wilson tells us: 'The epithets "old mole", "pioner" and perhaps "truepenny", refer to the common superstition that devils might work like miners beneath the ground and that their rumblings could be heard.'[1] I think we may more exactly reach the meaning of 'old mole' by turning to a passage in an Interlude called *Jack Juggler*,[2] which ran into three editions between c. 1563 and 1570. Jack Juggler is the Vice in this Interlude and he starts it off (after the stately Prologue) with a lively address to the audience:

> ... And now if all things doo happen right:
> You shall see as mad a pastime this night.
> As you saw this seuen yeeres, and as proper a toy
> As euer you saw played of a boy.
> I am called Jack Jugler of many an one:
> And in faith I wil play a iugling cast anone.
> *I will coniure the mole and God before:*
> Els let me leese my name for euermore.　　(104–11)

I have italicised one line: what can it possibly mean except '*I will make a compact with you*'(the audience) '*before the Devil and God*'? If, then, as it must seem, the word *mole* was in use in earlier Tudor times as a popular sobriquet for Satan, may it not well have so been used by Hamlet, in a jocose vein?

By the introduction of these phrases—'*hic et ubique*' and '*old mole*',

Shakespeare has carefully planted the suggestion that the Ghost's voice, *at this point in the play*, seems to Hamlet of diabolic origin.

The notion is further borne out by the abrupt change in the tone of Hamlet's discourse. From the first sound of '*Swear!*' coming up to him from below, he begins talking frivolously, facetiously, with a kind of hysterical familiarity:

> Ah ha boy, sayest thou so. Art thou there truepenny?
>
> (I, v, 150)

Art thou there truepenny? On which of these words should the stress of meaning fall? Should it not carry surprise, thus:

> Art thou *there* truepenny?

Meaning 'So it's down below you are!'; or possibly it might fall on *thou*:

> Art *thou* there truepenny?

Meaning 'So the devil is in this business too!' *Truepenny* is no way for Hamlet suddenly to address a father he revered, whose commandment he has just sworn should live 'Vnmixt with baser matter' within the book and volume of his brain. It is clearly a line expressing surprise and ridicule, a certain jocularity, quite out of keeping with the language he had addressed to the visible Ghost of King Hamlet, who is a 'gracious figure' to him, king, father, royal Dane.

But the proper way to treat a devil is to deride him, as mediaeval art and drama had insisted for centuries: Devils are comics: the right technique with them is one of mockery and this at once explains Hamlet's sudden change of tone; he believes himself, at this surprising moment, to be addressing a Fiend, not a Father. It's the ubiquitous Old Mole.

But, it might be argued, the text plainly says that it is the voice of the *Ghost*:

> *Ghost cries under the Stage.*

It cannot, then, be the Devil. This argument will not hold: Hamlet knew that the Devil has power to 'assume a pleasing shape' (II, ii, 595–6), so why not a pleasing voice? And if the Devil is to assume the voice of Hamlet's Father, then the actor playing the Ghost is the obvious man to do it for him. *Ghost cries under the Stage* is a direction to an actor, not to a reader.

There would be no difficulty in this idea for an Elizabethan audience: that an apparition or ghostly voice might be the Devil's work was a commonplace of the theology, whether Protestant or Catholic. It is an idea nowhere better expounded than by Chaucer in his *Friar's Tale*, which gives us the following conversation between a Summoner and a Fiend: the Summoner asks the Fiend what sort of shape he has in hell, if he is able to take the appearance of a man on earth:

> Ye han a mannes shap as wel as I;
> Han ye a figure thanne determinat
> In helle, ther ye been in youre estat? (160–2)

The Fiend replies:

> 'Nay certeinly!' quod he, 'ther have we noon;
> But whan us liketh, we kan take us oon,
> Or elles make you seme we been shape
> Somtyme lyk a man, or lyk an ape,
> Or lyk an angel kan I ryde or go.
> It is no wonder thyng thogh it be so;
> A lowsy jogelour kan deceyve thee,
> And pardee, yet kan I moore craft than he.' (163–70)

Elizabethans believed as Chaucer did in this respect.

We are coming closer, then, to the secrets of the stage-craft of this strange scene, and if there are some Romantics who still cling to the pseudo-psychological whimsy that when Hamlet says later on:

> The Spirit that I haue seene
> May be the Diuell (II, ii, 594–5)

he is merely thinking up a new excuse for a fresh procrastination of the deed he cannot do, they are ignoring the facts of the text.

In the general inference that I have sought to draw from our study of this moment of Shakespeare's stage-craft, I am glad to find support in the judgment of Dover Wilson who, approaching the meaning of the scene from a different angle, reaches an almost exactly similar conclusion: the audience, he says, like Hamlet himself

would wonder what to think before the vision appears; like him they would be overwhelmed by its apparition and accept it as the genuine spirit of the dead king while it is actually before their eyes; like him too they would be left baffled and bewildered by the cries from the cellarage. At the end of the first act, the Elizabethan audience could no more be certain of the honesty of the Ghost and of the truth of the story it had related, than the perplexed hero himself.[1]

The theatrical device, in Shakespeare's hand, creates a visual crisis as sensational as can be imagined, but it is a crisis in thought also: it gives huge expansion to the significance of the entire play, reminding us that if honest ghosts demand revenge, *Hell is on their side*.

It is interesting to measure Shakespeare's skill in using the ghost-under-the-stage device for the furtherance of his deepest meanings by comparing John Marston's use of it in *Antonio's Revenge*, which is the Second Part of his earlier play *The History of Antonio and Mellida*.[2] Both parts were published in 1602.

Antonio's Revenge reeks of *Hamlet* and it reeks of theft.[3] There is hardly a page that has not some echo out of Shakespeare bungled up in it, and particularly frequent are the echoes from *Hamlet*. It includes, among many familiar phrases and devices, an avenger-son of a poisoned father, the assumption of a fool's habit (the antic disposition), a bedroom scene in which his father's ghost appears to rebuke and forgive his former wife on the eve of her marriage to his murderer, a dumb-show much resembling its famous original, and, above all, a ghost under the stage. What is of interest, however, is not the origin of these ideas but the way they are put to use.

Marston uses the ghost-beneath-the-stage for its intrinsic, unexpected, supernatural thrill, as a *coup de théâtre* that has no further significance; not satisfied with one, he has two ghosts speaking in chorus. One is the Ghost of Andrugio (Antonio's poisoned father), the other the Ghost of Feliche, another victim of the same murderer. They interrupt, in a sort of unison, a soliloquy of Antonio's, as he stands by his father's tomb, reflecting on the villainy of the world; and their ghostly chorus is strengthened by a third voice, that of Feliche's father, Pandulpho, *who is still alive*, though not at the moment on stage. This makes the whole thing as preposterous as it is meaningless; but so it stands in the text: Antonio is moralising on Man:

> Still striuing to be more then man, he prooues
> More then a diuell, diuelish suspect, diuelish crueltie:
> All hell-straid iuyce is powred to his vaines,
> Making him drunke with fuming surquedries,
> Contempt of heauen, vntam'd arrogance,
> Lust, state, pride, murder.
>
> *And.* Murder. ⎫
> *Fel.* Murder. ⎬ *From aboue and beneath.*
> *Pa.* Murder. ⎭
>
> *Ant.* I, I will murder: graues and ghosts
> Fright me no more, Ile suck red vengeance
> Out of *Pieros* wounds. . .   (1103–13)

No further reference is made to these supernatural solicitings, for when Pandulpho reappears in the next act he offers no comment on the ghostly chorus, or how he came to have part in it.

Not satisfied with one use of the device, Marston attempts it again when Antonio murders Iulio, the little son of his adversary; this he does in his usual rhetorical style:

> Now barkes the Wolfe against the full cheekt Moone.
> Now Lyons halfe-clamd entrals roare for food . . .
> And now swarte night, to swell thy hower out,
> Behold I spurt warme bloode in thy blacke eyes.
>   *From under the stage a groane.*
> Howle not thou pury mould, groan not ye graues.
> Be dumbe all breath. Here stands *Andrugio's* sonne,
> Worthie his father.   (1178–89)

But this sepulchral groan has no more point than the murder-chorus. It will be clear from these showy ineptitudes how bungled a use of the ghost-under-the-stage motif Marston has made. The voice from below is simply a stolen stunt. It has no functional connection with the thought of the play, the shape of the theatre, or its theological implications. Shakespeare used all these in their vital combination.

Let us, for a moment, think of some other of his *coups de théâtre*: Falstaff shamming dead, or his buck-basketry: Lady Macbeth's sleep-walking: the witches' cauldron: the music of the god Hercules passing under the stage to signify that he is leaving Antony: the descent of Jupiter in *Cymbeline*: the resurrection of Hermione in *The Winter's Tale*: or, in the same play, *Exit pursued by a Beare*, which is a masterstroke of terror and comedy, exactly bridging the change-over from tragedy to comedy that takes place at this moment of the play.[1] These and half a hundred other of his startling uses of the facts and possibilities of theatre, to produce what no other art can attempt, are never gratuitous stunts. They are always vested by Shakespeare with important significances; they are theme-bearers.

In the scene from *Hamlet* that we have analysed, we have found that the stage-craft confirms and enriches Dover Wilson's interpretation of it; but there is another scene, even more crucial, where it does not, namely in the 'Nunnery scene' between Hamlet and Ophelia. Let us examine it again.

If we pay careful regard to their dialogue we will find it to contain a large number of absolutely certain, essential, but implied, stage-directions. I have italicised them in the relevant passage that follows from the First Folio, so as to isolate them for discussion:

Ham. Get thee to a Nunnerie. Why would'st thou be a breeder of Sinners? I am my selfe indifferent honest, but yet I could accuse me of such things, that it were better my Mother had not borne me. I am very prowd, reuengefull, Ambitious, with more offences at my becke, then I haue thoughts to put them in imagination, to giue them shape, or time to acte them in. What should such Fellowes as I do, crawling betweene Heauen and Earth. We are arrant Knaues all, beleeue none of vs. *Goe thy wayes to a Nunnery. Where's your Father?*
Ophe. At home, my Lord.
Ham. Let the doores be shut vpon him, that he may play the Foole no way, but in's owne house, *Farewell.*
Ophe. O *helpe him, you sweet Heauens.*

Ham. If thou doest Marry, Ile giue thee this Plague for thy Dowrie. Be thou as chast as Ice, as pure as Snow, thou shalt not escape Calumny. *Get thee to a Nunnery. Go, Farewell.* Or if thou wilt needs Marry, marry a fool: for Wise men know well enough, what monsters you make of them. *To a Nunnery go, and quickly too. Farewell.*

Ophe. O heauenly Powers, restore him.

Ham. I haue heard of your pratlings too wel enough. God has giuen you one pace, and you make your selfe another: you gidge, you amble, and you lispe, and nickname Gods creatures, and make your Wantonnesse, your Ignorance. Goe too, Ile no more on't, it hath made me mad. I say, we will haue no more Marriages. Those that are married already, all but one shall liue, the rest shall keep as they are. *To a Nunnery, go.*

Exit Hamlet (III, i, 121–49)

There are two distinct kinds of stage-directions given in these lines, one to prescribe Hamlet's movements, the other to prescribe his manner. Let us consider his movements first.

The 'line' that eventually takes him off the stage is *To a Nunnery, go.* In his preceding speech he has twice made use of just such a phrase, and each time he has added the word *Farewell.*

Farewell is also the last word of the speech before that. He has said *Farewell* four times in three speeches, and three times the word is associated with his advice to Ophelia to go to a nunnery; it is indeed Hamlet's last word to her, his exit-thought. That this is so is obvious and it becomes even more so when we glance at the 'Bad' First Quarto at this point; instead of Folio's reading:

Let the doores be shut vpon him, that he may play the Foole no way, but in's owne house. *Farewell.*

First Quarto reads:

> For Gods sake let the doores be shut on him,
> He may play the foole no where but in his
> Owne house: *to a Nunnery goe.*

This suggests that the pirate or tinker of the text of Q1 was at this point 'toiling painfully and conscientiously along the broken paths of memory' (to use Greg's description of his progress),[1] in this case a *visual* path: he remembered having seen Hamlet turn to go on

C 17

every occasion on which he told Ophelia to go to a nunnery: so he very naturally confused this advice with the idea of saying *farewell*, and made the substitution noted above, *to a Nunnery goe*.

Now *Farewell* is a word which inherently contains a stage-direction, a direction for a movement or gesture of departure, or leave-taking. An actor who did not 'make as if to go' on saying 'Farewell' simply would not know his job. It is a line to take a man off the stage, unless he is recalled by some other thought.

To make explicit the stage-directions that are implied in the dialogue, we may write them in thus, on their four occasions:

(1) . . . play the Foole no way, but in's own house. Farewell.
          (turns to go off upstage)
   Ophe. O helpe him, you sweet Heauens.
   Ham. (Returning) If thou doest Marry . . . *(etc.)*

(2) . . . not escape Calumny. Get thee to a Nunnery. Go, Farewell.
   (turns to go off upstage, but returns) Or if thou wilt needs Marry...
   (etc.)

(3)   To a Nunnery go, and quickly too. Farewell. *(turns to go)*
   Ophe. O heauenly Powers, restore him.
   Ham. (Returning once more) I haue heard of your pratlings too wel enough . . . *(etc.)*

(4) . . . I say, we will haue no more Marriages. Those that are married already, all but one shall liue, the rest shall keep as they are. To a Nunnery go.   *(Exit Hamlet)*

Such are his movements; now for his manner. The directions are given in three utterances of Ophelia's:

(1) O helpe him, you sweet Heauens.

(2) O heauenly Powers, restore him.

(3) O what a Noble minde is here o're-throwne? *(etc.)*

These tell us that Ophelia believes Hamlet to have suddenly run mad, to have been 'blasted with extasie', as by a *coup de foudre*. They also tell us the precise moment at which the actor playing Hamlet is to fall into that frenzy which makes her think him mad, and which is the motive of all those halted exits and swift returns that we have just discussed. The precise moment is when he hears Ophelia say

'At home, my Lord' in answer to his startling question 'Where's your Father?' At that point fury breaks forth.

It is not difficult to see why: she has lied to him, and he knows she has. But, it may be asked, how does he know this?

We have seen that his advice to her to seek out a nunnery is his last word to her, his exit-line; and at the end of the first speech in which he gives it, he must also turn to go, thus:

> We are arrant Knaues all, beleeue none of vs.
> Goe thy wayes to a Nunnery. (*Turns to go*)

The audience sees him turn up-stage: for the first time in the scene he is facing the arras behind which the audience knows his enemies to be ensconced: they are on edge for him to guess, to discover, to know what *they* know. There is no need of a crude effect, a fumbling Polonial hand, a protruding foot, a belly-swollen curtain: all that is needed for the audience to have their desire is that Hamlet, facing the arras, should suddenly stop short and stiffen, as might a pointer scenting a brace of partridges, and then turn back and ask the stunningly unexpected question 'Where's your Father?'

That this is his moment of enlightenment is certain, first from the sudden irrelevance of the question, taken in conjunction with the moves we have analysed, and secondly, from the rage that bursts from him when she tells him what he now knows to be a lie. He even senses that the King is there too in hiding: that is given in the line

> Those that are married already, *all but one* shall live

And why should he not know? He is no fool: a similar intuition teaches him later on to 'finger the packets' of Rosencrantz and Guildenstern, that night when he could not sleep, on his way to England with them. As Dr Flatter has so well said, Hamlet 'is always one jump ahead of himself. His mind does not walk, but moves by leaps and bounds.'[1]

These, then, are the mechanics of the second half of his interview with Ophelia in the nunnery scene: what of the first half? Dover Wilson, wishing to justify his conjecture that Hamlet had overheard the plot between the King, Queen and Polonius to spy on his meeting with Ophelia,[1] is forced to suppose that Hamlet knows from the start of the scene that Ophelia is betraying him to his eavesdroppers: our analysis of the directions for his moves and manner show this, of course, to be impossible: but there are other difficulties in such a view, in the language of the scene: Dover Wilson chooses four words for special comment and gives them an interpretation which they cannot support in the way he would wish: they are the words *nymph*, *orisons*, *honest* and *nunnery*.

The first two occur when Hamlet, breaking from his famous meditation on the ills of life, observes Ophelia for the first time. Polonius has said to her

> *Ophelia*, walke you heere. . . Reade on this booke,
> That shew of such an exercise may colour
> Your lonelinesse. (III, i, 43–6)

It would seem that it is visibly a prayer-book she is reading: perhaps, after walking back and forth once or twice, slowly, in what we have called 'the lobby' she falls to her knees in prayer (so as not, by movement, to distract the audience from Hamlet's soliloquy): be that as it may (for we cannot be certain) it at least seems to Hamlet, when at last he observes her, that she is in *prayer* over her book, for he says:

> Soft you now,
> The faire *Ophelia*? Nimph, in thy Orizons
> Be all my sinnes remembered. (III, i, 88–90)

Dover Wilson is forced to think (with Dowden) that *nymph* is a word of estrangement, that *orisons* is affected and that the rest is sardonic.[2] There is however no evidence in Shakespeare that he used the word *nymph* in such a way at any time: all the associations of the word (except when it is in the mouth of a blackguard) are favourable, and embody things that Shakespeare manifestly loved in women: chastity above all, for we hear of temperate nymphs, fresh nymphs, gentle nymphs, of chaste crowns for cold nymphs, of Dian circled with her nymphs: and of 'nymphs that vowed chaste life': a nymph can also inspire a torrent of love:

20

O *Helen*, goddesse, nimph, perfect, diuine,
To what my loue, shall I compare thine eyne!

(*Midsummer Night's Dream*, III, ii, 137–8)

The only users of the word that have ill-thoughted meanings for it are Aaron the Moor and Richard III, who associate it with wantonness; but certainly not with estrangement.[1]

Orisons is a rarer word, but I find it in the mouth of Juliet:

For I haue need of many Orysons,
To moue the heauens to smile vpon my state

(*Romeo and Juliet*, IV, iii, 3)

and in the mouth of Imogen:

or haue charg'd him
At the sixt houre of Morne, at Noone, at Midnight,
T'encounter me with Orisons, for then
I am in Heauen for him   (*Cymbeline*, I, iii, 32–5)

These, then, are tender words and our scene begins tenderly. It is not long before we come to the other two words, *honest* and *nunnery*, now to be discussed. Ophelia is seeking to return to Hamlet the 'remembrances' that he had given her:

Take these againe, for to the Noble minde
Rich gifts wax poore, when giuers proue vnkinde.
There my Lord.
Ham. Ha, ha: Are you honest?   (III, i, 100–4)

Dover Wilson believes this to mean 'Are you a whore?' But who ever heard of a whore returning the gifts of a man who has traded with her? It is perfectly clear that Hamlet has no such thought about this nymph at that moment: the question he asks is stung from him by a quite different suspicion. He thinks she is obeying the command of Polonius (as indeed she is) to give his presents back to him, and what gives rise to this suspicion in his mind is her Polonial wisdom, in the stilted aphorism:

Rich gifts wax poore, when giuers proue vnkinde.

He hears her master's voice in this, she is repeating a lesson: it is one of the old fraud's typical *sententiae* and it stings Hamlet into the sudden suspicion that is marked by his exclamation 'Ha, ha'. In order that the audience shall not miss this point, Shakespeare has underlined it with a rhyme: the only rhyme in the scene:

> for to the Noble *minde*
> Rich gifts wax poore, when giuers proue *vnkinde*.

But her total, innocent surprise at his exclamation allays his suspicions and he turns the conversation away from the dangerous ground, and towards what is to be his last advice to her, to shield herself from a world full of offence by entering a nunnery: he knows that their relationship must be ended, and like many men who try to disentangle themselves from a love-affair, he tries to persuade her of his unworthiness, which he hopelessly exaggerates in the usual way. But not before he has given her his best advice:

Get thee to a Nunnerie. Why would'st thou be a breeder of Sinners?

Wilson believes the word 'nunnery' in this scene carries the sense of a 'whore-shop', a house of ill-fame.[1] And there is some slender evidence that the word could have this secondary sense in Elizabethan and Jacobean times.[2] The word, however, cannot have been wholly smirched if Lovelace could later write of the nunnery of a chaste breast. Nor here, where Hamlet first uses it, can it mean anything except a holy house for christian nuns. The proof of that is the phrase 'Why would'st thou be a breeder of Sinners?' There is nowhere better than a brothel for breeding sinners, as Shakespeare knew very well: for Lucio, in *Measure for Measure*,[3] got Kate Keepdown with child in the brothel of Mrs Overdone; and the Bawd in *Pericles*[4] boasts of having brought up eleven bastards in the course of her profession, only to bring them down again later. When, therefore, Hamlet says

Get thee to a Nunnerie. Why would'st thou be a breeder of Sinners? ... We are arrant Knaues all, beleeue none of vs. Goe thy wayes to a Nunnery.

he can only mean it honestly and christianly.

But, as we have seen, the next time he uses the word is after his discovery of Ophelia's treason to him: it now comes to him in fury:

she will never escape calumny, let her go to a 'nunnery' at once and be done with it, and be like the other women to whom God has given one pace, but they make themselves another, they jig and they amble, they nickname God's creatures and make their wantonness their ignorance. When, at the end of this tremendous tirade, he comes back to his famous phrase, it may perhaps be imagined as charged with the disgust he feels in these thoughts: and it may be that the secondary meaning was intended to come uppermost with '*To a Nunnery* go, and quickly too. Farewell.'

If so, the astounding peripety of the scene hinges on this pun. It is a trick of Hamlet's character to speak in puns at the height of passion: they come easily to him in a rage.

We are now in a position to see the whole dramaturgy in this crucial scene, both in its visual and auditory effect, from just after the ensconcing of the King and Polonius, to the exit of Hamlet: it begins at the still centre of the play and, in order to prepare us for the only meeting of the lovers—a meeting that is also a parting— a mood charged with meditation on the sorrows and injustices of the world is created by the most intimate soliloquy ever written:

To be, or not to be, that is the Question:

Into the melancholy of this speech there moves the figure of Ophelia, seemingly in prayer; and it may be this that puts the thought of a nunnery into her lover's mind: both of them seem to know that they are meeting for a severance, for a farewell: and at first they are tender with each other: she returns his gifts, he gives her his best advice. They part. Then comes the discovery, the whirl-about: in the rage of his 'dispriz'd love' he seems to take the word *nunnery*—the word he had given her for a protection—and use it to stab her with, leaving her 'of Ladies most deiect and wretched'. This is at least a possible interpretation of what he says; but it is certain in respect of his sudden change of mood and movements.

It is a scene of stunning surprises of a kind only possible in the medium of theatre, a medium apt for plottings and concealments, violence of gesture, quick changes of powerful emotions, sudden discoveries, abrupt departure. Not one of these things is frivolously used; all are essential to the woven texture of meaning, to the economy of the play. I do not know a more cunningly constructed scene.

We have seen how a close following of gesture and movement that are given in the text, directly or by implication, can help to clarify meaning visually; but stage-directions cannot always be so easily inferred. At times, all that we can know is that one is missing. A ready example of this can be found in the last moments of *Lear*, at the point when he is kneeling over the dead body of Cordelia, hardly knowing what is being said to him:

> *Alb.* He knowes not what he saies, and vaine it is
> That we present vs to him.
> > *Enter a Messenger.*
> *Edg.* Very bootlesse.
> *Mess. Edmund* is dead my Lord.
> *Alb.* That's but a trifle heere:
> You Lords and Noble Friends, know our intent,
> What comfort to this great decay may come,
> Shall be appli'd. For vs we will resigne,
> During the life of this old Maiesty
> To him our absolute power, you to your rights,
> With boote, and such addition as your Honours
> Haue more then merited. All Friends shall
> Taste the wages of their vertue, and all Foes
> The cup of their deseruings: O see, see.
> *Lear* And my poore Foole is hang'd: no, no, no life?
> > (v, iii, 293–305)

I have italicised the stage-direction that fails to direct: we can never know what action of Lear's it should be that interrupts Albany's speech and makes him exclaim O see, see. If we could, it might shed light on the meaning of that strange and famous line 'And my poore Foole is hang'd.'

But there is another stage-direction in *Lear*, long lost, yet happily recovered through the insight of Sir Lewis Casson, working in conjunction with Harley Granville Barker, in their production of the play at the Old Vic in 1940. I wish to record it here for what I think it to be—as absolutely certain an insight into Shakespeare's meaning, as if he had written it into the text of *Lear* with his own hand.

It comes at a point where the story of blinded Gloucester flows back into the story of mad Lear. It is one of the turning-points of the play, an anagnorisis or recognition that begins the reassembling of the old King's scattered helpers and a restoration to royalty and love.

It is a recognition-scene in which the recognition is delayed, in a manner characteristic of Shakespeare's art: we see it in other plays, when, for instance, Sebastian and Viola meet at long last: or when Pericles, 'wild in his beholding', knows Marina for his daughter, restored to him after many years. It is in the delay that we taste the recognition most feelingly: for with our eyes we see that a longed-for thing is about to happen, even before it has begun: we see the certainty of a joy to come, delayed in order to prolong the thrill of having it in prospect. This is an experience in art that I think can most feelingly be given through the medium of theatre: it corresponds in music to those suspensions by which the longed-for concord is artfully withheld: we feel there must be a resolution and we strain for it, enduring the slow certainty of its approach with a kind of joy that is crowned as the discord melts into harmony.

In *Lear*, though it is used for tragic purpose, the recognition still carries a kind of joy: for it is as if we are seeing the fragments of Lear's kingdom begin to reunite and knit, or at least to shelter together: the scattered isolation of their hunted groups is over: help is coming from France: love and loyalty are raising head.

I do not know how to create for a reader the effect of the single gesture that marked this moment in the production of which I am speaking: it was the simplest gesture imaginable and exactly placed on the meaningful phrase here italicised:

> The tricke of that voyce, I do well remember:
> *Is't not the King?*   (IV, vi, 106–7)

As he said these words, Gloucester *knelt*, as any Elizabethan or Jacobean would kneel, finding himself suddenly in the royal presence. It was a strongly visual gesture of homage.

But the act of homage that brings Gloucester to his knees, a loyal subject, leaves him there a seeming culprit, for that is how Lear interprets the ambiguity in kneeling; and now Gloucester's guilt is to be thrust home:

> I, euery inch a King.
> When I do stare, see how the Subiect quakes.
> I pardon that mans life. What was thy cause?
> Adultery? thou shalt not dye: dye for Adultery?
> No, the Wren goes too't, and the small gilded Fly
> Do's letcher in my sight. Let Copulation thriue:
> For Glousters bastard Son was kinder to his Father,
> Then my Daughters got 'tweene the lawful sheets . . .
>
> (IV, vi, 107–16)

Unless we see Gloucester kneeling there before the unknowing Lear, the lines lose the sharpness of their application, their irony; I have heard them spoken, often enough, as though they bore no reference to him, but were part of some wild soliloquy, vaguely addressed to the audience while Edgar and Gloucester stood by. But everything depends on the explicit recognition of Lear by the blind Gloucester and on the blind recognition of Gloucester by the seeing Lear. And this can only be given by his kneeling as he recognises him.

We shall meet with kneeling as a crucial gesture again in *Othello*,[1] but it is used most of all in *Coriolanus*; Volumnia tells her son to kneel for the suffrages of the people, his knee 'bussing the stones'

> for in such businesse
> Action is eloquence, and the eyes of th'ignorant
> More learned then the eares . . .   (III, ii, 75)

He had already offered his mother his victory over the Volscians by kneeling to her, and he kneels to her again when she visits him in their camp, and loads his kneeling with rhetoric to mark it the more strongly:

> Sinke my knee i' th' earth,   *Kneeles*
> Of thy deepe duty, more impression shew
> Then that of common Sonnes   (v, iii, 50)

But before the play is over it is Volumnia's turn to kneel, and, with her, kneel Virgilia and Valeria and young Marcus:

Down Ladies: let vs shame him with him with our knees*
To his sur-name *Coriolanus* longs more pride
Then pitty to our Prayers. Downe: an end,
This is the last. So, we will home to Rome,
And dye among our Neighbours: Nay, behold's,
This Boy that cannot tell what he would haue,
But kneeles, and holds vp hands for fellowship,
Doe's reason our Petition with more strength
Then thou hast to deny't.   (v, iii, 168)
        * [*read* shame him with our knees]

It is time to turn from the fascinations of gesture and of sub-
merged stage-direction, however meaningful, to a larger aspect of
Shakespeare's visual dramaturgy, his art to create crises for the eye
as well as for the ear. How precise was his care can sometimes be
demonstrated from particular stage-directions such as those we
find in his *Henry VIII*, whose ritual pomp is dictated, detail by
detail, for the glory of England.

*Enter Trumpets sounding: Then two Aldermen, L. Maior, Garter, Cranmer,
Duke of Norfolke with his Marshals Staffe, Duke of Suffolke, two Noblemen,
bearing great standing Bowles for the Christening Guifts: Then foure Noblemen bearing a Canopy, under which the Dutchesse of Norfolke, Godmother,
bearing the Childe richly habited in a Mantle, &c. Traine borne by a Lady:
Then followes the Marchioness Dorset, the other Godmother, and Ladies. The
Troope passe once about the Stage, and Garter speakes.*   (v, v)

This is the work of a Master of Ceremonies, at the end of his life.
Here all is order, all is gravity, a visual order and gravity that celebrate a divinely ordered and consecrated moment of history, the
first christening of a protestant princess, Shakespeare's patroness,
the infant Elizabeth:

> This Royall Infant, Heauen still moue about her;
> Though in her Cradle; yet now promises
> Vpon this Land a thousand thousand Blessings,
> Which Time shall bring to ripenesse.   (v, v, 17-20)

But Shakespeare's eye for a stage-picture is no less powerful in
violence and horror. Who, in the theatre, has not felt an impulse to
turn away his look when Gloucester's eyes are put out? This was

a gift Shakespeare had from the start, to tell his story three-dimensionally, as well as in lines. Let us recall the horrific visual images of *Titus Andronicus* that overgo anything that has ever been imagined for the stage perhaps: as when Lavinia, raped and mutilated, her tongue torn out, tells her secret by visual means:

> *She takes the staffe in her mouth, and guides it with her stumps and writes.*
>
> (IV, i, 77)

Or let us remember the strange allegorical pictures in the same play when Titus and his friends and kinsmen all shoot arrows bearing letters to the Gods in heaven, demanding justice; or when Tamora and her sons, disguised as Revenge, Rape and Murder, visit Titus to make mock of him: these are essentially visual fantasies suited to the medium of theatre and loaded with the meanings of the play. What better visual image could be devised for madness seeking justice than to show a man shooting arrows at the gods?

As it may be argued that these and other highly pictorial scenes may have been in Shakespeare's undiscovered source for this play, let us watch his pictorial imagination at work upon a known source and see how it is transformed so as to make visible and to intensify the meaning of the action narrated. The undisputed source of *Romeo and Juliet* is Arthur Brooke's *Tragicall Historye of Romeus and Juliet*, published in 1562. Two examples of the Shakespearean transformation will be enough to make our point.

Brooke's poem begins with a topographical description of Verona:[1]

> Bylt in an happy time, bylt on a fertile soyle,
> Maynteined by the heavenly fates, and by the townish toyle.
> The fruitfull hilles above, the pleasant vales belowe,
> The silver streame with channell depe, that through the towne
>   doth flow, *etc.* (3–6)

and so we come to an equally general account of the uneasy situation between the Capelets and the Montagews.

> A wonted use it is, that men of likely sorte
> (I wot not by what furye forsd) envye eche others porte.
> So these, whose egall state bred envye pale of hew,

And then of grudging envyes roote, blacke hate and rancor grewe.
As of a little sparke, oft ryseth mighty fyre,
So of a kyndled sparke of grudge, in flames flash out theyr yre,
And then theyr deadly foode, first hatchd of trifling stryfe
Did bathe in bloud of smarting woundes, it re[a]ved breth and lyfe.
No legend lye I tell, scarce yet theyr eyes be drye
That did behold the grisly sight, with wet and weping eye.
But when the prudent prince, who there the scepter helde,
So great a new disorder in his common weale behelde
By jentyl meane he sought, their choler to asswage,
And by perswasion to appease, their blameful furious rage.
But both his woords and tyme, the prince hath spent in vayne
So rooted was the inward hate, he lost his buysy payne.   (31–46)

This generalised narration has little for a reader's inward eye: there
are grudging envies and black hates, but no men: there is the blood
of smarting wounds and the wet of weeping eyes, but no particular
fight: there is a persuasive prince but we do not see him at work.

But with Shakespeare and the stage, all that is general becomes
particular, all that is abstract becomes human: the feud between the
rival houses flames out in a specific and visible brawl, into which
Tybalt hurls himself (we do not hear of Tybalt in Brooke until
nearly a thousand lines later in the story). In short, the play begins
with a violent picture of a faction fight fanned up out of nothing in
which every detail is sharply visualised:

> *Offi.* Clubs, Bils, and Partisons, strike, beat them down
> Downe with the *Capulets*, downe with the *Mountagues*.
> *Enter old Capulet in his Gowne and his wife.*
> *Cap.* What a noise is this? Giue me my long Sword ho.
> *Wife.* A crutch, a crutch: why call you for a Sword?
> *Cap.* My Sword I say: Old *Mountague* is come,
> And flourishes his Blade in spight of me.   (I, i, 70–6)

This is the dialogue of a man with eyes, and who can make
images that work instantly upon a stage for other eyes. It was a
talent of his to start his plays with something visually stunning, the
image of an idea.

But a more striking example than that which shows us the enmity of Capulet and Montague in being is that which shows us Romeo and Juliet falling in love. Arthur Brooke describes the scene with embarrassing ineptitude at considerable length. When he reaches the point, we are offered the preposterous picture of Juliet seated, with Mercutio gripping her right hand, and Romeo her left hand; Mercutio began it:

> With frendly gripe he ceasd* fayre Juliet's snowish hand . . .
> As soone as had the knight the vyrgins right hand raught
> Within his trembling hand her left hath loving Romeus caught . . .
> Then she with tender hand his tender palme hath prest,
> What joy trow you was graffed so in Romeus cloven brest?
>
>   * [read seized]   (259–68)

This absurd group of three hand-holders is nothing to Shakespeare's purpose, and shows nothing of the forces that empower the tragedy. At Shakespeare's dance, music plays—for on a stage we can have music—and we see the bumbling *empressement* of Capulet's hospitality: next we are aware of Romeo:

> What Ladie is that which doth inrich the hand
> Of yonder Knight?
> *Ser.* I know not sir.
> *Rom.* O she doth teach the Torches to burne bright, *etc.*
>
>   (I, iv, 39–41)

and his soliloquy is his declaration of love over the background of the music and the dancing: but it is overheard by Tybalt, and his rage, hardly governed by Old Capulet, brings back the dangers of the opening street-brawl and remakes the image of hatred from the midst of which, at this instant, love is to spring: for as Tybalt storms angrily out, the dance has brought Juliet to where Romeo is standing, which, since he has just been in soliloquy, I take to be down-stage, out on the apron.

And now they are together, and they kiss: and their kiss is so important to them that they weave a sonnet round it, and are almost into a sonnet-sequence, when the Nurse interrupts them. A kiss is the visual image of love, the simplest, the oldest, the most beautiful, the easiest symbol in the art of theatre: here, at the beginning of the story, we see this kiss, instantly following upon Tybalt's rage, juxtaposed images of the two great passions that power the play, and which in the end destroy one another. It is a meaning that can be *seen*.

CHAPTER II

UNIFICATION

How it staggered me to see the fine things in their ore! inter-
lined, corrected! as if their words were mortal, alterable, dis-
placeable at pleasure! as if they might have been otherwise, and
just as good! as if inspiration were made up of parts, and these
fluctuating, successive, indifferent! I will never go into the
workshop of any great artist again.

(Charles Lamb, Oxford in the Vacation, footnotes,
London Magazine, October 1820)

A source-study of certain structural elements in Pericles *and* A Midsummer Night's Dream, *to show that Shakespeare was at pains to give
unified shape of a meaningful kind to the plays he composed, and some of
the means he used to do so.*

Lamb had been shown the holograph of *Lycidas,* full of Milton's
corrections, that is at Trinity College, Cambridge. He wished it
had been thrown into the Cam. To study the sources of a Shakespeare play is another kind of attempt 'to see the fine things in their
ore', and may therefore come under Lamb's condemnation; yet it
offers an approach, sober and factual enough, to the elusive mystery
of imagining, or at least to the sight of a craftsman at work trans-
forming a discrepancy of basic materials into a new and single thing.

We are told by Coleridge that the imagination is a creative power
within us that 'struggles to idealize and to unify'[1] the materials upon
which it is at work; he says also that this faculty may co-exist with
the conscious will. In such fragmentary things as the note-books of
Beethoven, in which are scribbled down the earlier forms of many
musical ideas to be perfected later, or in the preliminary sketches
Picasso made for his *Guernica,* something can be seen (when they
are compared with the final works) of the part played by the conscious will in this struggle; and although no comparable jottings (if
he made any) have come down to us from Shakespeare, his sources

are perhaps no more than one stage further off; more and more of them, from time to time, come to light.[1] In the cases of *Pericles* and *A Midsummer Night's Dream* there are some sources, not yet noticed in detail, if at all, that serve our purpose well.

Coleridge, as I have said, tells us that the work of imagining may be carried on in co-existence with the conscious will: but it is not always possible or even profitable to distinguish between what is 'willed' and what 'inspired' in the struggle to idealise and to unify. We can only feel sure that the will is a controlling factor when we can recognise the use of a traditional technique. I do not, for instance, find it possible to believe that Shakespeare's use of the Three Unities in *The Tempest* was unconscious, nor can I think it a coincidence that so many of Shakespeare's plays are shaped in some conformity with the rules of 'Five-Act Structure'.[2] Where a known discipline is manifestly in use, we may infer a conscious will in command. But there are many other methods or skills that have no particular name which Shakespeare used to give unity to his work; almost every play has its own unifying devices.

Pericles, Prince of Tyre and *A Midsummer Night's Dream* make an interesting pair for study, not only because the sources for them that I mean to discuss have as yet had no detailed consideration, but also because the unity of *Pericles* seems to me the most precarious, and that of *A Midsummer Night's Dream* the most consummate in the whole canon of Shakespeare's work.

The pristine source of Shakespeare's *Pericles*, as is well known, was the story of Apollonius of Tyre in John Gower's *Confessio Amantis*:[3] it is a story to baffle dramaturgy. It stretches out, with many a slipped disc, over the life of a virtuous but shadowy Prince, in journeyings often, in perils of the waters, in perils of the city, and with other adventures even more miraculous than those of St Paul. The years pass by, the storms beat down, while the gossamer of narrative passes and repasses the seas, threads its way through one town after another, treating of kings, princes and governors, bawds and murderers, heroines and whores: there are unnatural separations and mystical reunions, incest in a palace, chastity in a brothel, a burial at sea, a tournament at court: famine and treachery stalk through the story for no particular or likely reason; yet the story struggles on in Gower's placid octosyllables to a divine intervention and a moral ending. How could such a story be told upon a stage? What trick was there to create a continuity for it, a sense of narrative coherence? *Antony and Cleopatra*, so recently completed, had wandered securely over the Roman world in the strength of its central conflict, but what could sustain a tale that sprouted so many strange themes in so many strange places?

Shakespeare found the device he needed in Lydgate's *Troy Book*. He may well have come upon it six or seven years before while he was occupied with those thoughts on the Trojan War that became *Troilus and Cressida*; for the play has several slight touches from Lydgate's poem, though none so striking as the idea I think he took from it to strengthen *Pericles*. It was the device of resurrecting John Gower to compère the action.

Gower is no ordinary Prologue or Chorus; he is an ancient poet who appears to re-tell a tragic poem of his while it is enacted in dumb-show before him, gesture by gesture, at whatever points in the story this method of narration seems the best. This is a technique of narration which Lydgate himself seems to have used for his Mummings, such, for instance, as the colourful Mumming at Hertford (c. 1430), about hen-pecked husbands. The matter of it comes mostly from the Wife of Bath, with a few touches from *Piers Plowman*, and concerns the struggle for mastery in marriage carried on by Robyn the Reeve and Beautryce Bittersweete, Colyn Cobeller and Cecely Soure-Cheere, Berthilmewe the Bochier and Proude Pernelle, Thome Tynker and Tybot Tapister, and lastly Colle Tyler and Phelyce the Wafurer. That these appeared and, presumably, enacted in dumb-show the poem that Lydgate recited may be inferred from such stage-directions as *demonstrando vj rusticos* in the margin of the poem.[1]

This method of presentation was continental at that time, and probably long before; the splendid Terence manuscripts in the Arsenal and Bibliothèque Nationale[2] in Paris show it in operation, in their frontispieces, which are almost identical. If we set one of them beside what Lydgate says of Trojan theatrical practice, we can see at once how the Middle Ages imagined classical Comedy and Tragedy to have been performed by the ancients (see Plate III). It also becomes clear that this tradition was the source from which Shakespeare took his unifying idea for *Pericles*.

> And whilom thus was halwed the memorie
> Of tragedies, as bokes make mynde,
> Whan thei wer rad or *songyn*, as I fynde,
> In the theatre ther was *a smal auter*
> Amyddes set, that was half circuler,
> Whiche into the Est of custom was directe;
> *Vpon the whiche a pulpet was erecte,*
> *And therin stod an awncien poete,*
> *For to reherse* by rhetorikes swete
> *The noble dedis,* that wer historial,
> *Of kynges,* princes for a memorial, . . .
> *And whil that he in the pulpit stood,*
> With dedly face al devoide of blood,
> *Singinge his dites,* with muses al to-rent,
> *Amydde the theatre schrowdid in a tent,*
> *Ther cam out men gastful of her cheris,*
> Disfigurid her faces with viseris,
> *Pleying by signes in the peples sight*
> *That the poete songon hath on hight;*
> *So that ther was no maner discordaunce*
> *Atwen his dites and her contenaunce* . . .
> *So craftily thei koude hem transfigure,*
> Conformyng hem to the chaunteplure.[1]
>
> (*Troy Book*, Bk II, 860–914, my italics)

This vivid and entertaining way of telling a story to eye as well as to ear seems to derive from Isidore of Seville,[2] and was therefore fully a thousand years old by the time Shakespeare took it over. In the fifteenth book of Isidore's *Etymologies* (xv, ii, 35), he tells us about classical amphitheatres. They were circular, he says, being formed by joining two semi-circular theatres together. The *scena*, he adds in a later book (xviii, lxii, 2), is a place below the theatre, built in the manner of a house with a pulpit, which was called the Orchestra (*in modum domus instructa cum pulpito, qui pulpitus orchestra vocabatur*). Into this pulpit, the poets of Comedy and Tragedy, he says, used to ascend to vie with one another, and 'to them singing, others made gestures' (*hisque canentibus alii gestus edebant*).

This is the history of the Gower device in *Pericles*. It is not easy to say for certain how far back Shakespeare went to find it; no further than Lydgate, I suspect. But it may not have been so far, for too many Elizabethan plays have been lost for us to say it could not have survived in plays other and earlier than *Pericles*. At least one survives in plot-form; it seems to have all the essential elements—a tent, an ancient poet, a dumb-show:[1]

> A tent being plast one the stage for Henry the sixt. he in it A sleepe...
> Henry Awaking ... to him Lidgate ... Then Enuy passeth ouer the stag. Lidgate speakes ...
> Henry and Lidgat speaks. Sloth passeth ouer ...
> Henry speaks and Lidgate Lechery passeth ouer the stag ...
> Lidgate speaks to the Audiens and so Exitts.

I think it possible that this *Tent*, described in Lydgate's *Troy Book* and in use in this play of *The Secound Parte of the Seuen Deadlie Sinns*, and to be seen in the Paris manuscripts of Terence, may be an ancestor of the tent which some scholars have reasonably supposed to have been a feature of the Elizabethan stage, for plays in which a cell or 'inner room' is needed.[2]

There is no doubt Gower was a great success with his first audiences, for the prose version of the story, printed in 1608 by George Wilkins, sought to recommend itself by asking readers 'to receiue this Historie in the same maner as it was vnder the habite of ancient *Gower* the famous English Poet, by the Kings Maiesties Players excellently presented'.

Gower is indeed a feature of the play, a star-part. 'He colours the whole action', as Mr Maxwell has truly said.[3] He makes seven lengthy speeches, three of which have dumb-shows to grace them with illustrative action, and it is clear that on a fourth occasion the stage begins to fill as he finishes off his speech:

> At *Ephesus* the Temple see,
> Our King and all his companie.

That he can hither come so soone,
Is by your fancies thankfull doome.   (v, ii–iii. Q)

At other times he is off-stage and his 'chaunteplure' yields to the actors and their dialogue. But there is something endearing in his appearances and the doggerel chattiness of his preposterous 'Olde Englysshe' (which he often forgets to keep up for lines at a time) as he announces, describes, expounds, prophesies, tells of the passage of time and of the seas, takes us into his confidence, recapitulates and moralises. His mere presence supplies a personal continuity in this bewildering story.

It is hard for us to imagine how effective a device it may be, because the play is now so seldom acted. To imagine in the study what it would be like on the stage is not easy; for though we can picture Gower, in a pulpit perhaps, and hear the tones and cadences of his voice with our inward ear, we cannot easily tell what effect such a compère will have in framing, distancing and giving continuity to the play; the convention is too unfamiliar; moreover, to the seventeenth century, Gower was still a 'famous English poet'; but in the twentieth he has been forgotten; so much so that it has been possible, without public outcry, to represent him, at Stratford-upon-Avon too, as a Negro calypso-singer. What such a figure had to do with the story of Pericles was beyond conjecture: but it was taken on trust as culture. Chaucer's friend, whom he called 'moral Gower', the ancient poet who was to re-enact the traditions of Lydgate and Isidore of Seville, remained asleep in Southwark cathedral, his head resting on the three volumes of his forgotten works.

More usually, the unity of a Shakespeare play is pervasive; *ex pede, Herculem.* In every branch and twig flows the sap of its meaning. The shape of the fable declares implicit judgments of value that are amplified and reinforced by the epiphanies, contrasts and inter-relationships of the characters, by the gist of discourse and (more subtly) by the image-patterns of the poetry, in any given play. Each tends to be the 'closed system' which Professor Auden says a poem must be,[1] within which all these elements cohere. It is a system of meaning and the quality of this meaning is moral. I do not

37

mean that it is a demonstration in ethics, but that it offers a completed spiritual vision of values; this cannot be fully recognised and apprehended without a deep joy, often painful. This joy is also pervasive, like the meaning itself, and feels as if it were a part of it: it is often called 'pleasure' or 'delight', but I find these words insipid. The experience of which I am attempting to speak is greater than (because it can include) imaginative grief; it can include tragedy.

The elements that compose a play come together in this kind of experience of it, which, though it may take two or three hours, is essentially timeless, as is every experience in art. It is felt as timeless because no desire is aroused (and so no restlessness) except the level desire to contemplate and receive it totally and understandingly. It is true that in a play or a novel there can be a disturbing narrative impatience, a hankering to know what will happen next, that takes contemplation from its eternal present and nags it into a possible future (that is, back into a sense of time): but this is a minor impurity that a single performance or reading (in the case of a novel) will eject. After the first time, one can contemplate the unfolding of the story without this itch.

The union of diverse elements into a timeless experience is partly an effect of craftsmanship; for though the First Cause (in the author) is the fable-vision itself, the Efficient Causes (in the writing) include many skills; it is characteristic of most of Shakespeare's work that a play of his is all of a piece, and is experienced as a unity, created in its proper and sufficient shape. Some of the skills that have helped to complete it can be noted, and to note them helps to show us how meaning is born and what meaning to look for and where.

I am not speaking of such meanings as can be entirely found out by consulting dictionaries and learned notes, but of that sense of unknowns newly comprehended (unknowns like love, envy, fear of death, forgiveness, renewal, magnanimity, etc.) through the sense-images of sight and sound created to embody them, as well as in words and their penumbra of suggestion that goes beyond all dictionaries.

The elements in the experience of a play that I have been discussing (vision, meaning, joy, timelessness, unity) combine in a total engagement of the imagination, with all else ousted from consciousness (our comfort, discomfort, neighbours in the theatre, our personal affairs, etc.); so that a relationship with the play is created which resembles the relationship between friends, a thou-and-me relationship, like that described by Montaigne when attempting to give the explanation for his affinity with Etienne de la Boétie: *Parceque c'était lui, parceque c'était moi.*

There are those who say that seeing is believing: Coleridge, on the other hand, speaks of 'that suspension of disbelief which constitutes poetic faith'.[1] I would rather wish to say that to enter into the imagination is to go beyond belief and disbelief into a region where it would be truer to say 'seeing is being' or 'seeing is becoming', at least during the timeless act of contemplation.[2]

When we listen to a symphony, hearing is being; or when we feel ourselves held by a painting, nothing else (for that moment) exists in our consciousness, and I do not find it misleading to describe the experience as one in which the self becomes the shapes and colours of sound, the shapes and colours of pigment; for it is an experience of knowing oneself in those terms and what they can signify, and (at that instant) in no other. It is true that this profound attention cannot be easily or long sustained, but it is the real thing, the thing we should always hope for and perhaps attempt to achieve by conscious effort. This is how art can be said to teach, for it reshapes us in accordance with a pervasive meaning and knowledge of value, and a joy in these.

The experience, at its most successful, always has the character of unity, of a prime number. It is indivisibly known in the whole synthesis of its supposed parts; these parts can only be taken in isolation by ceasing to imagine and by returning to critical discussion; for although they do not exist as parts in the imagination, they can in history. Critical attention may take stock of them by speaking historically; for there was a time when the sources of a play were still undiscovered by Shakespeare, and some of these can be sometimes known in their undiscovered state and compared with his plays. To watch their conversion, one might say their disappearance, into the new unity of a work of art is profoundly interesting; it is to follow craftsmanship to the brink of vision itself, and to 'throw light on the process of artistic Making'.[1]

I do not think this can be seen in the case of *Pericles*; the unity supplied by Gower is factitious, imposed from outside; many themes have been sensed in the play; resurrection, the mystical union between child and parent; life seen as a voyage over strange seas and through many a storm, that ends in reconciliation and divine showing forth; chastity as natural and all-subduing, in contrast with unnatural defilement, and how Heaven deals with these. But I do not think it can be said that they coalesce into a single experience of meaning of the kind I have tried to describe as especially Shakespearean; the conversation of common soldiers and very grave-diggers in *Hamlet* is pregnant with its major themes—the rottenness of Denmark, the pocky corpses; the theme of death itself and judgment, which supply macabre jesting over Ophelia and her grave, and which also preoccupy Hamlet in soliloquy. But this inweaving I cannot find in *Pericles*; the fishermen, for instance, that bring up armour out of the sea for the Prince, talk like fishermen, it is true, in the convention of peasant-comedy and make their usual jokes; but they say nothing to the purpose. Indeed they contradict themselves, for whereas their talk is about the likeness between fish and men:

The great ones eate vp the little ones   (II, i, 28)

yet they are presently saying to Pericles that their good King Simonides deserves to be so called for his peaceable reign and good government.

Though *Pericles* lacks pervasive unity, *A Midsummer Night's Dream* is a masterpiece of interweaving; the major theme is omnipresent, all the actions cohere, the fable in outline moves towards what the whole celebrates, the imagery creates and sustains the atmosphere, and at the end we reach a profoundly completed harmony of all classes of men in nature, with a blessing spoken upon it. It is an entire entertainment that deepens into a ritual out of gravity, comedy and farce; the world of the play is delicately united with the world of the audience at their natural meeting-place in the imagination, as well as in natural superstitions and in the most natural of human wishes, for happy love and fair posterity.

Let us begin our consideration of it by reaffirming Lamb's assertion that inspiration is not 'made up of parts': if its operation can be described at all, it may be said to be made up of timeless impulses and intuitions, moments of sudden creative discernment, such as can happen in dreams; it is not at all a process of assemblement by some mechanical or jigsaw method, though it can be polished and adjusted by taking thought, that is, by intellectual activity that does not need to wait on inspiration.

Shakespeare achieved a synthesis by means unimaginable to us who are not Shakespeare; but we, in tracing his sources are attempting an opposite process, of analysis; and because of this it is natural and convenient to think in terms of parts that we are able to separate out and discuss. By doing this we may come to the edge of the gulf that separates analysis from synthesis and (though it is impassable) look across a little further to the other side.

What we shall see, or at least what I shall try to show, is the *coalescence* of a number of entirely different works of literature, known to Shakespeare, and especially of two, as different in substance as they are in quality and genre, namely *The Knight's Tale* by Geoffrey Chaucer and *John a Kent and John a Cumber*, by Antony Mundy.[1]

It is easier to begin with Mundy than with Chaucer, because Mundy's work is a play, and so provides the kind of medium or vehicle of play-structure which a narrative poem does not. But before we can examine this structure there is another problem to consider; it is a matter of dates.

In a convincing article called *The Significance of a Date*,[2] Mr Shapiro has argued that *John a Kent and John a Cumber* should not be ascribed to the year 1595, as it was by Collier, nor to 1596, as it was by Greg, but to 1589. The manuscript, which is in Mundy's hand and signed by him, bears a date in another hand, written in a different ink: the date, under magnification, reveals itself as 1590. Shapiro assigns the composition of the play to a date 'not later than August 1589'. From this new reading, he has drawn some swift but cautious conclusions, from which I quote the following:

... Because the antics and malapropisms of Turnop and his companions in *John a Kent* resemble those of Bottom and his fellow-"mechanicals", because the malicious humour of Shrimp seems to reflect that of Puck, and because both plays are primarily concerned with the difficulties and misadventures of two pairs of lovers, it has been argued that *John a Kent* is influenced by, and later than, *A Midsummer Night's Dream*. Unless the date of the latter play is to be pushed back earlier than has hitherto been suggested, we shall have to suppose either that the parallels between the plays are fortuitous, or that Shakespeare may have taken hints from Mundy...

If we 'push back' *A Midsummer Night's Dream* to some time before the new date for *John a Kent* (that is, from 1594/5 to 1589) we topple the structure of Shakespearean chronology that scholarship has so carefully built, and this would be unreasonable. It is, in my opinion, impossible to suppose the parallels to be fortuitous; we are therefore left with the conclusion that Shakespeare, fishing like his contemporaries in the common pool of Elizabethan stage-devices, took these ideas from Mundy, if not from his manuscript, then from some performance of his play.

Mundy in his own days was held to be 'our best plotter': for so Francis Meres calls him in *Palladis Tamia*: he is thought to be 'Poste-haste' in an anonymous lampooning play called *Histriomastix*,[1] revised by John Marston from a version thought to have been given in 1589; and, as a nickname, Post-haste certainly suits him for his work in *John a Kent*: he scatters and squanders his bright notions skimmingly across the surface of his shallow but pleasing play, whereas Shakespeare grafts them to the living tissue or core of what he is showing us. Just as we have seen that Marston took no care, or perhaps did not know how to take care, in the matter of the ghost-under-the-stage motif, whereas Shakespeare linked it organically with his deepest theme of good and evil in revenge, and with the nature of the medium of theatre, so Mundy, the casual Post-haste, did not know how to plant the seeds of his invention; but Shakespeare knew, and, like the trees on railway embankments, the seeds he took from Mundy sent down their roots to make all firm below the surface, while their beauty proliferated above. All this I hope to show in detail: but since Mundy's play is little known, I must first give some account of it.

John a Kent and John a Cumber would, I think, have been many times reprinted, and would have deserved to have been revived, at least for the more experimental audiences of universities, if its manuscript had been complete: but, unhappily, it is damaged: folio 13 is torn across and is in part indecipherable: we have effectively lost the last hundred lines or so of the play. All that can be recovered from it has been printed by Miss St Clare Byrne in her edition for the Malone Society, published in 1923.

The play begins as the story of Sidanen and Marian, niece and daughter of the Earl of Chester: it is the eve of their wedding and they are to be married the following morning to two young nobles, the Earls of Morton and of Pembroke, respectively.

These suitors are their parents' choice, forced upon them against their true inclinations: for Sidanen loves and is beloved by Sir Griffen Meriddock, Prince of South Wales, and Marian loves and is beloved by Lord Geoffrey Powis. From the point of view of the audience, there is nothing to choose between these four young men, whether in virtue, nobility, or in the quality of their affections: but inasmuch as two of them are loved by our heroines, and the other two are the nominees of a tyrannical parent, our sympathies are slanted towards the former and against the latter. Let us call them the True Lovers and the Rivals, for convenience.

The True Lovers, unwilling to gain their loves by force of arms and the use of the private armies they have gathered, engage the services of a famous Welsh magician, John a Kent, to abduct the girls from Chester Castle, where they are immured. The wizard, adopting the disguise of an aged hermit, easily gains admission to the Castle and persuades them and the Countess of Chester that unless they wash their 'lily hands' in 'St Winifred's fair spring' before their wedding, hard fortune will befall them. Quickly convinced of this, the ladies allow John a Kent to lead them off through moonlit woods towards the wishing-well; but instead he leads them to their True Lovers who take them off to a castle of their own.

This abduction having gone without a hitch, John a Kent feels himself a little thwarted: it has all been too easy:

> but must these ioyes so quickly be concluded?
> Must the first Scene make absolute a play?
> no crosse? no chaunge? what? no varietie?   (529–31)

He resolves to make complications for the True Lovers he has just assisted by rousing the Earl of Chester and informing him of their elopement.

So he summons, out of the air, a magic boy or attendant sprite called Shrimp, and sends him off to raise the alarm. Shrimp is by nature full of mischief and has no difficulty in rousing the Earl's household and setting him and his family by the ears. A pursuit of the runaways is ordered.

Meanwhile there appears from Scotland a rival magician called John a Cumber: he is enlisted on the Earl's side. In addition to these, who are the main characters, there is a crew of Clowns, tenants of the Earl, who dodge in and out of the play under the leadership of one Turnop: they have organised themselves into a bucolic reception committee, first to offer a sort of Masque of Welcome to the Rivals and secondly to offer a serenade to the heroines.

The action proper now begins, and what seemed to be a rivalry of lovers now turns into a rivalry of wizards. The love story is advanced and retarded alternately, not for its own interest, but as the motive for the battle of wits fought out between John a Kent and John a Cumber, who use the Lovers and their Rivals, not to mention Turnop and his crew, as pawns in their games with each other. So dizzy does this become that at one point, without a word of warning to the audience, John a Kent enters disguised as John a Cumber, and John a Cumber enters disguised as John a Kent. It is anybody's guess which is which.

At last, at the climax of the fourth act, John a Kent seems finally to have routed his opponent and the cause of true love to have triumphed over that of forced marriage. But, as there is still a whole act to go before the play can end, John a Kent hands the heroines over to John a Cumber and the Earl of Chester, and the contest, for the third if not fourth time, starts all over again.

Needless to say, John a Kent is once more victorious, though precisely how we shall never know, for it is at that point that the manuscript is defective; that it all ends happily for True Love can easily, however, be inferred from what remains of it:

> t]hanke thee Iohn a Kent . . .
>]er, be not thou displeasde,
>]least these amourous cares hath easde.
> t]o be disgraste by thee,
>]r bothe of mine and me.
>]des, and euer more heerafter
>]vow continuall looue.
> f]ortune was not euill,
>]ouermatchte the deuill.
>   *exeunt.*
>]is.   *Anthony Mundy*
>   (Decembris 1590)

The worst, most crushing fault of this composition is that it changes purpose quarter-way through. It starts as a love story, which is a serious thing, and degenerates into a contest of conjurors, which at best is facetious: in spite of Mundy's skill in dialogue, his skill in manipulating the plot and his shower of viable motifs, there is something puerile about it.

Yet although the pranks of magicians have usurped the interest of what might have proved a promising play, *John a Kent* has some elements of a structural kind, well-suited to theatre, that need not have been wasted on such a silly theme. It is a kind of vehicle that could be put to better use, and this is essentially what Shakespeare saw in it, took over and recreated; and being at that time in his most Chaucerian mood,[1] he drew also on Chaucer to do so.

First, however, let us see what he found useful in Mundy. Mundy's most powerful, most naturally realised invention in this play is the rustic reception committee I have mentioned, namely Turnop and his troupe. They appear at the end of Act I:

Enter Turnop wth his crewe of Clownes, & a Minstrell.

This company of comics, tenants to the Earl of Chester, break in upon the play to show their feudal zeal by getting up a Masque of Welcome to his friends and nominees, the Rival Lovers (Lord Morton and Lord Pembroke), on their arrival in Chester. They consist of Turnop himself, Hugh the Sexton, Tom Taberer, Spurling and Robert; the form of entertainment they have devised is a kind of Dumb Crambo with an Oration to follow. For the Dumb Crambo, Spurling is disguised as a *Moor* and carries a *tun*, in delicate compliment to Lord Morton and, by a like visual pun, Robert holds a porringer full of water with a pen in it, in honour of Lord Pembroke (pen/brook). But who is to speak the 'roration', as Hugh the Sexton calls it? Shall it be he or Turnop? That is the subject of their excellent prose dialogue:

> Turnop. Nay neuer talke of it, Hugh the Sexten stutters, let him read the first lyne, or see if he can say the speeche, that dawes our Churchwarden made in prayse of his Mill horsse.
>
> Hugh. It makes no matter, I thinke my selfe the wisest because I am Sexten, and being Sexten, I will say the speeche I made my selfe.
>
> Tom Tabrer. heare ye Hugh, be not so forward, take a little vise of your minstrell.
>
> Omnes. And well sayd Thomas Tabrer, you haue scression, speak on.
>
> Tom. One of the wisest of vs must speak, and either [he] it must be Hugh or Turnop. Now, Hugh is Sexten, an office of retoritie I tell ye.
>
> Turnop. yea, thats when he is in the Belfrie, not else.
>
> Omnes. Hugh, Hugh, Hugh shall speak the speache to the Lordes.
>
> Tom. But Turnop beeing my Lordes man, his hogheard, his familiaritie seruant, he in my minde is not only fit, but also accessary for the ration making, then Turnop say I.
>
> Omnes. Turnop, Turnop, weele haue none but Turnop.   (334-50)

So Turnop it is and he takes command:

> Then let vs set forward, for now it is vppon the Lordes coming. Thomas, firk it with your fiddle. Spurling, you play the Moore, vaunce vp your Tun, and Robert, holde your porrenger right, least you spill the conceit, for heere they come.   (364-7)

The Lords appear and Turnop 'speaketh the Oration' in the manner of Christopher Marlowe:[1]

Lyke to the Cedar in the loftie Sea,
or milke white mast vppon the humble mount. . .   (372–3)

and the Lords respond to it, as Oswen, the Earl's son, bids them,
with courtesy:

> *Oswen.* My Lordes, my fathers tennants after their homely guise,
>   welcome ye with their countrey merriment,
>   How bad so ere, yet must ye needes accept it.
> Pemb. Else Oswen were we very much to blame,
>   thankes gentle freendes, heere drinke this for my sake. . . (389–93)

It is a lively, well-invented scene, very actable: it is built on good
bone. The structure or recipe for it, in analysis, is a troupe of peasants doing a grotesque but seriously intended honour to their
feudal overlord, in the hope of a largesse, on the occasion of a wedding. This is obviously the same comedic structure as that used by
Shakespeare for his 'mechanicals' in *A Midsummer Night's Dream*.
It reappears, with variations, in *Love's Labour's Lost* and *Two Noble
Kinsmen*; but the resemblances are greatest in the first of these;
Oswen's advice to Pembroke, in the passage I have quoted, anticipates what Theseus has to say, though falling short of it in poetry:

> For neuer anything
> Can be amisse, when simplenesse and duty tender it.
> (*Midsummer Night's Dream*, v, i, 82)

At their next incursion into the play, Turnop and his fellows
attempt to repeat their success by serenading Marian and Sidanen.
This time their performance is thrown into confusion by Shrimp,
the imp, who ensorcels their song so that the words they are to sing
are magically changed as they sing them, and give warning to the
Earl of Chester that his niece and daughter have eloped, to join their
lovers. This, in analysis, is the notion or motif of rustic entertainers
interrupted and routed by a mischievous fairy spirit.

After this the Turnop troupe disappears from the main action of
the play until it occurs to John a Cumber to rope them into a 'play
or interlude' he is arranging and in which he means 'to flout, scoff
and scorne at John a Kent': they agree to help him and he promises
to give them 'apt instructions' according to the purpose he intends.

47

However he omits to do so, and even to warn them that he means to disguise himself as John a Kent: so neither they nor the audience know, when the time comes, that it is not John a Kent that they are 'flouting, scoffing and scorning', but John a Cumber, who, hoist by his own petard, has a fool's coat clapped onto him by Turnop and Hugh Sexton: and they dance him off the stage.

This is their last appearance: they never had more than a sketchy connection with the main fable and this detachability allows their exit to oblivion at the end of the fourth act. But if the material has been somewhat wasted, it is good material: a play within a play, performed by clowns, is a good idea, and so is forcing a fool's habit on a dupe, if something more could be made of it, a new twist given to it. Why not, for instance, 'an Asses nole'?

Shrimp is another excellent idea: to speak functionally of him, he is a child-actor playing fairy-servant to a master of magical powers, whose errands cause the 'turbations' of the plot.

Shrimp is used by Mundy in ways that are echoed not only in Puck but also in Ariel: of course he never rises to the poetry of Puck or to the elemental character of Ariel, for Mundy was a mediocre poet with an imagination of more dexterity than range. But he had a theatrically inventive gift, which he used wastefully, like an improviser, or an amateur squandering his flourishes on a charade: he is like a foreigner in drama who does not know the value of the currency.

To make good these criticisms, let us compare the detail of the uses to which this fairy-imp idea is put by Mundy and Shakespeare.

We neither see nor hear anything of Shrimp until the magician, John a Kent, summons him out of nowhere to start up trouble: having succeeded, at the end of the first act, in pairing off the True Lovers, and feeling that his triumph has been too easy, the magician wishes he might have some opponent worthy of himself, to make things more difficult and enable him to stretch his art:

> O that I had some other lyke my selfe,
> to driue me to sound pollicyes indeed. (541–2)

But in default of such an opponent, he must play his game of chequers with himself and the next move must be to rouse the Earl of Chester; so he summons Shrimp to do it for him: it is the first time Shrimp is mentioned:

> But since my selfe must pastime wth my selfe,
> Ile anger them, bee't but to please my selfe.
> Sirra Shrimpe.   Enter Shrimp a boy.
> Shrimp. Anon Sir, what is your will wth me?
> Iohn. Thus Sirra. To Chester get ye gon,
> They are yet asleep, that shall be wakte anon.
> Shrimp. I goe sir.   *exeunt* seuerally. (547–53)

At his first appearance, then, Shrimp flashes on and off, with nothing to explain who he is or where he comes from, on an errand only half made clear; the audience, having no previous knowledge of him, has hardly had time to see or to gather what he is. Mundy simply had not thought him out, or given him a place in the cosmos of the play: he is its only supernatural being, and has no context, whether fairy or human, other than the commands of John a Kent. Let us compare Puck.

Puck appears for the first time with an equal suddenness and with his opening question to the First Fairy,

> How now spirit, whether wander you?   (II, i, 1)

he plunges us at once into a full exposition of Oberon's world. In the five and twenty lines that follow, the moon and flower imagery create the world of nature that is tended by fairies, whose stature is suggested by the fact that they think cowslips 'tall', and that they can creep into acorn-cups; we are told of the wrath of Oberon against Titania, and its cause, a little Indian Prince. The information is swiftly given, specific yet mysterious; we are scarcely aware that this is *exposition* because it is also *action*; Puck has come to clear a way for Oberon's arrival; Titania must not come within his sight. The dialogue has the double function of expounding and furthering the plot in the fairy world; complete in itself, yet it has connection with the world of the audience, through its theft of the little human Prince from the most distant, opulent and mysterious of continents, India. We are now fully prepared for the entry of Oberon and Titania:

but Shakespeare delays it, because there is another job to be done first: we have a context of Titania and her Fairy, but what of Puck? Oberon and Titania must wait for another twenty lines of necessary exposition: we learn that Puck is the knavish spirit that frightens the girls of the village: he is Oberon's Jester, who whinnies to horses, or, in the likeness of a three-foot stool, slips from the bum of a wise aunt telling her most serious story. This is more than exposition, more than anecdote and amusement for us: just as Oberon and his anger have been tethered to the most fabulous palaces of our audience-world by the gossamer thread of the little Indian Prince, so Puck and his mischief are tethered to the homeliest cottages of Athens, one might say of England, and the fields about them, by familiar folklore. The fairy world of the play and the homely world of the audience grow together at their meeting place in the mirror of imagination. The remote and the invisible are brought to our doors.

So powerfully creative is the poetry of the fifty lines I have been discussing that we cannot think easily of their technical function until we pause and force ourselves to do so: the comparison with Shrimp makes clear Shakespeare's professional mastery as a playwright.

Shrimp improves upon acquaintance, though we never learn more of him than is strictly necessary for the immediate conduct of the play: Puck of course spills over and, like all good art, is far more than functional: unless we say he has the function of plenitude. Yet Shrimp is lively and sufficient in merriness and mischief: he can wriggle through keyholes:

> Sirra, get ye to the back gate of the Castell,
> and through the key hole quickly wring thee in . . .
> Shrimp. I fly Sir, and am there alreadie   *exit* boy. (983–99)

and he has a Puck-like exultation:

> Why now is Shrimpe in the height of his brauery
> that he may execute some parte of his maisters knauery.
>
> (577–8)

and we get the stage-direction

Enter Shrimpe skipping.   (1011-12)

He is entering to announce the performance of a play, as Puck
enters to Oberon (*Midsummer Night's Dream*, III, ii, 9):

> Sir, yonder's great preparation for a play,
> which by the shaddowes of the Lordes and Ladyes,
> heer on the greene shall foorthwith be enacted.   (1013-15)

Shrimp must have lived a long time at the back of Shakespeare's
memory, for there is some of him in Ariel too: he can lead people
by an invisible music and charm them asleep, a beautiful device of
theatre: the fourth act begins:

> Enter Shrimp playing on some instrument, a pretty way befo[
> the Countesse, *Sydanen*, *Marian*, *Oswen* and *Amerye*.
> *Oswen*. Madame, this sound is of some instrument

In a similar situation, Trinculo remarks:

> This is the tune of our Catch, plaid by the picture of No-body.
>   (III, ii, 121)

Later, Shrimp and his victims are thus directed in the text:

> The boy trips round about *Oswen* and *Amery*, sing[
> chyme, and they the one after the other, lay them[
> vsing very sluggish gestures, the Ladyes amazed[
> about them.   (1145)

This is a well-found visual and musical effect: unfortunately
Mundy was too pleased with it and repeated it in the very next
scene: once again the wretched Oswen and Amery are led in by the
unseen musician and kept circling round a tree until they can hold
up no longer:

> Enter Shrimpe leading *Oswen* and *Amery* about the tree.
> *Oswen*. were euer men thus led about a Tree?
> still circkling it, and neuer getting thence?
> My braynes doo ake, and I am growen so faynt,
> that I must needes lye downe on meere constrynt.
>   he lyes do[
> *Amery* This villayne boy is out of doubt some spirit,

still he cryes follow, but we get no further . . .
In all my life I neuer was so wearie.
follow that list, for I can goe no longer.

        he lyes down[

        (1395–1402)

In addition to his carelessness with ideas, Mundy has this fault of repeating them: John a Kent begins by disguising himself as an old hermit, later he disguises himself as John a Cumber: John a Cumber disguises himself as John a Kent: the Earl of Chester and his faction disguise themselves as Antics. Twice John a Kent, and once John a Cumber achieve total victory over each other, and each time the contest is made to start all over again, with baffling tediousness. Turnop and his gang are used three times for like purposes—an address of welcome, a serenade, an interlude: Shrimp, as we have noted, has only one trick that we are allowed to see, namely the trick of becoming an invisible musician to lead the enemy astray and leave it exhausted. In none of these adventures and manipulations is there any inward logic or compulsion: they remain teasing tricks.

Yet evidently the play bristles with lively notions, apt to the medium of theatre and easy to re-work into other fables: let us attempt to list them.

Lovers in flight from parental opposition to their love.
Moonlit woods through which they flee to join their lovers.
A mischievous fairy imp, in service to a master of magic.
A crew of clowns who organise buffoonish entertainments, in honour of their territorial overlord, on the occasion of a double wedding. Contention for the leading part. Malapropisms.
Young men led by an invisible voice until they fall exhausted.
A 'happy ending' with True Lovers properly paired and wedded.

All these notions in combination make a dramatic vehicle, a *schema*;[1] they supply a main shape or formula for a stage-action that does not need a contention of conjurers to keep it moving, since the lovers themselves will supply conflict enough on the way to their concluding nuptials. The magical element that in Mundy properly belongs, in the person of Shrimp, to one of the conjurors, can exist in its own right in moon-lit woods such as Mundy invented but made no use of. So can characters like Turnop.

It was love that Mundy's play lacked; he had two pairs of lovers, but nothing to say of their condition. Here it was that Shakespeare's reading in Chaucer brought invention to him; it poured in from *The Canterbury Tales* and the *Legend of Good Women* in all its freshness, beauty, tangle, farce and gravity. In Chaucer, Theseus had married Hippolyta,

> With muchel glorie and greet solempnytee
> > *(Knight's Tale, 12)*

and the notion is taken up by Shakespeare at the opening and close of his play. Theseus is to celebrate his wedding

> with pompe, with triumph, and with revelling.   (i, i, 19)

The 'solempnytee' is to last a fortnight:

> A fortnight hold we this solemnity.
> In nightly Reuels; and new iollitie.   (v, i, 358–9)

From the *Knight* in the *Prologue* and from his *Tale* steps forth also Duke Theseus, heroic, humane, magnanimous and sardonic, mature in love and yet indulgent to beginners at it, authoritative, considerate to his inferiors, kindly spoken, taking the will for the deed. He is the only character Shakespeare took over whole from Chaucer: for Troilus, Pandarus and Cressida have suffered change: but Theseus, in Chaucer as in Shakespeare, is a piece of warm greatness and stability, the unmoved mover of the human side of both stories.

Yet, something else clung to the name of Theseus in Shakespeare's memory: he had read North's rendering of Plutarch, where he found a rather different account of him: Plutarch is comparing him with Romulus (my italics):

Theseus faults touching women and ravishments, . . . had the lesse shadowe and culler of honestie. Bicause Theseus dyd attempt it very often: *for he stale away Ariadne, Antiope* and Anaxo the Troezenian. . . . *Romulus nowe in a contrarie manner, . . . chaunged this violent force of ravishement*, into a most perfect bonde and league of amitie. . . Furthermore, time hath geven a good testimonie of the love, reverence,

53

constancie, kyndeness, and *all matrimoniall offices that he established* . . .
betwext man and wife. . .[1]

These useful accusations of 'ravishment' Shakespeare retained for
Oberon's anger with Titania, whom he rebukes for loving Theseus;
it is his retort to her insinuation about 'the bouncing Amazon',
Hippolyta:

> Didst thou not leade him through the glimmering night
> From *Peregenia,* whom he rauished?
> And make him vvith faire Eagles breake his faith
> With *Ariadne,* and *Antiopa?* (II, i, 77–80)

In doing this, Shakespeare lightly linked the world of the court of
Theseus to the court of Oberon, while repudiating the charge of
'ravishing' as the forgery of jealousy. But the solid virtues of
Romulus, establisher of matrimonial bonds, Shakespeare trans-
ferred to Theseus the ravisher, as more fitting to Chaucer's Theseus,
perhaps, and to the fable forming in his own mind. To this North
may have made another contribution:

> . . . Yet for all that, he [Theseus] suffered not the great multitude that
> came thither tagge and ragge, to be without *distinction of degrees and or-*
> *ders.* For *he first divided the noble men, from the husbandmen and artificers.* . .[2]

Here was sounded a feudal note that harmonised as well with
Chaucer's Theseus as with Turnop, whose interlude could be used
to grace these 'matrimonial offices' ascribed to Romulus.

It must, as in Mundy, be something preposterous, of course; it
must have the Turnop touch: but instead of pictorial puns and a
'roration', Shakespeare found what he wanted in Chaucer once
again: of course he could have got it from Ovid and other places,
but I think as Chaucer was in his hand, he may have found it there,
in *The Legend of Good Women,* which retells the whole story of
Pyramus and Thisbe; or perhaps he took the suggestion from *The*
Merchant's Tale:

> By Piramus and Tesbee may men leere;
> Thogh they were kept ful longe streite overal,
> They been accorded, rownying thurgh a wal. . .
>
> (*Merchant's Tale,* 884–6)

for it is in *The Merchant's Tale* that we find another motif—the motif of a dispute between the King and Queen of Fairyland, whom Chaucer calls Pluto and Proserpine, but Shakespeare Oberon and Titania. For the name of Oberon, he had a journey to make into other regions of memory or reading: it comes in Lord Berners' *Huon of Bordeaux*, in the twentieth chapter (my italics):

When Huon heard Gerames, then he demaunded further of him if he could goe to *Babilon*. Yes, sir, (quoth Gerames) I can goe thether by two wayes . . . but I councell you to take the longe way, for if you take the shorter way, you must passe thorow a wood about sixteene leagues of length, but *the way is so full of Fayryes* and strange things, that such as passe that way are lost, for *in that wood abideth a King of the Fayryes named Oberon*. . .

How are we to imagine this figure that, in some fluid way, seems to have identified itself in Shakespeare's mind with Chaucer's Fairy King Pluto, in dispute with Prosperpine? It is a tenuous link: let us lay Berners' account of Oberon beside what we know of him from Shakespeare:

he is of height but of three foote, and crooked shouldered, but yet *he hath an Angell-like visage*, . . . and if he see that you will not speake a word unto him, then he will be sore displeased with you, and before you can get out of the wood, *he will cause raine and wind, hayle and snowe, and will make marvelous tempests, with thunder and lightenings, so that it shall seeme unto you that all the world should perish*. . .[1]

Here are many things of interest: the crooked shoulders and the anger at not being spoken to are forgotten or ignored, but the dimension of three feet gives us something of the scale of Shakespeare's fairies—the enamelled skins of snakes are wide enough to wrap fairies in—and that, taken with the angel-face, suggests a child-actor for Oberon; perhaps the entire fairy world in this play was played, in Shakespeare's day, by children; to do so was well within the medium of Elizabethan theatre, and the capacity of its child-actors.

All that is certain, however, is the name, and the power over the forces of nature associated with the Fairy King. The rains and tempests, the threatened ruin of a world, become the signs of Oberon's dispute with Titania over the Indian boy, and are further linked with Shakespeare's first audiences by their recent memories of the disastrous floods of 1594: so when Titania yields the boy to Oberon, as she does in her infatuation with Bottom, the way is clear for a restored harmony in nature, that will bless the human marriage-bed with increase:

> To the best Bride-bed will we,
> Which by us shall blessed be:
> And the issue there create,
> Euer shall be fortunate:
> So shall all the couples three,
> Euer true in louing be...　　　　　　　　(v, i, 392–7)

So the forces of nature enter into the *solempnitee* of human marriage.

The three worlds of woodland, court and audience are in these ways profoundly interwoven: there remains the Turnop world of Bottom the Weaver to consider.

The link between the Mechanicals and the court of Theseus is an axiom of feudality: loyalty earns largesse. But how were the Mechanicals to be linked with the fairy kingdom? That they could somehow be taken over by the forces of magic is the notion present in *John a Kent*; the Clowns are involved with Shrimp and, later, with John a Cumber, but their involvements are casual. Those of the Mechanicals are organic, not only because their actions are more cunningly interlaced with the other actions in the play, but because of their relationship to the theme at its core—romantic love. It is their function to embody its fantastic and farcical aspects, its infatuations and heroics.

Bottom's adventure with Titania, like his impersonation of Pyramus, may also have been prompted by Chaucer; his most preposterous character, Sir Thopas, had just such a dream as Bottom had:[1]

> Me dremed al this nyght, pardee,
> An elf-queene shal my lemman be
> And sleep under my goore.
> 　　　　　　　　(*Tale of Sir Thopas*, 77–9)

It is thus that Bottom is linked in depth with the fairy world: not simply part of a conjuror's prank, as Turnop is in *John a Kent*, but as the chief instrument for the restoration of concord in the world of nature; for that is how the 'translation' of Bottom by an ass-head works upon the story; he is the root of reconciliation as Oberon perceives:

> Ile to my Queene, and beg her *Indian* Boy;
> And then I will her charmed eie release
> From monsters view, and all things shall be peace.
>
> (III, ii, 375–7)

Perhaps we have enough considered these fluid echoes and elements of coalescence that seem to have united, at various levels, in the huge context of Shakespeare's memory, conscious and unconscious, ready to arise in his imagination unified and dovetailed, either of their own accord, or when he willed them to do so. It does not seem possible to get much nearer by this road to the processes of his dramaturgy: yet it is possible to represent the action of that mysterious inner logic in terms of some axioms of his comedy.

Very early in his career, a 'comedy' came to mean, for Shakespeare, a love-story: fresh from his first creations in comic form, *The Comedy of Errors*, *Two Gentlemen of Verona* and *Love's Labour's Lost*, he knew it was safe to plot a play on the mutual loves of Jack and Jill. This was his democracy of love: one man, one girl; from the first, whatever the turbations on the way, Shakespeare's firm comic formula was:

> *Iacke* shall haue *Iill*, nought shall goe ill...
> (*Midsummer Night's Dream*, III, ii, 461)

For that is romantic love, and odd man out is not.

But in *John a Kent* there are four Jacks and two Jills: so two Jacks must go hungry, and that is not happy, therefore not comic. In *The Knight's Tale* there are two Jacks to one Jill; so one Jack has to die, and that is not comic either.

The coming together of *John a Kent* and *The Knight's Tale* made these odds all even: the four indistinguishable young lovers of the former melted into two, and were renamed Lysander and Demetrius. Sidanen and Marian, being a pair, took over from the solitary Emilya and were called Hermia and Helena. As in *John a Kent* we know which pair out of the four lovers to back, because we know which way the girls' affections have gone forth; so in the *Dream*, and for the same reason, we know from the beginning which man is marked out for which girl, and because Lysander is Hermia's choice and Demetrius Helena's, that is how we wish it to be; for a second axiom of Shakespeare's comedy is that love sees most clearly through the eyes of a girl; and a corollary is that no nice girl, after choosing her lover, changes her choice.

We, in the audience, are unconsciously persuaded of these axioms too, if only for the purposes of the play, and upon that persuasion is built our enjoyment of the turbations in the loves of Lysander and Demetrius. When the possible permutations have been completed, Puck leads them back into their proper pairs, ready for the great solempnitee, into which the entire cosmos of the play is logically integrated: for had not Theseus planned his feast, Bottom would never have gone to the woods: and had he never gone to the woods, Oberon would never have been reconciled with Titania: and had they not been reconciled, the forces of nature would still have been at war and the new amity would never have come about that brought Oberon and Titania to

> Dance in Duke *Theseus* house triumphantly,
> And blesse it to all faire posterity. (IV, i, 86–7)

And thus the ducal succession in Athens is partly the work of Bottom. Bottom is a weaver.

Let us now look at the *solemnitas* itself: we have noted how Posthaste Mundy, relying on his ingenuity, had no compunction in working his tricks over and over again: they were not related in any organic way to his fable, for the fable itself has no central core or theme to give them unified vitality. But with Shakespeare every climax is new and rises directly from the deepest theme in the play and its relation to the audience.

Love we see as gravity in Theseus, as comedy in Demetrius and Lysander, as wild fantasy and dream in Bottom, as the harmony of nature in Oberon and Titania: it has still to be seen as farce; and that is best kept for the end, for it will make the easier stepping-stone from the ridiculous to the sublime at the close. Shakespeare chose it for the subject of the Interlude that we have seen in rehearsal from the start, *Pyramus and Thisbe*: but what we see performed in the last act bears no resemblance to the text of the play as it was rehearsed in the woods: it appears to have been entirely re-written by Quince at the last moment. Likelihood has been rightly sacrificed to the surprise of fresh invention. The play is a roaring success and is crowned with a Bergomask: as the dance ends, the Solemnity concludes with the heavy stroke of midnight:

> The iron tongue of midnight hath told twelue.
> Louers to bed ...   (v, i, 352)

Any other playwright in the world would have stopped here, and if Shakespeare had done so, he would still have written the most delicate, poetical and unified comedy in our language: but he went on, for there were more linkages to express in this world of his creation. For as the lovers had all gone out from the palace into nature, so now, on their return, nature follows them in from the woods to the palace, and the fairy troupe surprises them with nature's blessing: here is true insight into the use of a medium, a schema. Nothing is forgotten, all the motifs unite in one central thing and theme:

> *With this field dew consecrate,*
> *Euery Fairy take his gate,*
> *And each seuerall chamber blesse,*
> *Through this Pallace with sweet peace ...*   (v, i, 404-7)

Yet there is still the audience-world to have their participation in the experience acknowledged; so Puck, as familiar in a palace as in a cottage with his broom, speaks the Epilogue, last of Shakespeare's surprises, and tells the audience to think the whole dream was *theirs*: this is not stage-craft but audience-craft:

> Thinke ...
> That you haue but slumbred heere,
> While these visions did appeare.

And this weake and idle theame,
No more yeelding but a dreame...

It may be thought that the figure of Theseus has been somewhat left out of our count: but although he is little on stage he is central: to him is given the great speech on the imagination towards which the whole play moves and by which it is to be understood: for by it all the fantasies of the play are seen to be the imagery of a poet bodying forth the forms of things unknown.[1] That unknown thing is love and the images show it to be the holy bond of things, as Chaucer calls it.[2] So, at the heart's core of the play there is a moral vision of the fantasy, mystery and constancy of things hymeneal, of an epithalamy, in which all things concur and are interlocked in our human society in the bond of love under the fantastic hand of nature. Some six years before, George Puttenham had summed all this in the twenty-sixth chapter of the first book of his *Arte of English Poesie*, and perhaps there could be no clearer statement of Shakespeare's theme and intention:

...Wherefore the Ciuill Poet could do no lesse in conscience and credit, then as he had before done to the ballade of birth, now with much better deuotion to celebrate by his poeme the chearefull day of mariages aswell Princely as others, for that hath alwayes bene accompted with euery countrey and nation of neuer so barbarous people the highest & holiest of any ceremonie apperteining to man; a match forsooth made for euer and not for a day, a solace prouided for youth, a comfort for age, a knot of alliance & amitie, indissoluble: great reioysing was therefore due to such a matter and to so gladsome a time . . . and they were called *Epithalamies*, as much to say ballades at the bedding of the bride...

CHAPTER III

JUXTAPOSITION OF SCENES

JUXTAPOSITION, in fine: and what is juxtaposition?

(Amours de Voyage, VI, Arthur Hugh Clough.)

A chapter to show some of the effects achieved by Shakespeare in disposing the sequence of his scenes.

Whatever may seem arbitrary or haphazard in the plan of a Shakespeare play commonly derives from his habit of taking a story for his structure, sometimes two or even three stories, and running them abreast or tandem. Though it often makes for an appearance of careless untidiness, action with him is always paramount; theme, character, discourse and imagery[1] (to take them in the order of their dramatic importance) all issue from the intrinsic shape and quality of the story as, after some meditation, he had come to conceive it. The narrative is the *donné* and the succession of scenes is determined by Shakespeare's basic skill as a story-teller.

In all the stories he chose to dramatise, the corporate structure of a whole society is always indicated. Even in his most hurried, most parochial play, *The Merry Wives of Windsor*, the entire borough is somehow embroiled in the amours of Sir John; and the Histories, crowded as they are with high personages and affairs of state, make time for their Bulcalfs, their Warts, their drawers, gardeners, porters, grooms and citizens, and can find place for the consciences of common soldiers, and even of common murderers.

The multiplicity of scenes, long or little, that results from these working habits of his imagination, seems to observe no law but that of the time sequence; they are as unpredictable in number as they are variable in mood and milieu, and pass from one group of characters to another, and from place to place, as he pursues his story on its several levels. To minds nurtured in the *liaison des scènes* this is chaos; certainly such a way of composition forfeits the unrelenting tension of a more classical style, such as we experience in *Oedipus* or in *Phèdre*. These are not narrative-plays in the sense that Shakespeare's are, but depict a situation out of the inner logic of which the catastrophe unfolds itself.

Yet there are other effects of power that are made possible by Shakespeare's profusions; though his scenes seem to follow on each other by random frog-jumps from one tussock in the story to another, there is often a concealed art in his choice of the tussock on which next to alight. A good example may be found in *Julius Caesar*, where we find the murder of Cinna the poet immediately followed by the first meeting of the Triumvirs. When he was plotting the play, he must have read of the lynching of Cinna twice, once in the life of Julius Caesar, once in the life of Brutus, as North tells them. He also came upon the story of the Triumvirate proscriptions twice, once in the life of Brutus, once in that of Mark Antony. The life of Brutus is the only one that has both incidents, and in it they are well separated.

Yet, when Shakespeare came to write his play, he picked these incidents out and set them together, as if both were the immediate consequences of the assassination of Caesar. First we see and hear a frenzied mob tearing a poet to pieces; then, instantly after, we see and hear the mob's three masters, quietly at work upon their own murdering, but coldly and judiciously. To gain this contrast he had to make a horizontal jump in time and a vertical jump in the social scale. The result is more than swift story-telling, it is a demonstration in morals and politics. A whole society is cracked open before our eyes and laid on the table like a rotten nut, plebs and patricians, side by side. It is an epiphany of Rome in forty lines.

Look here upon this picture, and on this is a thought silently present in many such a juxtaposition of scenes; they comment upon each other, mutely. Let us take other instances. In *The Merchant of Venice* we hear Jessica say she is ashamed to be her father's child; we see her disobey him, rob him and leave him. In all these things she calls for our sympathy, and we accord it to her, yet with a tug of reluctance: we wish her to leave him, yet we think the less of her for doing so. A moment later we are watching Portia submit herself to the caprices of her father's will, while Morocco hovers round the caskets; she too has our sympathy with that touch of reluctance; we wish her to obey, yet we also wish her to follow her heart in love and to break free from her father, like Jessica; but we think the more of her that she does not. The scenes echo each other in reverse and the ethos of Venice is silently paired and compared with that of Belmont.

An example of like subtlety, but more complexity, opens *Twelfth Night*. Here Shakespeare has three delicate differentiations in melancholy to establish—Orsino's, Viola's and Olivia's. A glance at his sources (if such they can be called when he has so greatly altered and enriched them) shows that he invented these several sorts of melancholy to endow and distinguish his characters with: then he set them side by side for us to judge them. The play begins with the love-melancholy of Orsino, musical, flowery, full of changes, nurtured by private instrumentalists and herbaceous borders, a safe, comfortable melancholy which he indulges, embellishes and exaggerates: he is proud of it.

Against this mood, which in its own way is genuine and beautiful enough, luxurious though it be, is instantly set the starker grief of Viola for her lost brother, drowned, as she fears, in the storm from which she herself has barely escaped and which has left her wrecked on doubtfully hospitable shores. Her recognition and reunion with this lost brother is to be the climax of the play.

Lastly there is Olivia's assumption of grief, also for a lost brother. But, for all the mourning rings and black mantillas she may wear, her sorrows are a sham, as we are meant gradually to perceive. The first hint we get is from Sir Toby; he cannot understand this obstinate ostentation:

What a plague meanes my Neece to take the death of her brother thus? I am sure care's an enemie to life.

It is Feste, however, who breaks the bubble: subtler than Sir Toby, he perceives the true nature of her affectation and, by a stroke of audacity, picks upon it to jest his way back into her favour by submitting it to a quick dose of chop-logic.

Clo. Good Madona, why mournst thou?
Ol. Good foole, for my brothers death.
Clo. I thinke his soule is in hell, Madona.
Ol. I know his soule is in heauen, foole.
Clo. The more foole (Madona) to mourne for your Brothers soule, being in heauen. Take away the Foole, Gentlemen.

This is a joke that no one could have made to Viola in her loss, yet Olivia thinks well of it:

> What thinke you of this foole *Maluolio*, doth he not mend?

for the fact is that her 'veiled walks' and 'eye-offending brine' are tricks for keeping Orsino at arms' length, a courteous way of indicating that he does not attract her: we hear no more of them once she meets Viola; promptly she falls in love and the dead brother is as much forgotten as if he had never been. The juxtaposition of these three melancholies shows us what each is worth in terms of the others. All are weighed, none condemned; but it is Viola's that we take seriously. Meanwhile the comedy has started, as comedy should, in an atmosphere of sadness and anxiety which it will be its business to convert into one of joy, and has prepared us for the carefreedom of Sir Toby and the acuity of Feste.

The first play in which Shakespeare used this principle of juxtaposition throughout is *Henry IV*, Part I. It is the simplest case, the prime example of the method by which a succession of scenes is made to tell a complex story, while their alternation creates a structure of argument that is not concluded until the last act. Because of the simplicity of its design, it is specially rewarding to analyse, not so much to clarify the theme and meaning of the play—for these, perhaps, are not in serious doubt—as to show the principle itself at work.

The play is made out of three contending and contrasted elements all of which we are made to sympathise with, even to admire, in turn. I call them (for convenience) Throne, Tavern and Rebels. They run neck and neck and neck together all through the play. At first sight this seems a purely narrative arrangement, turn and turn about:

ACT I. Throne—Tavern—Rebels.
ACT II. Tavern—Rebels—Tavern.
ACT III. Rebels—Throne—Tavern.
ACT IV. Rebels—Tavern—Rebels.
ACT V. Throne—Rebels—BATTLE.

It might be the serial-story structure of a Dickens novel, with its variations in tempo, locality, groups of character, moods and manners, all jostling the story along. But soon we sense something more than narrative in the organisation of these scenes, we are made to feel their complex bearings on each other and we notice interwoven passages of commentary made by the contenders upon each other, both explicitly and by implication.[1]

The King comments on the glory of Hotspur and the dishonour of Hal. Hotspur comments upon the 'ingrate and canker'd Bolingbroke' and upon 'the sword and buckler Prince of Wales'. Hal comments on Hotspur as 'one who kills me some six or seven dozen of Scots at a breakfast'. Falstaff dresses up as the King, taking a joint-stool for his throne, a dagger for his sceptre, a cushion for his crown. He makes his comment in something like the style of a political cartoon.

So the alternations become alternations of different moral worlds, each irresistible whenever it appears; not one of them is felt to be the enemy, for each claims the sympathy of the audience in virtue of the feelings it can rouse in it—the loyalty and compassion called for by the King, the violence and chivalry that Hotspur communicates, and the priceless explosions of laughter that Falstaff touches off. So we are cajoled into backing each horse in turn, as it takes its momentary lead, and feel the call of Rule, of Riot and of Rebellion, ready to cast our vote for each as it solicits us.

Soon we are made aware that these three elements meet in a single word, in terms of which the whole play is planned. The word, of course, is *Honour*, and it is given to Falstaff to pose the crucial question: 'What is Honour?' The answer to this question is gradually and dramatically revealed; the argument is at last clinched by an enacted *exemplum*; we are *shown* honour. The obvious narrative structure has embodied a secret dialectic.

F   65

But before we reach this point, there is a fourth element of which our analysis must take note. Inwoven in the play, like the passages of comment that each group makes upon the others, there is a chilling reminder of times past. The ghost of Richard II stalks through it as formidably as the ghost in *Hamlet*. He casts the shadow of unforgettable guilt that darkens equally the minds of the King and of the Rebels, and will indeed stretch far beyond Shrewsbury to the eve of Agincourt itself, to lay a cold finger on Hal's heart too:

> Not to day, O Lord,
> O not to day, thinke not vpon the fault
> My Father made, in compassing the Crowne.
> I *Richards* body haue interred new,
> And on it haue bestowed more contrite teares,
> Then from it issued forced drops of blood.   (IV, i, 288–93)

But now, before Shrewsbury, it is Hal's father who is oppressed by that memory: he feels himself punished for it in his son, to whom he confesses it, pointing out the terrible similarities, the apparent repetitions of history:

> And then I stole all Courtesie from Heauen,
> And drest my selfe in such Humilitie,
> That I did plucke Allegeance from mens hearts,
> Euen in the presence of the Crowned King.
> > (*1 Henry IV*, III, ii, 50–4)
> For all the World,
> As thou art to this houre, was *Richard* then,
> When I from France set foot at Rauenspurgh;
> And euen as I was then, is *Percy* now: . . .
> He hath more worthy interest to the State
> Then thou, the shadow of Succession. . .   (III, ii, 93–8)

The King, in his time, has been a rebel himself; the rebels are also thinking of the part they played at Ravenspurgh:

> He presently, as Greatnesse knowes it selfe,
> Steps me a little higher then his Vow
> Made to my Father, while his blood was poore,
> Vpon the naked shore at Rauenspurgh: . . .

In short time after, hee depos'd the King.
Soone after that, depriu'd him of his Life:

(IV, iii, 74–7 and 90–1)

Hotspur is speaking, making what case he can against the usurper, but the guilt is lodged in his soul too. So it comes about that Hotspur's honour and Henry's honour and Hal's stand rooted in dishonour. But for all that, as the fifth act will show us, Hal's honour comes nearest but one to the truest honour shown us in the play—that of Sir Walter Blunt.

When at last we reach the battle we will find that Shakespeare has planned it as a succession of single encounters, each of which presents its own comment on the basic theme; in order that we may have no doubts as to what honour is and who has it, we are first given the paradigm to contemplate in the integrity of Sir Walter's behaviour. Shakespeare has quietly groomed him for this demonstration by showing him as a peacemaker on his earlier appearances (I, iii, 70 and IV, iii, 30). His 'deservings and good name' are openly envied by Hotspur (IV, iii, 35). This should warn us that Sir Walter is also to bear a part in the argument of honour.

It is he who is chosen to open the battle of Shrewsbury: disguised as the King, so as to draw the King's danger upon himself, he meets with the Douglas and dies at his hands without revealing, or even hinting at his own identity: his sacrifice is as selfless as it is unostentatious in its loyalty. Presently in comes Falstaff; all that he can see in this noble death is a confirmation of his own philosophy:

there's Honour for you: (v, iii, 31)

And so it is indeed, high honour; it turns Falstaff's jibe against himself.

Presently it is Falstaff's turn to meet the Douglas: true to his code, with a hilarious buffoonery, he falls down and shams dead: the juxtaposition could hardly be more tellingly presented, and lest the irresistible laughter it occasions should incline us too much to Falstaff's side, when he rises from his position of preposterous indignity, he gores the body of Hotspur to give colour to his claim that he has overcome him in battle. Who can avoid the thought 'There's

Falstaff for you!'? His views on honour have been shown to be those of a buffoon, of an old, *je-m'en-foutiste* rapscallion, beyond honour, beyond cowardice, beyond mortal respect, unquenchably comic as he is. He may not have honour, but he has fun.

Of Hotspur's honour the play has given us many foretastes before we see it in action. It is of the kind that can be taken from him by defeat, as children playing conkers take the total of its victories from a defeated conker and add it to the victor's total. It is a showy kind of honour while it is worn, and it breeds boasting. We heard no boasting from Sir Walter Blunt; he merited his name. In contrast we are given this word-battle of glory from Hal and Hotspur:

> I am the Prince of Wales, and thinke not *Percy*,
> To share with me in glory any more:
> Two Starres keepe not their motion in one Sphere,
> Nor can one England brooke a double reigne,
> Of *Harry Percy*, and the Prince of Wales.
> *Hot.* Nor shall it *Harry* for the houre is come
> To end the one of vs; and would to heauen,
> Thy name in Armes, were now as great as mine.
> *Prin.* Ile make it greater, ere I part from thee,
> And all the budding Honors on thy Crest,
> Ile crop, to make a Garland for my head.

This kind of talk, even while it offends modesty, yet has a stirring-power that rouses some archetypal cravings in us all, for it goes back to our earliest poetic of primitive heroism. We find it in *Beowulf*, where one of the finest things that can be said of a man is *bēot he gelǣste*—he fulfilled his boast, he was as good as his word.[1]

Hal reaps his honour, conker-wise, from Hotspur; but he reaps it more lastingly in other ways, and the last scenes of the play are expressly designed so that he may be seen doing so. He comes off well in honour, second to Sir Walter Blunt. The scenes are arranged so that he is heard to rebuke Falstaff for trifling in battle; though wounded we see him decline help and respite; he protects the King his father from the Douglas, driving him off in flight: he even allows Falstaff the 'honour' of his own victory over Hotspur:

> For my part, if a lye may do thee grace,
> Ile gil'd it with the happiest tearmes I haue. (v, iv, 156–7)

His last act is to allow the Douglas to be delivered from his captivity, 'ransomlesse and free', in recognition of his valour and 'high deeds'. These things show him to have generosity and humour as well as filial feeling, patriotism and soldiership; his courage, of course, has never been in doubt. The three contending elements have thus been steered into a final clash where each gives the right measure of the others in a perfectly designed exhibition of contrasts in honour, the theme that is sounded at the outset of the play, and thus concludes it.

For the moment, in these last scenes of glory, the ghost of Richard II is allowed no intrusion; it may be, however, that an attentive ear, not easily overwhelmed by heroics, may hear a distant Ricardian laughter through the closing eloquences of the usurper-King: irony is hard to shout down.

> Rebellion in this Land shall lose his way*
> Meeting the Checke of such another day:
> And since this Businesse so faire is done,
> Let vs not leaue till all our owne be wonne.
>
> *[read sway?]

The Second Part of *Henry IV* is less symmetrically shaped, and its multiple themes are less clearly (as they are less easily to be) expressed in terms of simple juxtaposition. This is because of the nature of the story it tells. The First Part, as we have seen, unites its three narrative-elements in a single theme, fully declared and concluded in the contrasted actions in battle that end the play. This makes a shapely unity. But the Second Part, inheriting the elements of Rebellion and Riot, loses the former by the scattering of the rebels in the fourth act, and is forced by the facts of history to reorientate itself to the further but different climax of the coronation of Prince Hal, which has no organic narrative-connection with the actions against the rebels. Moreover, as the rout of the rebels was (in history) achieved by a treacherous betrayal (the blame for which fortunately fell on the cold shoulders of Prince John of

Lancaster), Prince Hal has to be withdrawn from this left-over action, although he is presently to be the play's true protagonist.

He has equally to be withdrawn from the scenes of Riot, to decontaminate him from Falstaff, in preparation for his coronation. For want, therefore, of the unifying presence of the Prince, Riot and Rebellion no longer make the kinds of contrast that can be brought out by juxtaposition: they simply alternate in the telling of the story. To sharpen the contrast that is to come at the end of the play between Riot and Rule, the sluttish felonies of Riot are more strongly presented, as has often been noted. We see Falstaff in cadging penury, drunkenness, whore-mastery, tavern-brawling and gross abuse of the press-gang. His parasitical interest in, rather than his love of, the Prince is stressed. Of course he remains as fat, as funny and as irrepressibly delightful as ever, even while we perceive him to be more than ever at home in the deepening dirt of his scenes; he even develops an endearing whore-house courage in defence of Doll Tearsheet; and it is somehow touching that in spite of his antiquity (at last acknowledged by him—'I am old, I am old'), she loves him in her boozy way. From all this Prince Hal is almost entirely withdrawn, as I have said.

Rebellion has lost its best visual image—Hotspur—but Riot still has Falstaff's glorious belly. What image could Shakespeare's invention discover that would be more powerful upon an audience than that vast rotundity and the harvest-moon face above it? Perhaps there was only one, but he found it in his sources, the crown of England. It is for this image that Prince Hal is reserved. That splendour alone could enter into competition with all that Shakespeare had created in Falstaff.

But it is also used for uniting father and son. By extraordinary luck, Shakespeare's sources gave him the story of the dying King Henry's obsession for his stolen crown that makes him command it to be placed upon his pillow, as well as the story of Hal's momentary filching of it, which leads to the climax of their relations with each other—reproach, repentance, explanation and loving atonement. The audience sees the golden round change heads, first surreptitiously, but in the end lawfully, and hears the two hearts bared to each other in a relationship more powerful than any Falstaff can create.

The next time we see this crown-symbol is at the coronation. The newly anointed King is leaving the Abbey to the sound of trumpets, and it is upon his head. At this point is staged the only juxtaposition, properly so called, in the play—a juxtaposition that includes and concludes Part I in Part II, in the celebration of England, with Rebellion put down and Riot rejected. For immediately before the bells and trumpets sound from the Abbey we are treated to a little scene which shows where drunken whoredom leads. It leads to murder. We see the arrest of the screaming Hostess and Doll Tearsheet and hear the accusation: 'There hath beene a man or two (lately) kill'd about her.'

This culmination of criminal squalor is set sharply against the newly sanctified majesty of England. In that majesty is included the justice which has to deal with such things as murder, and just as Hotspur was the image for Rebellion in Part I, so the Lord Chief Justice is the image embodying Justice in Part II. That is why he is introduced to confront Falstaff at the start of the play, to create the symmetry we perceive when he confronts him at the end.

For, once again, Shakespeare's sources had given him an anecdote, to supply what he needed, in the story of Hal and the Lord Chief Justice who committed the Prince to prison for having struck him, the King's representative. It may well have been a temptation to Shakespeare to show us this incident on the stage in Part I; but if it was, he set it aside, reserving it for the greater effect of the young King's confrontation of the Lord Chief Justice at the end of Part II, and his proclaiming the rightness of his action and the confirmation of his office. This is what empowers Shakespeare to use him as an image of Justice, to round off the last scene of all with a confrontation of Law and Riot:

> *King.* My Lord Chiefe Iustice, speake to that vaine man.

and

> *Ch. Iust.* Go carry Sir *Iohn Falstaffe* to the Fleete,
> Take all his Company along with him.

For once, Falstaff has nothing to say: but Pistol comes out with the tag for which he has already prepared us: '*Si fortuna me tormento, spera me contento*'.

Let us consider one more case of simple juxtaposition, more subtly moving to our feelings and probing more deeply into human nature. It is not one of Shakespeare's invention, like those we have discussed, for he found the juxtaposition in his source, though there it has no special significance; it is simply one in a train of events leading to Antony's death. North's version relates:

> Now he had a man of his called Eros, whom he loved and trusted much, and whom he had long before caused to swear unto him, that he should kill him when he did command him: and then he willed him to keep his promise. His man drawing his sword lift it up as though he had meant to have stricken his master: but turning his head at one side he thrust his sword into himself, and fell down dead at his master's foot. Then said Antonius, 'O noble Eros, I thank thee for this, and it is valiantly done of thee, to show me what I should do to myself, which thou couldst not do for me.' Therewithal he took his sword, and thrust it into his belly, and so fell down upon a little bed...

This is the only mention of Eros in Plutarch's story; it passes on at once to the discovery of the wounded Antony by his secretary, Diomedes, who has him carried to the monument, to join the Queen. She received him thus:

> It was a hard thing for these women to do, to lift him up: but Cleopatra stooping down with her head, putting to all her strength to her uttermost power, did lift him up with much ado, and never let go her hold, with the help of the women beneath... So when she had gotten him in after that sort, and laid him on a bed, she rent her garments upon him, clapping her breast, and scratching her face and stomach. Then she dried up his blood that had berayed his face, and called him her lord, her husband, and emperor, forgetting her own misery and calamity, for the pity and compassion she took of him...[1]

'*forgetting her own misery*'. Shakespeare had too deep an understanding of his 'triple-turned whore' to follow this description: it is too much the action of a mere heroine. So he changed it, and made her think first of herself and her own safety. To underline her temporisings, he worked up the contrast offered by the unhesitating act of Eros.

Plutarch seems utterly to have missed the significance of this name: the passage I have quoted reads as if he had no idea how well it suited the gesture of love that Eros performs in killing himself. A brief analysis of the relevant scenes will show how well this was understood by Shakespeare.

No art can present an action like that of the death of Eros so poignantly as the art of drama, or create that pang of amazement that an audience feels on *seeing* the boy fall 'dead at his master's feet' in simple self-sacrifice. That such an action should be performed by someone named *Eros* was a coincidence almost too apt: Shakespeare seems to have felt that the audience must be led to accept his presence in the play—without noting the special significance of his name until the time was ripe.

In Plutarch, as I have said, the Eros anecdote is self-contained: we hear nothing of him before or after. But Shakespeare was careful to build him into the play, well before the scene of his sacrifice, and plant his name in the most casual of contexts; 'How now, Friend *Eros*?' says Enobarbus, meeting him briefly, on his first appearance in a minor scene (III, v). After a suitable interval, we see him again, leading Cleopatra to make her peace with Antony, after the disgrace of Actium: he speaks in such a way as to make it clear he is highly placed with his master:

> Most Noble Sir arise, the Queene approaches,
> Her head's declin'd, and death will cease her, but
> Your comfort makes the rescue.   (III, xi, 46–8)

But in this scene the name is not used: not until later, when we see him arming Antony for his last battle, does the name begin to sound: it begins in Act IV, Scene iv, where it is five times heard:

> *Ant. Eros*, mine Armour *Eros*.
> *Cleo.* Sleepe a little.
> *Ant.* No my Chucke. *Eros*, come mine Armour *Eros*.
>   (IV, iv, 1–2)

and from then on more frequently, more insistently: it forces itself upon the dullest ear:

> shee *Eros* has
> Packt Cards with *Caesars*, and false plaid my Glory
> Vnto an Enemies triumph.
> Nay, weepe not gentle *Eros* . . .   (IV, xiv, 18–21)
>
> Vnarme *Eros*, the long dayes taske is done,
> And we must sleepe. . .   (*Ibid.*, 35–6)
>
>   Apace, *Eros*, apace;   (*Ibid.*, 41)
>
> *Eros*? I come my Queene. *Eros*? Stay for me,
> Where Soules do couch on Flowers, wee'l hand in hand,
> And with our sprightly Port make the Ghostes gaze:
> *Dido*, and her *Aeneas* shall wante Troopes,
> And all the haunt be ours. Come *Eros*, *Eros*.   (*Ibid.*, 50–4)

Twenty times in a hundred and thirty lines, like an irregular refrain in a long lament, the boy's name is repeated, always with affection:

> My good knaue *Eros*.   (IV, xiv, 12)

Shakespeare well knew that the repetition of a name can have special effect on a stage: he had used the device successfully at least once before in the scene where King Henry V is wooing Katherine of France. Henry discards the blank verse we have heard him speak so eloquently, and pleads his love in prose, in an affectation of 'plaine Souldier': he does not wish to appear 'one of those fellows of infinit tongue, that can ryme themselues into Ladyes favours'. It is a pose which gives great scope to an actor, and the style turns colloquial at the very point when it moves from verse to prose, from *Katherine* to *Kate*:

> O faire *Katherine*, if you will loue me soundly with your French heart, I will be glad to heare you confesse it brokenly with your English Tongue. Doe you like me, *Kate*?   (V, ii, 105)

and *Kate* is reiterated twenty-six times in two hundred lines of blunt prose, carrying in its sound, to an English audience, the doubled sense of *dainty*; for 'dainties are all *Kates*' as Petruchio says in similar circumstances.

So in *Antony and Cleopatra* the doubled sense of *Eros* is borne in upon us by reiteration; had the name been *Philo*, who can suppose it would have been thus repeated? But it is *Eros*, and his love is seen in his death and heard in the words he speaks:

> *Eros.* Turne from me then that Noble countenance,
> Wherein the worship of the whole world lyes. (IV, xiv, 85–6)

and again

> My deere Master,
> My Captaine, and my Emperor. Let me say
> Before I strike this bloody stroke, Farwell.
> *Ant.* 'Tis said man, and farewell.
> *Eros.* Farewell great Chiefe. Shall I strike now?
> *Ant.* Now *Eros*.   *Killes himselfe.*
> *Eros.* Why there then:
> Thus I do escape the sorrow of *Anthonies* death.
>
>   (IV, xiv, 89–95)

A moment later we see Antony borne to the Monument of Cleopatra, whose latest lie is the immediate cause of the death now upon him. He makes no reproaches, he only asks her for a last kiss; and she refuses it.

> *Ant.* I am dying Egypt, dying; onely
> I heere importune death a-while, vntill
> Of many thousand kisses, the poore last
> I lay vpon thy lippes.
> *Cleo.* I dare not Deere,
> Deere my Lord pardon: I dare not,
> Least I be taken...   (IV, xv, 18–23)

This is not North's Cleopatra who *'forgot her own misery'*, but the imperial whore that having made a ruin of Antony's life, and now brought him to his death, shrinks from his easy, last request, for fear of what might happen to her, were she to grant it. Eros made no such calculation and killed himself: but Cleopatra is not yet ready to die: she still has cards to play with Caesar.

Of course she kisses Antony in the end, but meanwhile the point has been made before our eyes—the simplicity of love in Eros has been contrasted with the devious twists in the Serpent of old Nile: once more we have been shown her shot-silk of love and treachery. She continues to calculate to the end what her chances are to be with Caesar: as yet she does not know, but she begins to do so when Dolabella tells her plainly that Caesar will lead her in his triumph through the streets of Rome. This is what she most fears. It is the entry of Caesar himself which confirms these fears, for he shows her plainly and at once that it does not lie in his character to be subdued by her magnetism. It is their first confrontation—their last, too—and in six words Shakespeare blasts her hopes; Caesar asks

> Which is the Queene of Egypt. (v, ii, 111)

If Caesar does not know a Cleopatra when he sees one, cannot distinguish her from other women, is immune to what North, in a marginal note elsewhere, calls 'flickering enticements',[1] what chance is left her? So she plays for time with him, putting on the little comedy of Seleucus to deceive Caesar into thinking that she wishes to live: and in this she succeeds. As soon as he has gone she makes clear to her women that she at last knows how to decide:

> He words me Gyrles, he words me,
> That I should not be Noble to my selfe. (v, ii, 190–1)

And so she sends for the countryman and the worm, and the robe in which to meet 'the curled Antony': her death is a wedding and a coronation for her, needing a woman's thought for her appearance. It is into this perspective of the feminine that the death of Eros, placed where it is, gives us a special insight that is relevant to the whole play. It is a study in empire and soldiership, but also in maleness and femaleness.

The play most rich in the use of juxtaposition, echo, balance, contrast and confrontation is *Troilus and Cressida*, perhaps the most complex in design and effect of all Shakespeare's plays. It has a structure of unique interest, full of surprises for every analyst. But before it can be examined from this point of view, there are other technical matters, of a different kind, that must involve us. We have to face what at first may seem a minor point in bibliography that can have little importance dramaturgically speaking. Yet I think it will appear that our whole understanding of *Troilus and Cressida* depends upon how we take this point; so it calls for a chapter to itself.

CHAPTER IV

A PROLOGUE AND AN 'EPILOGUE'

Nobody agrees with you, not those that are and were fighting
with you. Disillusionment in living is the finding out nobody
agrees with you not those that are fighting for you. Complete
disillusionment is when you realise that no one can for they
cant change. (Gertrude Stein, *The Making of Americans*)

This chapter offers reasons for believing:

(1) *That* Troilus and Cressida *was originally performed to public
audiences at the Globe in 1602/3, and that it then had neither the fierce
Prologue nor the salacious 'Epilogue' that are now an accepted part of
its text.*

(2) *That with these removed, the play begins to emerge as a Tragedy on
the heroic and traditional theme of Troy, in line with the belief that the
English were descended from the Trojans, that London was New Troy,
and that the Greeks were the enemy; that the play was therefore in no
sense intended as a Comedy, still less as a work of cynicism and disillusion, as some have thought; that it was a popular subject with the
London public.*

(3) *That it was revived for performance at one of the Inns of Court for the
Christmas Revels of 1608, and that Shakespeare, who is known to have
had trouble from undergraduate audiences at Christmas revels before,
attempted to protect the play, by the addition of the* Prologue *and*
'Epilogue', *from a bad reception by rowdy young cynics; and that in
doing so he has accidentally crossed the wires of criticism for the twentieth
century.*

The argument I propose is of some complexity and aims at modify-
ing current opinion about the history, and consequently the interpretation, of this enigmatic text. The easiest method to pursue is the
Euclidian: after stating what is to be proved, to assemble the data.
I proceed, therefore, to a concise tabulation of all the relevant facts;
then to a list of a number of necessary conclusions, drawn from

them by recent bibliographical scholarship;[1] and after that to some other inferences, which seem less certain. The new argument can then begin.

A. THE DATA

KNOWN FACTS ABOUT THE FIRST MENTIONS AND PRINTINGS OF THE PLAY

ENTRIES IN 'STATIONERS' REGISTER'[2]

The play was twice entered in *Stationers' Register* (the official method of claiming ownership and some protection) as follows:

1 1603. 7 februarii. Master Robertes. Entred for his copie in full Court holden this day to print when he hath gotten sufficient aucthority for yt, The booke of '*TROILUS and CRESSEDA*' *as yt is acted by my Lord Chamberlens Men* vj^d.

2 1609. 28^{uo} Januarii. Richard Bonion Henry Walleys. Entred for their Copy vnder thandes of Master SEGAR deputy to Sir GEORGE BUCKE and master warden LOWNES a book called *the history of TROYLUS and CRESSIDA*. vj^d.

RELEVANT PECULIARITIES OF THE QUARTO (1609)

The Quarto exists with two forms of title-page. The earlier, cancelled, form has survived in three copies and describes the play thus:

3 THE / Historie of Troylus / and Cresseida. / *As it was acted by the Kings Maiesties* / seruants at the Globe.

The later, substituted, form has survived in eleven copies and describes the play thus:

4 THE / Famous Historie of / Troylus *and* Cresseid. / *Excellently expressing the beginning* / of their loues, with the conceited wooing of *Pandarus* Prince of *Licia*.

THE PREFATORY EPISTLE TO QUARTO

Quarto is prefaced by a perplexing 'Epistle', headed:

A neuer writer, to an euer / reader. Newes.

In some 420 words it makes the following points:
It is a play that has never been performed.

5 *ETernal reader, you haue heere a new play, neuer stal'd with the Stage, neuer clapper-clawd with the palmes of the vulgar . . . refuse not, nor like this the lesse, for not being sullied, with the smoaky breath of the multitude. . .*

It is a satirical comedy.

6 [The play is] *. . . passing full of the palme comicall; for it is a birth of your braine, that neuer under-tooke any thing commicall, vainely . . . Amongst all* [Shakespeare's Comedies] *there is none more witty then this: And had I time I would comment upon it, though I know it needs not, (for so much as will make you thinke your testerne well bestowd) but for so much worth, as euen poore I know to be stuft in it. It deserues such a labour, as well as the best Comedy in* Terence *or* Plautus.

It is above the comprehension of grave-minded, dull-witted world-lings, interested in pleas, rather than plays.

7 *. . . And were but the vaine names of commedies changde for the titles of Commodities, or of Playes for Pleas; you should see all those grand censors . . . flock to them for the maine grace of their grauities. . . And all such dull and heauie-witted worldlings, as were neuer capable of the witte of a Commedie, comming by report of them* [Shakespeare's Comedies] *to his representations, haue found that witte there, that they neuer found in them-selues. . .*

It has made escape from its proper owners.

8 *. . . but thanke fortune for the scape it* [the text of the play] *hath made amongst you. Since by the grand possessors wills I beleeue you should haue prayd for them rather then beene prayd. . .*

QUARTO AND FOLIO ON WHETHER IT IS A COMEDY, A HISTORY OR A TRAGEDY

(There is no agreement in the original texts on this point. They contradict themselves and each other.)

9 *Quarto title pages* (a) THE Historie of Troylus and Cresseida
(b) The Famous Historie of Troylus *and* Cresseid.
Quarto Running titles: The history of Troylus and Cresseda.
Quarto Epistle insists it is a Comedy, none wittier.

1623 Folio title-page and first three running-titles:
The Tragedie of Troylus and Cressida.
Subsequent running titles: *Troylus and Cressida.*

THE PROLOGUE AND 'EPILOGUE'

10 The Prologue is printed in Folio only and not in Quarto. It occupies a whole page, unlike any other Prologue in Folio, on the recto of an unpaginated leaf; on the verso the play begins.

The so-called 'Epilogue' which begins at the last entry of Pandarus at the end of Act V, is both in Quarto and in Folio but can be shown to be an afterthought in both.

B. SOME AGREED CRITICAL POSITIONS

(1) Peter Alexander, Philip Williams and Alice Walker give us reason for believing that the Folio text was printed from a copy of Quarto, collated with Shakespeare's 'foul papers'.

(2) Miss Walker has explained the appearance of a second entry in Stationers' Register on the hypothesis that Bonian and Walley made their application to the Court at a time when Robertes' allowance, made six years before, was held to have lapsed.

(3) She believes the text of Quarto to derive from a transcription, perhaps made from Shakespeare's 'foul papers', for a private reader, not for theatrical purposes. In this she is supported by Philip Williams. She thinks it not impossible that the transcription was made from the playhouse copy.

(4) The play appears in Folio, thrust in, without pagination, between the Histories and the Tragedies; this fact has no bearing on the present enquiry, but may be worth mentioning as a peculiarity. The reason for it has been fully accounted for by Greg.[1]

C. SOME MORE DOUBTFUL POINTS

Was the play ever performed in public at the Globe?
What kind of play is it?
These questions are interlocked. Professor Alexander was the

first to suggest that the play was perhaps performed 'at one of the Inns of Court': I quote from his article in *Library IX*, No. 3 (1928):

(1) ... the deliberate flouting of the tradition as established by Homer and Chaucer would have been intelligible only to instructed spectators.

(2) ... It is unlikely that this play was ever performed at the Globe. [He regards the play as a Comedy] ... excellent fooling for Clerks.

W. W. Greg followed Alexander's lead, but with characteristic caution:

(3) ... one cannot help suspecting that *Troilus and Cressida* would have been caviare to the generality of playgoers at the end of Elizabeth's reign. ... But there is one audience that we may readily believe would have understood both the high seriousness of the doctrine of 'degree' and the impassioned poetry of love, and have at the same time savoured the salacious seasoning of bitter wit... That audience was the termers of the Inns of Court.[1]

Miss Walker, in her edition, accepts and advances Alexander's view, citing the *Gesta Grayorum*[2] in its support, from which she draws the picture of a high-spirited audience of young men (such as those at Gray's Inn); but, contrary to Greg, she imagines them as 'in the forefront of the revolt against sugared love-poetry' and 'not likely to waste an evening's fun sighing over Troilus.'[3] She too classes the play as a Comedy and thinks 'a mixture of satire and irony with farce and scurrility would presumably have catered for the tastes of both Benchers and Termers. But whatever the occasion for which *Troilus and Cressida* was written, it can never have appealed to anything but a limited audience, for burlesque and irony are sophisticated tastes.'[4]

E. K. Chambers expressed the view:

(4) ... it is just possible that the only performance had been at court, or as Alexander suggests, at an Inn of Court... But I think there is sufficient, although not much, evidence to indicate that *Troilus and Cressida* was known by about 1604, and if known, it must have been performed ... [i.e. in public].
... It might have been classed as a comedy... It is in fact a tragedy, having no kindly ending, as all the comedies have.[5]

A NEW ARGUMENT

We have now tabulated all the factual data and critical opinions that are necessary at the moment and our argument may begin. The first step must be to reopen the question whether the play was ever performed in public at the Globe, and if so, when.

The first entry in Stationers' Register (**1**, page 79, above) and the first (cancelled) title-page of Quarto (**3**, page 79, above) both positively state that it was performed in public by Shakespeare's Company, and Quarto adds 'at the Globe'. These two statements are wholly independent of each other, being made by two different authorities, six years apart. This is evidence too strong to shrug off. There would be no advantage for Robertes in making such a statement if it were untrue; his title was already shaky: why should he jeopardise it further by a gratuitous lie, that could immediately have been checked, before a full Court whose very business was to know about such things?

The entry says '*as it ys acted*'. This does not, and cannot, mean 'as it *was* acted'. It does, and can only, mean 'as it is now being acted', that is, repeatedly, or anyhow several times, in 1602 to 1603.

The entry is dated 3 February 1603, that is, seven weeks before the death of Queen Elizabeth (24 March 1603). But the statement on the cancelled title-page reads: *As it was acted by the Kings Maiesties seruants*: that is, during the reign of James I. Unless we suppose (and there is no reason why we should) that this statement also was a pointless lie, by a different liar, the evidence is strong that the play was given an unspecified number of times in the last months of the reign of Elizabeth and, later, in the reign of James.

Against this we have the highly emphatic and colourful language of Bonian and Walley (**5**) to the Ever-reader, three times protesting, in one brief publisher's blurb, that the play had never before been given to the public. But they protest too much. It is manifest that the *Epistle* is a device to interest a special class of buyers—a class which disdains the sweat and tobacco of the multitude.

But their first title-page is indisputably in head-on collision with their Epistle. The cancellation was made in mid-issue, therefore urgently and of a sudden, and the Epistle added just as quickly in support of the new title-page, which, together, mark a complete change in sales-policy, as if on the spur of some favourable moment. Instead of addressing the general public that would be impressed by mention of the Globe, Bonian and Walley have turned to a snob audience whom they flatter by the suggestion that this audience had somehow inspired the play (6); and they further titillate it by a special mention of Pandarus and his 'conceited wooing' on the title-page, in harmony with their claim in the Epistle that the play is a witty comedy (4, 6).

What can have dictated this sudden change in their salesmanship? Can it have been to cash in quickly on the play's success at some such Christmas performance as has been suggested? Can it have suddenly become the talk of the town? The second entry in Stationers' Register is dated 28 January 1609, which is certainly close to Christmas. Yet it would leave time to allow for a transcription of the text, after a Twelfth-night performance. The challenge of the Epistle is to young wits: the enemy are a stuffy lot of 'grand censors' more interested in *pleas* than in plays. This suggests the barristers and benchers in authority over the young wits. On one memorable occasion, as we shall see, these had interfered to prevent further Christmas revelling by having the stages taken down. It seems possible that after Bonian and Walley had filched their copy of the play (8), set it in type and issued some copies, news reached them of some repercussion in the Inns of Court from its performance that set the students at odds with their seniors and so created a sudden market for a quick sale to the former. This, however, is nothing but a conjecture: what does however seem certain is that Bonian and Walley were lying when they said it had never been performed before 'the vulgar', and they knew it.

There is, however, some dramaturgical evidence, supported further by a freak of text, this time in Folio, to mitigate this charge against them and suggest that what they said in their title-page and *Epistle* was only a half-lie. After all, half a lie is sometimes half a truth, and that would be truth enough for men who knew, and indeed in a sense admitted, that they were not the real owners of the play, however they may have managed to secure the authority of Master Segar, deputy to Sir George Bucke, and Master Warden Lownes (**8** and **2**). We shall come to this again at the conclusion of the subject.

Our argument from these texts has led us to believe that on the point whether the play had or had not been given public performance, more credence should be given to the first entry in Stationers' Register and the first (cancelled) title-page of Quarto, than to Bonian and Walley and their 'Never Writer' and his hastily substituted title-page.

We may then provisionally suggest that the play was several times performed in public, probably at the Globe, by Shakespeare's Company, towards the end of the reign of Queen Elizabeth and perhaps in the reign of James I too: that it is likely enough also to have been specially performed at one of the Inns of Court during their Christmas revels in 1608: and that this performance owed some element in it to the students themselves, *for it is a birth of your braine*. This phrase is taken by Alexander, in his article, to refer to Shakespeare's brain: but the grammar of the passage will not bear this construction. It is not Shakespeare who is in the vocative. The 'Never Writer' is clearly addressing 'The Eternal reader', and buttering him up with praises for his comic undertakings. How comic these could be at Christmas in an Inn of Court we shall presently see from the *Gesta Grayorum*. A performance put on at their request, especially one altered a little to suit their tastes, could easily deserve such a phrase, at least in a piece of sales-talk.

We have now to meet the objection that *Troilus and Cressida* is not the sort of play that could have appealed to a Globe audience. If it can be fully met, it will be logical to trust the first entry in Stationers' Register and the first title-page of Quarto against Bonian and Walley, for the *only* corroboration yet advanced for their statements lies in this objection. If there could also be found something that would give it a kind of half-truth justification to Bonian and Walley at the same time, we might be in a position to put forward a hypothesis consistent with all the evidence so far adduced, instead of only with a part of it.

THE TRADITION OF TROY

Troilus and Cressida in no way 'flouts' any Chaucer tradition then continuing (in 1602–9), nor any Homeric tradition either. (See C. (1), (2) and (3), above.) Cressida's reputation had long since gone the way of Henryson's imagination—she was a harlot turned leper. This picture of her downfall had even been attributed at one time to Chaucer himself, for Thynne printed his *Testament of Criseyde* as if it were a poem of Chaucer's, in his collected edition of Chaucer's works (1532). The poem was reprinted in 1593 by Henry Charteris:[1] by the end of the century, Criseyde's moral decline, to her sad death among the beggars and their leprosy, was so well-known that Feste could throw off a quick allusion to it—'Cressida was a beggar'[2]— and be sure it would be caught. There is other proof of this, as we shall see presently. The fall of Pandarus had been even swifter: by 1530 his name had become the noun for a pimp. Sir David Lindsay classes 'pandars' with 'pykethankis, custronis and clatteraris'[3] (sycophants, eunuchs and scandal-mongers). Shakespeare inherited him in an advanced state of decomposition.

As for the Homeric tradition, there was no such thing in 1603: and what does not exist cannot be flouted. Chapman's *Iliad* was not published in full until 1611. There did exist, however, a powerful *anti*-Homeric tradition, streaming down in great strength from the early Middle Ages. There is no reason at all to believe that Shakespeare's play would have been 'caviare to the generall' (see C. (3), page 82, above) for the Troy story was an old favourite with London and had been for centuries, certainly since the fourteenth, to go no further back for the present. Every literate and many an illiterate person knew something of it: Helen of Troy had trodden the public stages in successive productions of *Dr Faustus*: Hector was one of the Nine Worthies, even the arms he bore were widely known: *Sable, two lions combatant Or*:[4] Troy was London itself and had been so by romantic tradition since the reign of Richard II at least.

The tradition stemmed from one Walter, an Oxford archdeacon, from whom Geoffrey of Monmouth said he had received an ancient book, written in the British language; the tradition asserted that

Britain was a Trojan colony and London was a New Troy. Britain itself had taken its name from a great-grandson of Aeneas, Felix Brutus. The legend came into full poetic flower in the late fourteenth century; *Sir Gawain and the Green Knight* opens with a stanza of triumph, declaring how 'Ennias the athel and his highe kynde' had conquered provinces in Europe and become the patrons of almost all the wealth of the western isles, and how

> fer ouer the French flod Felix Brutus
> On mony bonkkes ful brode Bretayn he settez
>   wyth wynne . . .

and Chaucer, in the last year of his life and the first of the reign of Henry IV, addressed a poem on his empty purse to him, flattering him with 'O conquerour of Brutes Albyon!' Nor was it only a poetic legend. Walsingham's *Historia Anglicana* alleges a serious attempt by a leading London citizen, Sir Nicholas Bramber, to seize power and rename London 'Little Troy', for which (we are told) he was executed in 1388. The continuator of Higden's *Polychronicon*, writing of the disorders following on the Peasants' Revolt of 1381, refers to the *Trinovantani*, meaning the Londoners. The story is discredited in Polydore Vergil's official history, *Anglicae Historiae Libri sex viginti* (1534–55) but is given the full treatment by Holinshed's chronicle (1577). This tells how Brutus landed at Totnes in the year 1116 B.C., sixty-six years after the fall of Troy, and how he put down the giants that then inhabited this island of Albion, and renamed it after himself. The story reappears in the *Mirror for Magistrates* (1574) and to this popular work, *The Lamentable Tragedie of Locrine* (c. 1591, first published 1595), also popular, is thought to owe something.[1] In its opening scene we meet with King Brutus himself, whose brother, Corineius tells him:

> The Troyans glorie flies with golden wings,
> Wings that do soare beyond fell enuies flight.
> The fame of *Brutus* and his followers
> Pearceth the skies. . .   (i, i, 56–9)

There is a record of a play called *Troy*, by an unknown hand, with Trojan horse and all, performed by the Admiral's Men in June

1596,[1] but now lost, and there is the prompter's 'plot' of a play of *Troilus and Cressida*,[2] by Dekker and Chettle, acted, probably about 1599, by the Admiral's Men. Fragmentary as this 'plot' is, it shows us that the cast included:

Ulisses, Priam, Hector, Deiphobus, Menelay, Diomede, Cassandra, Antenor, Pandarus, Paris, Troylus, Achillis, Aiax wth patroclus on his back, Polixinia, and *Cressida wth Beggars.*

Here is evidence that Cressida was her fully fallen self long before Shakespeare showed her in the act of falling, and that popular audiences knew all about it, together with all the great names in the story. A dozen years later, Dekker was composing his *Troya Nova Triumphans* to celebrate the election of Sir John Swinnerton as Lord Mayor of London, with a pageant in its praise.[3] It is true this pageant says nothing about the Troy story, but its title shows that the popular identification of Troy with London was still strong enough to conjure with.

This tradition was not only pre-Homeric (in England) but *anti-*Homeric. Lydgate had put posterity on its guard in the matter in his *Troy Book*. The Greeks were the enemy and Homer was a Greek, whose evidence was not to be trusted:

> And al for he with Grekis was allied,
> Ther-for he was to hem fauourable
> In myche thing, whiche is nouȝt commendable. . .
>
> (*Prologue*, 280)

Much that has seemed barbarous to classical scholars in Shakespeare's treatment of the great Greek heroes is explained by this long and popular tradition.

It is clear, then, that plays of this character not only could be, but were performed before the general public towards the end of the reign of Elizabeth and later. There was no caviare about it. We are therefore strengthened to believe in the conjecture, formed for other reasons, that Shakespeare's *Troilus and Cressida* was indeed acted at the Globe by his Company, since his theme, so far from being esoteric, was popular, Henrysonian and anti-Greek. We are now free to begin a consideration of the evidence from the play's structure.

THE PROLOGUE AND THE 'EPILOGUE'

It is easier for our analysis to consider the 'Epilogue' first. The question to ask is not whether we like it, but what its function is, how it *works*. It begins at the unexpected entry of Pandarus on the battlefield, at the end of the play, where he meets the Trojans in retreat and despondency after the death of Hector: Troilus is still attempting to keep their hearts up, but he and they and the audience all know that their doom has sounded: he ends his address to his troops with a concluding couplet expressing the only hope left to them:

> Strike a free march, to Troy with comfort goe
> Hope of reueng shall hide our inward woe. (Q, v, x, 30–1)

The couplet has the ring of finality; all the same Pandarus comes bustling in and the epilogue begins:

> *Enter Pandarus*
> *Pan.* But here you, here you.
> *Troy.* Hence broker, lacky, ignomyny, shame,
> Pursue thy life, and liue aye with thy name.
> > *Exeunt all but Pandarus.*
> *Pan.* A goodly medicine for my aking bones . . . *etc.*
> > (Q, virtually the same in F)

It is clear that Pandarus in his sudden and unlikely appearance is supplied with no stage-motive; his entry has no purpose in connection with the play proper and its stage-craft, except to give opportunity for the brusque but unnecessary dismissal he receives. It is unnecessary because he has already been dismissed in the same terms at the end of Act V, Scene iii, line 114. What he is really brought on for is *to address the audience*. After lamenting that bawds are so ill-requited, he tells his hearers there are pimps among them and bequeathes to them his venereal diseases:

> Good traiders in the flesh, set this in your painted cloathes,
> As many as be here of *Pandars* hall,
> Your eyes halfe out weepe out at *Pandars* fall.
> Or if you cannot weepe yet giue some grones,
> Though not for me yet for my aking bones:

Brethren and sisters of the hold-ore* trade,
Some two monthes hence my will shall here be made,
It should be now, but that my feare is this,
Some gauled goose of Winchester would hisse.
Till then ile sweat and seeke about for eases,
And at that time bequeath you my diseases.

(Q, virtually the same in F)
* [*read* hold-door]

The functions of this harangue may be analysed as follows:

(1) The creation of a violent jar by the juxtaposition of salacious comedy in the music-hall style on what seems a closing couplet in the tragic vein.

(2) Under the general cover of comic insult, Pandarus draws any possible *groans* or *hisses* (both clearly expected in the text) towards himself and away from the play, particularly away from Troilus. The very violence of the jar will interrupt and divert attention. It is to be noted that what Pandarus has to say about pimping and venereal disease has nothing to do with the play itself. It changes the subject.

If an author anticipated a mocking reception, this would be a way of laughing it off: he would himself be starting the laugh, against the audience. It is evidently an audience foreseen as obstreperous. There is no parallel in Shakespeare for this treatment of his public. He loves to woo his audience as he leaves it. Puck, at his last entry, so carefully prepared, hopes there may be no hissing, asks for the hands of his hearers. Feste concludes *and wee'l striue to please you euery day*. The King in *All's Well* confesses himself a beggar for applause, and also promises a strife to please future audiences: Rosalind, in her Epilogue, says that to beg will not become her, but she will conjure her hearers into liking *As You Like It*. Prospero, in his, asks not only for the applause but also for the prayers of his audience. This kind of Epilogue is a Shakespearean topos, his invariable audience-craft. It must be concluded that the 'Epilogue' in *Troilus and Cressida* is designed in a lewd vein to titillate some particular and unwonted audience, expected to give trouble. This could not be the Globe audience. If our previous argument suggesting that the play must have been given more than once at the Globe may be trusted, then it follows that the 'Epilogue' must have been thrust in later at the end of the play to protect it against some special danger from an audience elsewhere. It is a device added on, for a precise but ephemeral occasion, to a play already complete.

This argument from dramaturgy, by a freak of text in Folio, is fully confirmed. Before this 'Epilogue' was tacked on to the play by Shakespeare, he had arranged for the dismissal of Pandarus in Act V, Scene iii, where he enters to perform a real function (in relation to the story) namely to deliver a letter from Cressida to Troilus: this entry is in no way incongruous; it is indeed subtly prepared for. It comes at the point when Priam, Cassandra and Andromache have failed to persuade Hector not to go out that day to fight: Troilus is there too, armed like Hector for battle, and fierce in his rage to fight, after having witnessed (with the audience) the treachery of Cressida in her scene with Diomede.

A link with that scene is deliberately made by Shakespeare to prepare the audience for this entry of Pandarus, who comes to deliver the letter from Cressida. To remind the audience of the scene of her treachery, Troilus is given a sudden outburst against Diomede, occasioned by an *Alarum* (which has no other purpose than to give Troilus this opportunity). He uses Diomede's name and speaks of the sleeve that had once been his, but which we have seen Cressida in her wantonness allow Diomede to snatch from her. Here is the link:

> *Priam.* Farewell: the gods with safetie stand about thee.
> *Alarum.*
> *Troy.* They are at it, harke: proud *Diomed*, beleeue
> I come to loose* my arme, or winne my sleeue.
> *Enter Pandar.*
> *Pand.* Doe you heare my Lord? do you heare?
> *Troy.* What now?
> *Pand.* Here's a Letter come from yond poore girle.
> *Troy.* Let me reade.
> * [*read* lose]

While Troilus reads the letter, Pandarus speaks of his 'rascally tisicke' that keeps him coughing, and of an 'ache in my bones': the latter symptom throws out a conventional hint of venereal disease, but goes no further. He then turns from the audience to Troilus and says 'What sayes shee there?'

> *Troy.* Words, words, meere words, no matter from the heart;
> Th'effect doth operate another way.
> Goe winde to winde, there turne and change together:
> My loue with words and errors still she feedes;
> But edifies another with her deedes.
> *Pand.* Why, but heare you?
> *Troy.* Hence brother* lackie; ignomie and shame
> Pursue thy life, and liue aye with thy name.
> > *Alarum. Exeunt.* (F, v, iii, 93–115)
> > * [*read* broker]

This concluding couplet (which does not appear in the Quarto text at this point) tells its own story. This was the place for the final dismissal of Pandarus before Globe audiences: but for some particular occasion, for the benefit of an audience less civilised if more sophisticated, Shakespeare hooked it out of its proper place and tacked it on at the end, with some smut added, for the reason we have analysed, but forgot to cancel the tell-tale couplet about a 'brother' lackey in his foul papers. So it found its way into Folio twice.

The Prologue is a device that balances and resembles the 'Epilogue' in many ways: it is powerfully ironical if not offensive, particularly in its use of language. The sardonic tone is achieved by the use of a high diction deliberately punctured by colloquialisms: what the Prologue has to say teems with proud, rare words and wanton inversions that tower up above common speech, only to culminate in a plain, blunt, mocking phrase:

> *Sixty and nine that wore*
> *Their Crownets Regall, from th'Athenian bay*
> *Put forth toward Phrygia, and their vow is made*
> *To ransacke Troy, within whose strong emures*
> *The rauish'd Helen, Menelaus Queene,*
> *With wanton Paris sleepes, and that's the Quarrell.*

Just as the 'Epilogue' protects Troilus' final *exit*, so the Prologue protects his first appearance: it is '*A Prologue arm'd*'. Ben Jonson had also used an armed Prologue to defend *The Poetaster* (1601) from possible rough-house work of sophisticated audiences:

> If any muse why I salute the stage,
> An armed *Prologue*; know, 'tis a dangerous age:
> Wherein, who writes, had need present his *Scenes*
> Fortie-fold proofe against the coniuring meanes
> Of base detractors, and illiterate apes,
> That fill vp roomes in faire and formall shapes.
> 'Gainst these, haue we put on this forc't defence:
> Whereof the *allegorie* and hid sence
> Is, that a well erected confidence
> Can fright their pride, and laugh their folly hence.

Can fright their pride, and laugh their folly hence. Shakespeare took this device out of the common pool of theatrical tricks for what seems to be the same purpose, and with a like, ironical defiance for his 'faire Beholders', he virtually tells them to take it or leave it.

> *Like, or finde fault, do as your pleasures are,*
> *Now good, or bad, 'tis but the chance of Warre.*

The Prologue has no other function but this, apart from announcing the Trojan setting with its familiar theme. Just as there is no other such Epilogue in Shakespeare, there is no other such Prologue. Together they wall the play with ironical and defiant protection, against some troublesome audience. It is evident that they make a matching pair: we *know* that the Epilogue was an afterthought, clean contrary to Shakespeare's habit and nature, destructive of the carefully prepared effect of an earlier scene and making no sense with the play where it occurs. Such an afterthought cannot be a casual whim: it must be the effect of an unforeseen but overriding purpose, and we may conjecture, as a not unreasonable corollary, that the Prologue was an afterthought too, added to protect the beginning of the play, as the Epilogue was to protect the end: for these are a play's two most obviously vulnerable points, where rowdy audiences are concerned: a play must get a hearing, a play must conclude to applause. Ben Jonson had led the way to a show of force to get hearing from a particular section of his audience, and Shakespeare followed his lead.

He had, after all, had experience of the kind of trouble to be expected from the Inns of Court. At the Christmas Revels held at Gray's Inn in 1594,[1] the young Grayans had elected to themselves a *Prince of Purpoole*[2] and a whole mock Court to serve him (some three score of them, each with his own fancy title); a play was to be given before the 'Prince' and his guest, the 'Ambassador' of *Frederick Templarius*, Emperor of the Inner Temple, that ancient, neighbouring and friendly 'State'. The play was 'a Comedy of Errors (like to *Plautus* his *Menechmus*)' to be 'played by the Players'. But unhappily the occasion passed the bounds of normal revelry; the *Gesta Grayorum* reports:

. . . there arose such a disordered Tumult and Crowd upon the Stage, that there was no Opportunity to effect that which was intended. (p. 22)

The 'Ambassador' and his train departed in discontent and dudgeon.

. . . After their Departure the Throngs and Tumults did somewhat cease, although so much of them continued, as was able to disorder and confound any good Inventions whatsoever. (p. 22)

The Comedy of Errors eventually got its hearing but only after some 'Dancing and Revelling with Gentlewomen' had quenched a little their Purpoolian libido: but the esteem in which they held Shakespeare and his Company may be inferred from what happened on the following night, when a Sorcerer, the supposed cause of the Inconvenience, was indicted by the 'Clerk of the Crown' for having (among other things)

. . . foisted a Company of base and Common Fellows, to make up our Disorders with a Play of Errors and Confusions; and that that Night had gained to us Discredit, and it self a Nickname of Errors. (p. 23)

All this facetiousness was fun for the Purpoolians, but not, perhaps, for Shakespeare and his Company. He may have resolved that if he should ever again be called upon to offer a play at a student Christmas Revel, he would take steps to ensure a hearing. When the time came, as we are supposing it did, Jonson's device was ready to hand to start the play off. As for the end of the play, a show of force would be no use; a touch of salacity might be better. If this was how Shakespeare thought, the evidence is that his guess was right: the Grayans had a taste for smut, as is shown by some of the titles bestowed on the courtiers of the Prince of Purpoole:

Ruffiano de St. *Giles's* holdeth the Town of St. *Giles's* by Cornage in *Cauda,* of the Prince of *Purpoole...*

Cornelius Combaldus, de Tottenham, holdeth the Grange of *Tottenham...* by rendering to the Master of the Ward-rope so much Cunny-Furr as will serve to line his Night-Cap...

Bawdwine de Islington holdeth the Town of *Islington...* rendering, at the Coronation of his Honour, for every Maid in *Islington,* continuing a Virgin after the Age of Fourteen Years, one hundred thousand Millions, *Sterling.*   (pp. 12–13)

If *Troilus and Cressida* was in danger from such an audience, Pandarus was clearly the man to save it.

While we are considering the students of the Inns of Court, there is one more passage that may be quoted from the *Gesta Grayorum.* Miss Walker has drawn our attention to it already as recording the official consequences of the 'Night of Errors'.[1] We learn that the Prince of Purpoole 'was much disappointed by the Readers and Ancients of the House'. He had devised 'two grand Nights ... at his Triumphal Return' but had to abandon further entertainments 'for Want of Room in the Hall, the Scaffolds being taken away, and forbidden to be built up again' by the Readers and Governors, that is, by the benchers and barristers in authority (p. 53). It seems possible that the 'Never Writer' of the Preface to Quarto may have had such authorities in mind when he mentioned 'those grand censors' who (it would seem) preferred pleas to plays and were not up to the livelier wits of such as he was urging to buy his book (7).

To sum our argument so far: advancing from the findings of Professor Alexander and Miss Walker, we have reached the hypothesis that *Troilus and Cressida* was originally written for and performed to public audiences at the Globe in the reigns of Elizabeth and James I from 1602/3 and onwards, and then had neither Prologue nor 'Epilogue'. Later, possibly for the Christmas Revels in 1608 at some Inn of Court, it was revived and, in anticipation of the kind of treatment the *Comedy of Errors* had received, it was given an armed Prologue and a lewd, laughing 'Epilogue' to protect it. This hypothesis is consistent with all, not merely with some, of the known facts and is in itself likely enough. Where certainty can never be reached, we must trust the simplest conjecture that satisfies all the circumstances as we know them.

Certain footnotes may be added in corroboration, and in defence of Bonian and Walley: the quality of the play is enormously altered by the addition of the 'Epilogue', so much so that it leaves a strong flavour of low comedy as its last effect, quite out of proportion to its length. Moreover, if the play had never been given in public with this addition, it would be a sort of half-truth to say it had never been clapper-clawed by the vulgar: for without the 'Epilogue' it is virtually a different play. That they sensed the importance of his last, mocking speech may have suggested the alluring mention of *Pandarus*, Prince of *Licia*, on their second title-page. And if the Epilogue of Pandarus was specially written to protect the play from the audience, it would be fair enough to say that it was, to that extent anyhow, 'the birth of your braine', for they had occasioned it.

Our hypothesis will also allow us to understand how the Prologue came to be in Folio only, whereas the 'Epilogue' is in both Folio and Quarto. For the 'Epilogue' involves two actors (Troilus and Pandarus) and therefore two cues; and so it would be the concern of the prompter and would have to be entered in his book. But the actor playing the Prologue would need no more than the loose sheet on which Shakespeare had written it; at most he would need to hand this to the prompter (in case he should 'dry') as he walked on, and take it back again on his way out.[1] It would then be returned to Shakespeare's 'foul papers', from which, as Miss Walker has shown, Folio text was partly set up.

One of the questions posed by our data remains outstanding (**9** and C. (4), page 82, above): was *Troilus and Cressida* imagined as a Comedy, a Tragedy or a History? To this we cannot present a full answer until we have attempted a structural analysis of the play as a whole; and that must be the step taken in the chapter which follows; but we can already make the following points. If the 'Epilogue' was the afterthought we have seen it to be, added some six years later, then the play originally ended on a note of tragic grief, spoken by the chief survivor of the doomed city of Troy, with which all London was in sympathy. It is clearly impossible to suppose that anyone could think this intended to be comic. This, however, is only a provisional answer (based on the evidence so far adduced) to the sick criticism of our sick century, that is perpetually seeking corroboration from Shakespeare for its cynicism and disillusion. This kind of criticism rests its case not only upon Pandarus and his 'Epilogue' but on much else it claims to find in the play. That the play should have been designed to end on the heroic note

> Strike a free march to Troy, with comfort goe:
> Hope of reuenge, shall hide our inward woe.   (F, v, x, 30)

weakens but does not destroy the case for a cynical interpretation. To destroy it we must proceed to our structural analysis, beginning at the black heart of the matter, that is, with Thersites.

CHAPTER V

MORTE HECTOR: A MAP OF HONOUR

Ah thou, the Modell where old Troy did stand,
Thou Mappe of Honour. . . .

(Richard II, v, i, 11-12)

This chapter attempts a structural analysis of Troilus and Cressida, *to show the conflict of values between materialism and idealism which the play presents; how this conflict is organised dramatically by a series of designed contrasts, balances, confrontations and echoes; and how our sympathies are secretly directed in favour of Troy in the overthrow that impends for it; and the relevance of this to Shakespeare's contemporary world, and to our own critical understanding of the play.*

A. THERSITES

Thersites does not come in Dares or Dictys, whose supposed works were the chief foundation on which the Troy Legend was built; nor does he come in Caxton or Lydgate; he has no part in the mediaeval matter of Troy. He first appears in English (so far as I know) as 'a ruffler foorth of the Greeke lande' in 1537, in an interlude attributed to Nicholas Udall. He is not our Thersites, though he springs equally from Homer's man; he is a farcical braggart-hero of the same name in an interlude that Shakespeare may never have read. No Thersites appears in the 'plot' of the Dekker-Chettle play of *Troilus and Cressida*; the plot is, of course, fragmentary, but there is enough of it to make us reasonably sure he did not figure in it. There was no tradition about him, as there was about Pandarus and Cressida.

Shakespeare no doubt took the character from the Second Book of Chapman's *Iliad*, published in 1598,[1] where he is described as a 'jester'. Chapman only meant thereby that he made jokes. Shakespeare, however, took the hint in the word and imagined him as a fester (in the sense that Touchstone is a jester) to Achilles, and that is the reason why he is called 'a privileged man' (II, iii, 54). Chapman, coarsely but on the whole accurately, translated Homer's description as follows, and that was what Shakespeare had to go on:

... he the filthiest fellow was of all that had deserts
In Troy's brave siege: he was squint-eyd and lame of either foote,
So crook-backt that he had no breast, sharpe-headed, where did shoote
(Here and there sperst) thin mossie haire. . . .   (*Iliad*, Bk II, 186–9)

This gives us some idea of his probable make-up in an Elizabethan production and of the kind of comic loathsomeness he should present. 'Mossie haire' is good, as Polonius might say.

Shakespeare uses Thersites for a choric device. He takes no part in the action proper: he is only there to talk. His function is to create vilifying laughter against the Greeks and to cry down their war, which he says is a war for a placket. He is, of course, himself a Greek and has a further function of voicing the philosophy they stand for, as we shall see later. Not one among the Greeks escapes his blistering imagination. Agamemnon is a fool with less brain than ear-wax: Ajax a mongrel, beef-witted lord, an elephant, a very land-fish, and much else: Achilles is a fool too, a valiant ignorance: Patroclus is Achilles' brach: Menelaus is the primitive statue and oblique memorial of all cuckolds, Diomed a false-hearted knave, a whore-masterly villain: Nestor a stale old mouse-eaten dry cheese, Ulysses a dog-fox. And, after she has gone over to the Greeks, Cressida is a dissembling, luxurious drab.

It is to be noticed that he never lays his tongue on Troy or Trojan, except once to call Troilus a 'scurvie foolish doting knaue', but that is nothing to what he calls Diomed in the same breath—'that dissembling abhominable varlet Diomede' in the battle of the sleeve (V, iv, 1–5). Thersites even has a kind of admiration—as much as his envious nature is capable of—for Hector, who he expects will knock out Ajax' brains (III, iii, 298) and Achilles' too (II, i, 97). To this extent, then, Thersites is *an anti-Greek device*; he is there to direct antipathies; he seems to be a Greek, but in respect of his *function* he is really on the side of Geoffrey of Monmouth and King Brutus.

But although he is anti-Greek, he is, as I have said, a Greek too, and the most degraded of them all. He is bottomlessly base, and knows it. Shakespeare contrives a meeting in battle between him and Hector on purpose to expose him:

Hect. What art thou Greek? art thou for *Hectors* match?
 Art thou of bloud, and honour?
Ther. No, no: I am a rascall: a scuruie railing knaue: a very filthy roague.
Hect. I doe beleeue thee, liue.   (F, v, iv, 25-8)

This is an epiphany of them both: if Hector's manner is grandiose, it is not contemptible; but Thersites is shown in a cowardly crawl. Shakespeare arranges a further confrontation for Thersites with a bastard son of Priam, to whom he proclaims an affinity, in that he is bastard-begot, bastard-instructed, bastard in mind, bastard in valour, in everything illegitimate (v, vii, 16).

How then does this choric device work? In the first place, like other jesters, Thersites makes us laugh: he does so by making everything Greek the subject of unforgettable scurrilities. But for him one might think nobly of the affection that is pictured between Achilles and Patroclus[1]—the only sign of affection in the whole Greek army—but Thersites finds a word to degrade it for us:

> *Ther.* Thou are said to be *Achilles* male varlot,
> *Pat.* Male varlot you rogue whats that.
> *Ther.* Why his masculine whore.   (Q, v, i, 14)

In the second place he voices the view that in the war for Helen, all the argument is a cuckold and a whore (II, iii, 68), which is, of course, a possible view. It is in fact the basest possible view, fitting the basest possible Greek. If Homer had thought so there would have been no *Iliad*.

Hector is killed, Thersites survives: in this they are nicely balanced, for each gets what he most desires: Hector saves his honour, Thersites saves his skin, and the couplet of Chrestien de Troyes is fulfilled:

> Qu'ancor vaut miauz, ce m'est avis,
> Un cortois morz qu'un vilains vis.[2]

A dead lion is better than a live rat. But that is not the opinion of a rat.

By that reversal of values that seems to begin with the *Confessions* of Jean-Jacques Rousseau, this rat is usually taken, in modern productions, as the moral spokesman of the play. Shakespeareanly speaking, an actor's business is to make him as odious to the audience as he knows how, but nowadays he is usually presented as a Jesus-Underdog who alone discerns the truth about our filthy world. So totally has the Romantic Movement, at its fag-end, reversed the values of heroism and of the gutter in the aftermath of two world wars. The pose of realist self-denigration is the most romantic of all.

B. HELEN

We are now free to turn to the narrative organisation of the play. Three stories are driven through it abreast: the love-story of Troilus: the chivalric story of Hector: the political story of Ulysses. Behind these loom the story of Helen and the story of the Fall of Troy. Of these the Hector story is the most important, for it dominates and determines all the others. Hector alone suffers death —as we shall see, a tragic death—and this in itself confers dramatic eminence upon him. More yet, his death dooms Troy. Hope of revenge is all that remains after his murder by Achilles.

Second in importance must come the Troilus story, after which the play is named. Troilus is left alive, yet is at least as tragic as he is in Chaucer, the victim 'of purest faith unhappily forsworn'; we see him last in a rage of grief over the falsity of Cressida and the death of Hector, trying to rally his men in defence of the stricken city—a defence which the audience knows will be in vain.

The third, political, story of Ulysses peters out. It is there to embody something never dreamed of in Trojan philosophy, namely a Macchiavellian intelligence at work to win a war by cunning device; but the wiliness of Ulysses is allowed no victory by Shakespeare.[1] The master-mind, deployed upon Achilles, 'is not prou'd worth a Blackberry' as Thersites says (v, iv, 14). It is the passion of Achilles over the death of Patroclus, not what Ulysses has to say about the wallet at Time's back, that brings Achilles back into the war, and destroys Hector.

The enfolding story of the fall of Troy is indicated rather than treated in the play which moves towards a doom never quite reached. No problem is started by this story, but its inevitableness is fully known to every audience before they so much as enter the theatre. It is a *donné*. The first spectators of *King Lear* no doubt hoped for a happy ending,[1] but not the first spectators of *Troilus and Cressida*.

The story of Paris and Helen raises the first question of all: is she worth a war? The question had been raised by Homer and given an answer from which Shakespeare, following Chapman, took much, but not all:

> So (talking on the towre)
> These Seniors of the people sate, who, when they saw the powre
> Of beautie in the Queene ascend, even those cold-spirited Peeres,
> Those wise and almost witherd men, found this heate in their yeares
> That they were forc't (though whispering) to say 'What man
>   can blame
> The Greekes and Troyans to endure, for so admir'd a Dame,
> *So many miseries*, and so long? In her sweet countenance shine
> Lookes like the Goddesses'. And yet (though never so divine)
> *Before we boast, unjustly still, of her enforced prise*
> *And justly suffer for her sake, with all our progenies,*
> *Labor and ruine, let her go; the profit of our land*
> *Must passe the beautie.*' Thus, though these could beare so fit a hand
> On their affections, yet when all their gravest powers were usde
> They could not chuse but welcome her, and rather they accusde
> The gods than beautie. *For thus spake the most fam'd King of Troy;*
> '*Come loved daughter, sit by me and take the worthy joy*
> Of thy first husband's sight, old friends' and Princes' neare allyed,
> And name me some of these brave Greekes, so manly beautified.
>
> (*Iliad*, III, 163–80)

I have italicised the passages that Shakespeare seems to have pondered. They were much in his mind in 1602/3, for he throws Helen's worth into question in another play of this period, *All's Well That Ends Well*, in a song written for Lavatch:

> Was this fair face the cause, quoth she,
> Why the Grecians sacked *Troy*,

Fond done, done, fond was this King *Priams* ioy....

(I, iii, 66-9)

In *Troilus and Cressida* the question is posed by the Prologue, as we have noted, with characteristic irony: it is also raised in the opening scene, but in a mood of romantic passion, by Troilus; its importance is underlined by an alarum and a soliloquy—one of the few in the play:

Sound alarum

Tro. Peace you vngracious Clamors, peace, rude sounds,
Fooles on both sides, *Hellen* must needs be faire,
When with your bloud you daily paint her thus.
I cannot fight vpon this Argument:
It is too staru'd a subject for my Sword ...   (F, I, i, 88-92)

Colourful and dramatic as it would have been to have a scene in which Homer's two Trojan veterans made their famous comment on Helen's beauty as she passed across the stage, Shakespeare rejected the idea, perhaps as too favourable to Helen. If there is any value-judgment offered in this play on which Shakespeare intended us to have no doubts, it is the judgment that Helen is intrinsically worthless.

This, of course, is not the opinion of Troilus, or of Paris, for they are lovers. Helen is only a 'starved subject' for Troilus' sword in comparison with Cressida, and this is clear from his later declaration in council: her freshness, he thinks, makes stale the morning:

Is she worth keeping? Why she is a Pearle,
Whose price hath launch'd aboue a thousand Ships ...

(F, II, ii, 81-2)

and Paris, as one might suppose, is also of his opinion:

Well may we fight for her, whom we know well,
The worlds large spaces cannot paralell.   (F, II, ii, 161-2)

These extravagancies are balanced by the sober judgment of Hector:

Brother, she is not worth
What she doth cost the holding.   (F, II, i, 51-2)

And the same view is later echoed by Diomed:

103

> For euery false drop in her baudy veines,
> A Grecians life hath sunke: for euery scruple
> Of her contaminated carrion weight,
> A Troian hath been slaine ...   (F, IV, i, 71)

This echo of Hector, however, is itself ironically balanced against Diomed's actual behaviour: for all his righteous feelings about Helen, he will presently be seen doing battle for the contaminated carrion weight of Cressida. It is left to Thersites to develop the theme in his inimitable *canaille* language:

all the argument is a Cuckold and a Whore, a good quarrel to draw emulations, factions, and bleede to death vpon: Now the dry Suppeago on the Subiect, and Warre and Lecherie confound all. (F, II, iii, 68–71)

To confirm our judgment on Helen's worth, Shakespeare allows us to see and hear her in person. One glimpse is enough: we have expected a feather-brain from the anecdote about how she had spied a white hair on Troilus' chin (reported at great length to Cressida by Pandarus in an earlier conversation) but we do not taste her full inanity until the brief scene of her appearance, the chief function of which is that we may do so. The sex-charged gossip of the scene reaches its climax in her plea to Pandarus:

> Let thy song be loue: this loue will vndoe vs al.
> Oh *Cupid, Cupid, Cupid*.   (Q & F, III, i, 103)

Coming from the lips of the cause of the Trojan war, the phrase is an absolute of heartless, brainless, *silliness*. Hector, Diomed and Thersites, at their one point of agreement, are in the right.

Yet there is another thing the scene is built to show. However shallow she may be, and whoever she should belong to, Helen is happy and at home in Troy. This is a fact which may appeal only to those of whom Hector tells us are

> young men, whom *Aristotle* thought
> Vnfit to heere *Morrall Philosophie*:   (Q, II, ii, 166)

but, unless a woman is her husband's chattel, no law obliges the return of Helen to Menelaus against her will: and it is clear that she prefers to stay in Troy. No doubt she is an adulteress: but she has

I   The Swan Theatre, London, 1596 (after a drawing by Johannes De Witt).

facing p. 104

II   The people in the gallery of the Swan (detail of Plate I).

III How drama was done by the Ancients.
A fifteenth-century frontispiece to a codex of Terence, in the Arsenal
Library, Paris, showing how the artist imagined a play of Terence to
have been performed in classical times.

IV   The Ascension and Pentecost windows in the Church at Fairford,
Gloucestershire. The right-hand light is the perfect shape for its subject;
but in the left-hand light, this shape has compelled the artist to represent
the hill from which the Lord can be seen ascending as if it were a mushroom. This is the only kind of hill that could have fitted such a frame.
For the application of this to the character of Cressida, see page 106.
(The drawing is by Tamlyn Imison.)

cast her lot in with Troy and even if Priam is right in telling Paris that he speaks

> Like one be-sotted on your sweet delights   (Q, II, ii, 143)

the answer Paris gives is clear,

> I would haue the soile of her faire rape,
> Wip't of* in honourable keeping her,
> What treason were it to the ransackt queene,
> Disgrace to your great worths, and shame to me,
> Now to deliuer her possession vp
> On tearmes of base compulsion?   (Q, II, ii, 148–52)
>   * [read off]

The argument from prestige may be morally invalid, but so is the argument from matrimony: it would indeed have been a treason to Helen to send her back, for it is clear that she loves Paris and his family; the scene in which she appears ends with the request of Paris that she should help to unarm Hector, and clinches what we are supposed to think about her happiness in Troy:

> *Hell.* Twil make vs proud to be his seruant *Paris*?
> Yea what he shall receiue of vs in duty,
> Giues vs more palme in beauty than we haue.
> Yea ouershines our selfe.
> *Par.* Sweet aboue thought I loue her?*   (Q, III, i, 148–51)
>   * [read thee: (F)]

Helen was happy and beloved whether she was worth a war or not.

C. CRESSIDA

In presenting the character of Cressida, Shakespeare was faced by a difficult technical problem. He had to show Chaucer's Cressida on the way to becoming Henryson's, to catch her in mid-*dégringo-lade*. Now a main point in Chaucer's Cressida is her *gradualness*:

> For I sey nought that she so sodeynly
> Yaf him hire love, but that she gan enclyne
> To like hym first, and I have told you whi;
> And after that, his manhood and his pyne
> Made love withinne hire herte for to myne,

> For which, by proces and by good servyse,
> He gat hire love, and in no sodeyn wyse.
>
> *(Troilus and Criseyde*, II, 673–9)

She never sinks further than Diomed in his poem, though we have an inkling of a further fall in her weakly defiant

> To Diomede algate I wol be trewe.   (v, 1071)

But gradualness is not a quality that suits the medium of theatre, which is better suited to action and decisiveness: too much has to happen in this crowded play to admit of the almost imperceptible decline Chaucer could hint at in the last book of his long narrative poem.

An illustration of this principle in art—the accommodation of subject matter to medium—may be taken from a pair of lights in Fairford Church, of fifteenth-century work (see Plate IV). The subject matters are the Ascension of Christ and the Descent of the Dove. The intractable element in the medium is the shape of the light, dictated by the ogival apex and central mullion. The shape suits the Descent of the Dove without any forfeiture in realism: but from what kind of hill can Our Lord ascend into Heaven in such a frame? Only from one of mushroom shape, such as we see; to suppose the result is due to the quaint naiveté of an artist who did not know how to draw a hill, or to observe 'this hill is not like any hill I know' is parallel to a criticism of Cressida for the suddenness of her fall. Shakespeare has imagined the only kind of Cressida who can be thought of as hard to win; one who is constant in intention, but flighty in the event; by successive glimpses, these rapid modulations are let into the triple structure of the play.

It was necessary for Shakespeare's story that she should be won to the love of Troilus after long siege, but impossible (for lack of stage-time) to allow her the same long siege from Diomed, to whom nevertheless she must inevitably yield. He contrives to plant the idea that she was hard to win in the opening scene when she is not yet won; Troilus claims to have 'tarried' the grinding and the bolting and the leavening (I, i, 17–96): but after that things must move swiftly: there can be no 'tarrying' on stage, no interval of

months (as in Chaucer), because the other elements in the story
demand speed.

Yet to show her as a wanton from the start, therefore quick to
change, was not possible either: for what would be the point of
Pandarus, if she was so easy? As Troilus says:

> I cannot come to *Cressid* but by *Pandar*   (Q, I, i, 94)

Pandarus was part of the story too and could not be left out.

The solution found by Shakespeare to this dilemma was perhaps
the only one that could be made to work on the stage: it was to
imagine her as a chameleon-girl, who takes moral colour from
whoever she happens to be with; she responds at once to every
environment. When we first see her, she is gossiping with Pandarus: his presence elicits from her the kind of light salacity and
innuendo he so much enjoys. When next we see her, she is with
Pandarus again, but with Troilus too, and if she still has something
of her uncle's manner (for instance when she disclaims having
intended to beg a kiss in saying 'Stop my mouth') the presence and
passion of Troilus gradually win her to as nearly equal a height of
feeling (if we may judge by the words given to her) as she is capable
of reaching. She moves into blank verse from prose: she achieves
a kind of sincerity in acknowledging her changeableness of
impulse:

> I haue a kinde of selfe recides* with you:
> But an vnkinde selfe, that it selfe will leaue,
> To be anothers foole.   (F, III, ii, 144–6)
>
> * [*read* resides]

When she makes her great protestation, beginning

> If I be false, or swerue a haire from truth . . . (F, III, ii, 180–91)

she has taken up the tone and manner of Troilus and his mood of
passionate sincerity too: that what she says is ironical for an audience that knows what lies before her proves the point: for the irony
lies in the fact that they know, and she does not, that she will, in
fact, be false.

The mood of true love is still upon her when the next morning
she is torn from Troilus, and she is given lines that are clearly to be

spoken with sincerity: there is no calculation in them, for there is
nothing she can hope to gain by them:

> (*Cressida*) Ile go in and weepe.
> *Pan.* Do, do.
> *Cres.* Teare my bright haire, & scratch my praised cheekes,
> Crack my cleare voyce with sobs, and breake my heart,
> With sounding *Troylus*: I will not go from Troy.
>
> (Q, IV, ii, 104–8)

Yet when she steps into the Greek camp, she again takes on the
mood of her surroundings in the kissing scene. It seems the natural
thing for her to do. Shakespeare is here making dramatic use of an
old English custom:

> The curtesye of Englande is ofte to kys
> And of it selfe it is lechery where pleasure is
> All yonge folke remember this
> Intentio iudicat quenquam[1]

It does not appear that Cressida had any 'intentio' other than to
make herself agreeable in this English way. But the kissing is a convenient theatrical means to quicken the pace of her fall, and we are
made ready for the scene to come with Diomed, when she responds
to his hungers with the tantalising coquetry they call forth in her to
whet them: it is the practical down-to-bed realism of Diomed that
makes a 'whetstone' of her: again Thersites finds the damning
word. But she still has half a thought for Troilus, though her present mood retains its habitual command upon her:

> *Troylus* farewell; one eye yet lookes on thee;
> But with my heart, the other eye, doth see.
> Ah poore our sexe; this fault in vs I finde:
> The errour of our eye, directs our minde.   (F, v, ii, 105)

To respond to one's company is a pleasant characteristic, but
obligingness can be overdone. That Cressida should overdo it was
the best, perhaps the only, way of characterising her so as to fit
plausibly with her story and the crowded actions of the play. To
make a smart, hard whore of her from the beginning, as some producers do, is to show great insensitiveness to Shakespeare's skill

in the contriving of her downfall. Except for those who have iron hearts and think like Milton, that all wickedness is weakness, she should seem, as Chaucer wished she might be, excusable for pity:

> Iwis, I wolde excuse hire yet for routhe.   (v, 1099)

She was not gone the whole way to Henryson's heroine yet, even though we know she will, like the girl in the old epitaph:

> Here lies my daughter,
> Weak as water.
> Never said 'No'
> To friend or foe.

Like Manon Lescaut she is designed to seem infinitely attractive to men, yet infinitely unworthy of the man with whom she is matched. In this she is to Troilus what Achilles is to Hector. These seemingly insoluble equations are among the balancings on which the play is built.

D. THE WAR

Shakespeare wrote of many other wars: but in none of them are the opposing forces sundered by any deep moral principle. Yorkists and Lancastrians alike believe in the same things—Christianity and genealogy: no moral value is ever thrown back into question: even Richard III knows himself to be a villain and decides to chance the consequences. So with the Romans and the Volscians: they are all the same kind of tribal savage at each other's throats, though some are patrician savages. Mark Antony does not differ from Octavius Caesar in principle: both want victory by the same sort of means, though Antony wants Cleopatra too. What to him is the nobleness of life, to Caesar is merely a tumble on the bed of Ptolemy: but that is a question of taste. Compared with this difference in temperament, the difference that sunders the Greek and Trojan camps is like a split in the Tree of Knowledge of Good and Evil.

For the Greeks are all what we have learnt to call Realists, or Materialists.[1] They believe that what matters is to *win*. The Trojans are what we call Idealists or Romantics: they believe that what matters is *a code of honour and loyalty*. It is in the nature of things that they should not always know where honour truly lies, or act up to the best of the loyalties that lead in one direction, when they feel the counter-tug of a different loyalty in another. It was so with Lancelot too.

This is the basic conflict of the play, maintained and exhibited through its structural devices; these make for a continual interplay of opposites (by juxtaposition, echo, confrontation, contrast, etc.) through the three stories of Ulysses, Troilus and Hector, that together compose the whole narrative.

E. THE ULYSSES STORY

We first meet Ulysses at the great Greek Council scene of I, iii, that so closely parallels and contrasts with the scene of the Trojan Council of II, ii. Whoever sees or even reads the play is made instantly aware of Shakespeare's main strategy of juxtaposition in these two scenes. It is interesting to note further that he uses the same 'movements' in them both too. Each scene is constructed on this pattern:

An inconclusive debate: a violent and contrasting interruption from outside: a back-summersault by the main speaker, leading to a decision of policy that solves the problem in debate.

The two scenes have been much discussed and I will try to avoid familiar ground as much as possible. The most noticeable thing about the Greek debate is that it concerns itself only with how to win the war. Whether Helen is worth it or not is never considered, in fact she is not so much as mentioned. How to bring Troy to destruction is their only thought.

Agamemnon begins with a pious platitude to explain their ill-success: the set-backs they have suffered have been sent to try them, they are

> the protractiue tryals of great *Ioue*,
> To find persistiue constancie in men.   (Q, I, iii, 20–1)

Nestor echoes the platitude with a trope or two of his own. Ulysses gravely declares that it should be written up in brass for all to see and admire, but at once embarks upon a speech of his own which makes nonsense of what they have said. What really ails the Greeks, he continues, is not Jove but their indiscipline:

> The Generall's disdain'd
> By him one step below; he, by the next,
> That next, by him beneath ...   (F, I, iii, 129–31)

and he overwhelms his hearers with his celebrated speech on degree, exactly the right kind of speech to be heard from public faces in public places. Never did Shakespeare write a more cunning piece of poetry for a politician; it is a real spell-binder.

The ideas it contains were no less commonplace than those put forward by Agamemnon and Nestor; but Shakespeare stretched his art to make it a masterpiece of rhetoric, suited to this superlative speech-maker; it is, indeed, unforgettable. But Ulysses has no thought of taking what he has said seriously. He moves like a crab, sideways. Having shown himself as the brains of the party and gained its attention, he leaves his hearers taken in and begins to move off on another tack. Agamemnon asks:

> The nature of the sickness found, *Vlisses*
> What is the remedie?   (Q, I, iii, 140–1)

Ulysses' plan, so far from being to re-establish degree, is to uproot it. He has no serious thought of appealing to the better feelings or corporate sense of anybody; it is appetite the universal wolf that is to be invoked, for Ajax is to be bull-frogged up into a rival to Achilles; but this we are not yet told, for Ulysses is not yet ready to reveal his true design; first, he must whet his colleagues into hatred for Achilles; so he turns Agamemnon's question aside and begins to soften up the ground for an attack to be delivered later, by launching into an account, highly mortifying to his hearers, of how Patroclus' gifts in mimicry are used for their derision and the entertainment of 'Sir Valour', that is, of Achilles. Of course he tells them these wounding things with the proper tones of sympathetic deprecation.

Into the unfinished debate of these adult realists break the trumpets of romance. The young Aeneas enters and, with a courtesy so extreme that the Greeks take it for mockery, calls for a champion to defend the honour of his lady, in single combat with Hector, against that of Andromache:

> *Hector* in view of Troyans and of Greekes,
> Shall make it good, or do his best to do it:
> He hath a Lady, wiser, fairer, truer,
> Than euer Greeke did couple in his armes . . . (Q, I, iii 273-6)

Single combat is not at all the kind of warfare envisaged by Ulysses, who is a planner—one of those who

> know by measure
> Of their obseruant toyle the enemies waight. (Q, I, iii, 202-3)

The confrontation of two opposed principles could hardly be more suddenly or sharply presented; the trumpets, the banners, the youth, the high language of formal courtesy, in their sudden apparition, are a stunning use of the medium of theatre, that create a contrast such as no other art could even attempt: the anxious, calculating, ill-combining Greeks appear as if they were being visited by spirits from some other, finer world of family unity, delicate breeding and *panache*.

Menelaus says nothing to this boyish challenge: after all, the whole war is about his wife. Ulysses says nothing either, but it is clear that he is thinking; for Troy has unexpectedly played into his hand. He seems to be standing down-stage, for, as the Council and its Trojan visitors file off to end their part in the scene, he calls Nestor back:

> *Nestor.*
> *Nest.* What saies Vlisses?
> *Vlis.* I haue a yong conception in my braine,
> Be you my time to bring it to some shape. (Q, I, iii, 310-2)

Like Ulysses, Nestor knows that Hector's challenge, though expressed in general terms, 'relates in purpose only to Achilles'. If degree is to be the order of the day (as Ulysses has taught him to believe) it is Achilles who should take it up.

This is the moment for the back-somersault of Ulysses. To get

Achilles back into the war (which is his main concern) he sees that what is wanted is not degree but emulation. So let the blockish Ajax be chosen as their best man and let Achilles be slighted; it is no more than the simple matter of faking a lottery:

> No, make a lottry
> And by deuise let blockish *Aiax* draw
> The sort to fight with *Hector*.   (Q, I, iii, 374–6)

And Nestor, who always echoes the last speaker, sees the point with glee:

> Two Curres shal tame each other, Pride alone
> Must tarre the Mastiffes on, as 'twere their bone.
>   (F, I, iii, 391–2)

The scene then has these functions: to oppose the realistic approach to war of the Greeks and the romantic of the Trojans: to show Greek disharmony and Trojan unity: to exhibit the Macchia-vellian mind of Ulysses: to start the Hector story.

Nestor's cur-imagery is used again by Shakespeare, to recall this scene, in the mouth of Thersites, much later in the play:

that stale old Mouse-eaten drye cheese *Nestor*: and that same dogge-foxe *Vlysses*, is not proou'd worth a Black-berry. They set mee vp in pollicie, that mongrill curre *Aiax*, against that dogge of as bad a kinde *Achilles*. And now is the curre *Aiax*, prouder then the curre Achilles, as will not arme to day.   (Q, V, iv, 10)

Thus neither degree nor anti-degree have had the slightest effect on the winning of the war. For all his wiliness the 'closet-war' of Ulysses comes to nothing.

Yet the realism of Ulysses is not a mere matter of his cunning in politics and the will to win: it is not a thing given him for the con-venience of one scene in the story, but is a constant trait of his in all circumstances: he is the brain of realism in this play, what Henslowe might have called 'a Matchevel'. He is brain without bowels: lofty contempt is as high as he can go in the emotional and imaginative scale: he can see nothing in Cressida but that her foot speaks, she is a daughter of the game to him. Shakespeare makes use of the char-acter he has endowed him with in this way to prepare us for the

speed of Cressida's fall, for which other pressing and more important themes leave him so little playtime. But perhaps the ingrained
realism of Ulysses is best seen in his famous colloquy with Achilles:
he starts it by discussing a book he has with him, in which

> A strange fellow here
> Writes me, that man, how dearely euer parted,
> . . . Cannot make boast to haue that which he hath . . .
> Nor feeles not what he owes, but by reflection

(F, III, ii, 95-9)

This view he then proceeds to elaborate into the vulgar materialist
dogma that a man's value is what it is in market reputation, that
his honour is a matter of continual publicity, and not an attribute
residing in him and seen in his behaviour. His argument is given
power by imagery. Time has a wallet at his back in which he puts
alms for oblivion: time is like a fashionable host that slightly
shakes his parting guest by the hand. It is the doctrine that to be
forgotten is to be a failure, a nobody: the doctrine that nothing is
of worth but what is esteemed 'contemporary'. This is all Ulysses
knows or thinks of heroism: it is heroical to be *thought* a hero:

> *Achil.* Of this my priuacie,
>   I haue strong reasons.
> *Vlis.* But 'gainst your priuacie
>   The reasons are more potent and heroycall.

(F, III, iii, 190-3)

Ulysses' advice, in its most important aspect, is lost on Achilles. It
is not politics but passion of grief and rage over the death of Patroclus that brings him back into the war. His is a different kind of
realism, not an intellectual's, as is that of Ulysses, but a gangster's.
But at least he takes the point about publicity. After the gang-
murder of Hector, he takes all the credit for it:

> On *Myrmydons*, and cry you all amaine,
> *Achilles* hath the mighty *Hector* slaine. (Q, v, viii, 13-14)

Ulysses' most realistic scene, however, is his scene with Troilus,
which brings us close to the deepest things in the play; for Troilus,
it means initiation into tragedy.

F. THE TROILUS STORY

Troilus is designed as a passionately sensual idealist in the established tradition of courtly love. What he says of himself in these two regards is borne out by all else that he says and does in the play. When he is awaiting Cressida, he is giddy with desire:

> I am giddy; expectation whirles me round,
> Th'ymaginary relish is so sweete,
> That it inchaunts my sence: what will it be
> When that the watry pallats taste indeed
> Loues thrice repured Nectar? Death I feare me . . .
> (Q, III, ii, 17–21)

With this enravished sensuality he combines the ideal of truth, that is, of fidelity:

> I am as true as truths simplicity,
> And simpler then the infancy of truth.   (Q, III, ii, 165–6)

In these things he does not change in the course of the play. As well as being a courtly lover, he is also a chivalric knight, as is made clear in the opening scene, at the end of which, in spite of his love-melancholy, he decides to join 'the sport abrode', that is, to go out and fight at the request of Aeneas. He at first regards the war, as Hector does, that is, as an *honour-game*, in which the stakes may be death.

It is on this point that he turns sour during the course of the play: he comes, through his disillusion, to see things differently:

> *Troyl.* Brother, you haue a vice of mercy in you,
>   Which better fits a Lion then a man.
> *Hector.* What vice is that? good *Troylus* chide mee for it.
> *Troyl.* When many times the captiue Grecian falls,
>   Euen in the fanne and winde of your faire sword.
>   You bid them rise and liue.
> *Hect.* O tis faire play.
> *Troyl.* Fooles play by heauen *Hector*.
> *Hect.* How now? how now?
> *Troyl.* For th'loue of all the gods
>   Lets leaue the Hermit Pitty with our Mother,
>   And when we haue our armors buckled on,

The venomd vengeance ride vpon our swords,
Spur them to ruthfull worke, raine them from ruth.
Hect. Fie sauage, fie.
Troy. Hector then 'tis warres.   (Q, v, iii, 37–48)

Hope of revenge, the note on which he ends the play, has made a
realist of him: in a sense, like Cressida, he goes over to the Greeks.
The bitterness of his betrayal has undermined his moral nature. To
fight for revenge is a fall from fighting for honour. Revenge has
the approval of Hell, as we have seen in *Hamlet,* so close in the
chronology to *Troilus and Cressida.* Revenge calls the mercy of
chivalry in question, and that is why Hector calls his brother a
savage in this scene. Troilus retorts with the realist argument; *war
is war.* There are no holds barred. Thus Troilus is one who was once
a chivalrous lover, but who abandons chivalry when abandoned by
love. His essential function, however, in the play is something
more than to show this change wrought in him by despair; it is to
by-pass for us the whole question whether or not Helen is person-
ally worth fighting for, and this he does in the Trojan Council
scene, that is so manifestly to be weighed against that of the Greeks:
the Greeks, as we have noted, do not talk of Helen. The Trojans
talk of nothing else, for they are not thinking about victory, but
about what is honourable and right, so far as they can discern these
things. Troilus' arguments are worth following.

He begins with the argument from prestige:

> Weigh you on the worth and honour of a King
> (So great as our dread Father) in a Scale
> Of common Ounces?   (F, II, ii, 26–8)

But in his next speech he sheers away from argument by pouring
scorn on reason, because

> reason and respect,
> Make lyvers pale, and lustihood deiect.   (Q, II, ii, 49–50)

Yet he reasons on, and is well able to, asking a fundamental question
in reply to Hector's view of Helen as a war-aim:

Hect. Brother, shee is not worth, what shee doth cost the keeping.
Troy. Whats aught but as tis valued.   (Q, II, ii, 51–2)

The whole play is a weighing of values. Hector tells him in reply that it is mad idolatry to make the service greater than the god. Now courtly love is indeed a kind of idolatry; but it is too easy an assumption that the god of courtly love is a particular woman. Troilus holds it to be womanhood itself, that is, the power of womanliness to elicit from a man his whole virtue. Helen is more than Helen,

> She is a theame of honour and renowne,
> A spurre to valiant and magnanimous deeds,
> Whose present courage may beate downe our foes,
> And fame in time to come canonize vs ... (F, II, ii, 199–202)

Here epic and chivalric ideals are at one. To win a personal glory is not mere Hotspurism: the last word in praise of Beowulf is that he was *lofgeornost*, most eager to deserve praise. His adventures are such as show forth the virtues most highly prized in his society, a hero's virtues; and when epic merges into romance, the new vehicle serves the old purpose of glorifying male virtue.

If we look at the romances of Chrestien de Troyes we find what seem to be heroines, where there were none in *Beowulf*; but they are there to give new kinds of opportunity for the display of valour, constancy, humility and other knightly beauties of character. The importance of Guinevere, in Chrestien, as in Malory, is what she elicits, by simply existing, from Lancelot. We need not ask whether she was worth the pains he suffered at her behest; she is as bitchy as the best of them. Chrestien tells us that when Lancelot (fighting incognito) is winning all the honours of tournament, Guinevere (who guesses his identity) sends him her command to 'do his worst'[1]—that is, to make an exhibition of bad soldiership; and he obeys her, even to showing cowardice.

And the Queen, as she watches him, is happy and well-pleased, for she knows full well, though she does not say it, that this is surely Lancelot.

Malory reports King Arthur as saying

And much more I am soryar for my good knyghtes losse then for the losse of my fayre quene; for quenys I myght have inow, but such a felyship of good knyghtes shall never be togydirs in no company.[2]

Lynet does not persist in her insults to Sir Gareth because it is a trait in her character to be rude, but because it is a trait in his character to endure insults from a lady.[1] The wife of Sir Bercilak in *Sir Gawain* offers to seduce her guest, not to show us something of her own nature (of which the poem tells us virtually nothing); she is putting on an act to test the courteous chastity of Gawain.

So Helen is and is not Helen: not her 'carrion weight' (the realist's criterion) but what she inspires. It is this power in woman to elicit in man the things that he esteems as his glories which is at the core of courtly love: she is the catalyst of courage, of humility, of gentleness, of generosity, of mercy, of constancy and of many other virtues (many of them borrowed from Christianity) for any who is capable of love—as the villainous are not[2]—though these absolute ideals may be 'to the Greeks foolishness'.

For Troilus, it is Cressida who has this power: her beauty in rousing sensual desire rouses idealism, till he can almost believe that she too is touched with it:

> O that I thought it could be in a woman:
> As if it can, I will presume in you,
> To feede for aye her lampe and flames of loue.
> To keepe her constancie in plight and youth,
> Out-liuing beauties outward, with a minde
> That doth renew swifter then blood decaies ...
>
> (F, III, ii, 154–9)

and he wishes for a 'winnowed purity in love' from her to match his own. It is the romantic longing, which he craves to find realised in Cressida, having had it called forth in him by her. He is even willing to presume it is so.

This is our preparation for the counterbalancing scene when, piloted by Ulysses, he watches Cressida paltering with Diomed: she 'is and is not Cressid'. Ulysses voices common sense: '*Cressid* was here but now.' To him she is just a woman whose foot speaks. To Troilus she is the source of sanctimony itself:

> If soules guide vowes; if vowes are sanctimonie;
> If sanctimonie be the gods delight:

If there be rule in vnitie it selfe,
This is not she.   (F, v, ii, 137)

It is interesting how he here appeals exactly to that 'specialty of
rule' that gives order to the universe, to which Ulysses had so
eloquently attested in the first Council scene; it can scarcely be an
accident of dramaturgy that it is now cast back in Ulysses' teeth:
or, if an accident, one of those that happen only to genius.

> Instance, O instance! strong as *Plutoes* gates:
> *Cressid* is mine, tied with the bonds of heauen;
> Instance, O instance, strong as heauen it selfe:
> The bonds of heauen are slipt, dissolu'd and loos'd . . .
>   (F, v, ii, 153–6)

For Ulysses the harmony of heaven is a good theme for a political
speech: for Troilus it is what Chaucer calls

> Benigne Love, thow holy bond of thynges
>   (*Troilus and Criseyde*, III, 1261)

It is the same mystical bond that makes motherhood sacred:
Troilus pleads:

> Let it not be beleeu'd for womanhood:
> Thinke we had mothers . . .   (F, v, ii, 127–8)

Ulysses cannot see the connection, he is a rationalist; he asks:

> What hath she done Prince, that can soyle our mothers? (v, ii, 132)

She had done everything, of course, unless a man were spiritually
blind. This is the crucial juxtaposition, the sharpest in the play. It
is the head-on collision of the real and the ideal, so far as the discourse is concerned: it is visually reminiscent, however, of a very
different and very similar scene—the scene of the interchange, between Troilus and Cressida, of those vows which he is now watching her break. Both scenes are at night, and just as in the later scene
Ulysses watches the love-making of Diomed and Cressida, so, in
the earlier scene, Pandarus watches the love-making of Troilus and
Cressida. The positioning of these scenes can hardly fail to echo
each other visually, when the play is well staged, and produce a
pretty contrast in character: in Act III, Scene ii Pandarus fussing

round dirtily, but warm-heartedly: in Act V, Scene ii Ulysses, standing unmoved, clean and cold, watching Troilus break his heart. Pandarus in one pan of the weighing machine, Ulysses in the other. It is for the audience to take the reading.

G. THE HECTOR STORY

We must return to the Trojan Council. Its unresolved debate, like that of the Greeks, is violently interrupted by a contrasting entry: this time it is not idealism bursting in upon realism, but reality itself breaking in on ideals, with the entry of Cassandra, crying the doom of Troy. Every man in the audience knows that what she says will come to pass, and that the advice she gives will never be taken:

> Troy must not be, nor goodly Illion stand,
> Our fire-brand Brother *Paris* burnes vs all.
> Cry Troyans cry, a *Helen* and a woe:
> Cry, cry, Troy burnes, or else let *Helen* goe. (F, II, ii, 109–12)

Hector thinks this a divination that should move his brothers to follow his and her advice and let Helen go. He argues the sanctity of marriage:

> What neerer debt in all humanity,
> Then Wife is to the Husband? . . .
> If *Helen* then be wife to Sparta's King
> (As it is knowne she is) these Morall Lawes
> Of Nature, and of Nation, speake alowd
> To haue her backe return'd. Thus to persist
> In doing wrong, extenuates not wrong,
> But makes it much more heauie. *Hectors* opinion
> Is this in way of truth . . .   (F, II, ii, 175–88)

Here is an argument, not of expediency but of an ideal, that seems morally plausible; and indeed it would be so, if Helen were kept in Troy against her will; but, as we have seen, she is happy there and Hector's argument is false. He appeals to the 'law in each well-ordered nation' in asserting the natural debt of wife to husband; but what nation has extradition laws to curb adultery? Hector does not give his brothers a chance to make this obvious rejoinder, for it is the moment for *his* somersault. Seeing, perhaps, the weakness of his position—we are not told this, however—he makes his sudden *volte-face*; more likely it is due to the dismay he sees on the faces of his brothers:

> *Hectors* opinion
> Is this in way of truth: yet nere the lesse,
> My spritely bretheren, I propend to you
> In resolution to keepe *Helen* still;
> For 'tis a cause that hath no meane dependance,
> Vpon our ioynt and seuerall dignities.   (F, II, ii, 188–93)

He then reminds the audience of the challenge which, morals or no morals, he has had delivered to the Greeks:

> I haue a roisting challenge sent among'st
> The dull and factious nobles of the Greekes . . . (F, II, ii, 208–9)

He makes his somersault light-heartedly: it is the first of the three misguided actions taken by him that lead to his death; he should have listened to Cassandra and she makes her only other entrance to show him his death in her vision (V, iii, 80–7). But Hector had not heeded her enough to win him from the attractions of honour, brotherhood and prestige, so characteristic of the chivalric hero, that had brought about his sudden change of mind. The *volte-face* of Ulysses, in contrast, had sprung from his sharpness in cunning, his crab-movements, his double-dealing, his glee in malice. Weigh Hector against Ulysses and take the reading.

We are told by Ulysses (who may be believed in this) that Hector's challenge 'relates in purpose onely to *Achilles*' (I, iii, 323). Slowly the play threads its way towards the impending tournament; the Ulysses scheme for the selection of Ajax as the Greek champion is adopted: Achilles is nettled, but not stirred to do more than invite the Trojans to his tent after the combat to satisfy his 'woman's longing' to 'see great Hector'. His curiosity is allowed, later, to gain on him so far as to draw him to watch the duel. His presence at it is a part of Shakespeare's gradual building up of what may be called the *Morte Hector*. He comes bloody-mindedly enough, but holds himself in reserve (except for a solitary sneer to show his mood) until after the encounter of Hector and Ajax. Meanwhile old Nestor is given a speech in praise of Hector's clemency in battle (IV, v, 183): this anticipates what Troilus is later to say about Hector's 'vice of mercy', already quoted. The two speeches have the same function, of defining Hector as a paragon of chivalry and at the same time of preparing the audience for Hector's death: for it is partly, but precisely, this very 'vice of mercy' which brings his death about.

The speech comes appropriately in Nestor's mouth: he is an ancient of days who understands something about the old traditions: he alone among the Greek lords had fired up at Hector's challenge and offered his 'three drops of blood' in defence of his lady, 'fairer than his grandam and as chaste as may be in the world' (I, iii, 298): Nestor, in short, though a Greek and open to cunning, is not one of the New Men, the realists: he can appreciate *style*:

> I haue thou gallant Troyan seene thee oft,
> Laboring for destiny, make cruell way,
> Through rankes of Greekish youth, and I haue seene thee
> As hot as *Perseus*, spurre thy Phrigian steed,
> Despising many forfaits and subduments,
> When thou hast hung th'aduanced sword ith'ayre,
> Not letting it decline on the declined,
> That I haue said to some my standers by,
> Loe *Iupiter* is yonder dealing life.   (Q, IV, v, 182-91)

Achilles knows no such courtesy: he is a killer and he makes it clear that he is one. He demands to survey Hector once again after their introduction:

> *Achil.*   I will the second time,
> As I would buie thee, view thee lim by lim. (Q, IV, v, 237-8)

To this butcher's language, Hector replies in sportsman's terms, for war to him is tournament:

> *Hect.* O like a booke of sport thou'lt read me ore:
> But ther's more in me then thou vnderstandest.
>   (Q, IV, v, 239-40)

There is indeed: chivalry is beyond the comprehension of Achilles, who replies:

> *Achil.* Tell me you heauens, in which part of his body
> Shall I destroy him: whether there, or there, or there,
> That I may giue the locall wound a name,
> And make distinct the very breach, whereout
> *Hectors* great spirit flew: answer me heauens.   (Q, IV, v, 242–6)

This insult to God and man stirs Hector to a frank rage, instantly repented:

> . . . For Ile not kill thee there, nor there, nor there,
> But by the forge that stythied Mars his helme,
> Ile kill thee euery where, yea, ore and ore.
> You wisest Grecians, pardon me this bragge,
> His insolence drawes folly from my lips. . .   (F, IV, v, 254–8)

These are the planted omens of their last encounter: they are as sharp a confrontation of hatred and unhatred in war, as the confrontation of passion and rationalism in Troilus and Ulysses before the tent of Calchas.

In the last act, Hector's entry is delayed so that he may be just in time to see Troilus fighting single-handed against Diomed and Ajax.

> *Troy.* Come both you coging Greekes, haue at you both.
>
> *Exit Troylus*
> Enter Hector
>
> *Hect.* Yea *Troylus?* O well fought my youngest Brother.
>
> (F, v, vi, 10–11)

It is a cry of admiration from the touch-line. But at this moment, to bring an end to the sense of what is sporting, Achilles enters. It is to be inferred from the dialogue that he makes a set at Hector and, after some little fighting, shows himself out of breath. There are no stage-directions in either Q or F, but it seems clear what is to be imagined, so I supply them:

> Enter Achilles
>
> *Achil.* Now doe I see thee; haue at thee *Hector.*
>
> [*a long fight; Achilles gasps and falters*]
>
> *Hect.* Pause if thou wilt. . .   (F, v, vi, 13–14)

This is an enactment of what Nestor and Troilus have both told us about Hector's way of fighting ('Not letting it decline, on the declined' and 'Euen in the fanne and winde of your faire sword, you bid them rise, and liue') and it is the second of the acts of Hector that leads to his death. Achilles, true realist, despises him for it, but takes advantage of it:

> I doe disdaine thy curtesie, proud Troian...   (F, v, vi, 15)

He makes his exit.

Chivalry and courtly love have their ugly sides: Hector accepts the love of Paris and Helen, though it is adulterous, because it is a spur to valiant and magnanimous deeds and because what he sees as the honour of his family is involved. There is another aspect of chivalry, all too characteristic, of pillage. Yielding to the impulse for loot is the third fatal action taken by Hector: the incident is in Shakespeare's sources, which he a little reshapes to touch it with irony. There enters a man in gorgeous armour, whom Hector challenges to stand and fight: but he takes to his heels. Hector exclaims:

> ... wilt thou not beast abide?
> Why then flye on, Ile hunt thee for thy hide.   (F, v, vi, 30–1)

and makes his exit in pursuit of him. Almost at once he returns with the man's armour, remarking

> Thy goodly armour thus hath cost thy life.   (F, v, viii, 2)

Hector did not know that it would also cost his own life, for, thinking his day's work done in the securing of this trophy, he rests his sword:

> Now is my daies worke done: Ile take good breath:
> Rest Sword, thou hast thy fill of bloud and death.
>   (F, v, viii, 3–4)

It is the moment of his murder:

> *Enter Achilles and his Myrmidons.*
> *Achil.* Looke *Hector* how the Sunne begins to set;
> How vgly night comes breathing at his heeles,
> Euen with the vaile and darking of the Sunne.
> To close the day vp, *Hectors* life is done.

Hect. I am vnarm'd, forgoe this vantage Greeke.
Achil. Strike fellowes, strike, this is the man I seeke.

(F, v, viii, 5–8)

That there was a difference between killing and murdering was clear enough to Malory, though not to Achilles; he is a savage, who, in wreaking revenge on an unarmed enemy, wins the war and takes the credit.

On Myrmidons, cry you all a maine,
Achilles hath the mighty *Hector* slaine.   (F, v, viii, 13–14)

Let us contrast Malory

. . . than the kynge stablysshed all the knyghtes and gaff them rychesse and londys; and *charged them never to do outerage nothir morthir*, and all-wayes to flee treson, *and to gyff mercy unto hym that askith mercy*, uppon payne of forfiture (of their) worship and lordship of kynge Arthure for evirmore...[1] [my italics]

To show mercy to an enemy that asks for it is a virtue not only to be found in the higher types of men: it appears in the largest and most ferocious wolves. A male Canadian timberwolf who knows him-self defeated, will offer his jugular vein, in submission, to the snap-ping jaws of the victor; but the victor cannot, or does not bite.[2] Something in his nature prevents him. But nothing prevented Achilles and his Myrmidons.

H. SYNTHESIS

Our analysis shows the play to be a straight tragedy of the tradi-tionally anti-Homeric, anti-Greek kind, based on Caxton, Lydgate and Chaucer, and picking Thersites out of Chapman to assist in the disparagement of the Greeks. We have seen that this would have been familiar and popular in the London of 1598–1612, within which the play falls: all this accords with what the first entry in Stationers' Register and the cancelled title-page of Quarto together assert, namely that it was acted more than once by Shakespeare's Company, at the Globe. It is shapely and complete if taken to begin and close with the griefs of Troilus, following the Chaucerian suggestion of a 'double sorwe', and ending with the doom over-hanging Troy that closes his last couplet.

To this artistic entity, so carefully balanced in its presentation of values and of those who stand for them, at some time Shakespeare added the protection of a Prologue and 'Epilogue' to ward the play from a different kind of audience, on a special occasion (having had personal experience of its obstreperousness before) and framed it protectively, that it might be a tragedy still, defended from deriders by derision. This consorts with what we know of Gray's Inn, and with the second entry in Stationers' Register, the second title-page of Quarto and the Epistle of Bonion and Walley.

The device that was meant to save the play from the disillusioned and sophisticated in the seventeenth century has, by a nice irony, handed it over to them in the twentieth; for the sardonic tone of the Prologue and the salacity of the 'Epilogue' have united with the half-understood vituperation of Thersites to twist interpretation; when we hear that 'war and lechery confound all', we hear the voice of our own fears and guilts and it pervades our understanding of the play, to distaste it with bitterness and disenchantment: Pandarus a dirty, old man, half-pimp, half-voyeur: Helen brainless and characterless; Cressida with her speaking feet on the way to leprosy. How easy in our present mood and in such company to mistake Thersites and Ulysses (by a slip of attention) for our moral tutors!

It is only by going back to the roots of the play, that draw their sustenance from our first great civilisation, that we can see the topsy-turvidom of such interpretation. We must re-direct our judgment to think a Shakespearean thought.

It is the harder for us to do so in that the twentieth century has no sense of the identity of Troy and London. Perhaps William Blake was the last Londoner to feel it.[1] Heroism and high language are also out of fashion. Total war makes 'fair play' meaningless. The thought of lovers tied by the bonds of heaven, by vows that are 'sanctimonies', is less frequently a theme of dramatic poetry, or even of honest prose than it used to be. Realism is much admired.

Nevertheless we can attempt to see the tale of Troy as Shakespeare saw it and read his play as a tragic contemplation of the over-throw of a great tradition typified by two high secular ideals (secular for all their affinities with Christianity)—good faith and clear honour in war and love. These, next to catholicism itself, had given character to the old christendom from which England had broken free, ever since Ramon Lull's *Order of Chivalry* that Caxton translated, and the *Roman de la Rose* that Chaucer translated. They are the ideals chosen by Shakespeare from the Middle Ages to give the true character of ancient Troy, that is, of his own London, and make a map of honour for it. This was not a piece of antiquarianism on Shakespeare's part; he was writing a contemporary play about what was going on all round him, in terms of the old times when values were not in doubt.

We watch the code in the course of being overwhelmed by a ruthlessness that subordinates all values to the value of winning. We see the old ways fall, or about to fall, before the New Men of craft, lechery and murder, and the ideals that had been chiefly instrumental in the creation of what we call honour, nobleness, or magnanimity, derided, betrayed and defeated. Chaucer and Malory are out and Macchiavelli is in.

But this contemplation has a level gaze; the older values are not sentimentalised, the faults of the Old Order are shown just as they are in *Lear*, another play that in dealing with the same conflict (though in different terms) ends with a scene of desolation. Yet in *Lear* the old values are finally restored; in *Troilus and Cressida* they are about to be overthrown. This is a contemplation that has more to enthral us than the shallow railing of Thersites and the 'conceited wooing' of Pandarus; we are being shown a vision of the day when Odin meets with the universal Wolf,[1] when all the soldiers in Val-halla will not be able to shut their gates against it, 'so doubly seconded with Will, and Power'; force and fraud will be cardinal virtues and the lights of our first civilisation will go out; if that is matter for laughter, at what are we supposed to weep?

CHAPTER VI

SOLILOQUY

Alone? And talking to himself?

(John Dryden, *All for Love*, IV, i)

This chapter discusses some of the many uses Shakespeare made of Soliloquy, shows how he came in time to be chary of allowing it to others than protagonists, and to be careful to prepare for and build their soliloquies into the play, sometimes several scenes in advance. It then considers in detail some soliloquies of Brutus, Iago, Hamlet, and others, as examples of his use of this mode of discourse to create sympathy, and sometimes hatred, for the speaker.

I

The word *soliloquy* comes to us from St Augustine; his *Liber Soliloquiorum* brought the word into English in the fourteenth century and it was still being used in connection with him in Tudor times, to mean a private meditation of a religious character. Dr Johnson later defined it as 'a discourse made by one in solitude to himself': the divine Clarissa uses the word to describe her letters to Miss Howe (*Clarissa*, vol. I, Letter xxx); its use in connection with the theatre seems to be of later growth. There is no indication that Shakespeare knew the word.

There is, however, no play of his that does not use soliloquy as an instrument of discourse, nor any play of Marlowe's, nor any play of Lyly's. A continuous tradition of it poured into Tudor usage from the two great streams of classical and mediaeval drama and it was not until the late nineteenth and early twentieth centuries, and with the advent of the 'well-made play', that it began to cause embarrassment and came to be regarded as a clumsy and archaic device. Creizenach tells us 'the Elizabethan poets evidently knew nothing of the later artistic principle which ordains that during a soliloquy the dramatic fiction that the speaker has no hearers must be kept up.'[1] William Archer tells us 'In modern serious drama . . . soliloquy can only be regarded as a disturbing anachronism.'[2] But, in a footnote, with a perhaps unconscious humour, he allows the use of a telephone-soliloquy, provided the expedient is not abused. He had, however, a common-sense understanding that two great inventions—namely the proscenium arch and the master-switch—had driven their wedges between Elizabethan stage practice in the matter of soliloquy and that of his own time.

The proscenium arch began to divide actors from audience in the seventeenth century. Gas-lighting began to be introduced into London theatres between 1815 and 1817; gradual experiment divided the light on stage from the darkness in the pit, to create an illusion of a new and separate world behind the proscenium arch. The wonders that this illusion worked were at first the wonders of fantasy; Mary Shelley wrote about them to Thomas Jefferson Hogg (October 1824):

. . . Jane & I went two or three times to *Der Freischutz*. We liked the music, & the incantation scene would have made Shelley scream with delight, flapping owls, ravens, hopping toads, queer reptiles, fiery serpents, skeleton huntsmen, burning bushes; and a chorus made up of strange concords & discords produced a fine effect *in the, but for the stage, entirely darkened house.*[3]

I have italicised the novel sensation. But the real changes brought about by the new illusion were of an opposite kind and led, not to fantasy, but to *actuality* on the stage and began that process towards what is called 'realism' that has led from the drawing-room to below stairs and the kitchen sink. They created the eavesdropper audience and a stage-world in which actors spoke only to other actors and in which a total plausibility was the goal of drama; as Archer wrote:

. . . the glorious problem of the modern playwright is to make his characters reveal the inmost working of their souls without saying or doing anything that they would not say or do in the real world.[4]

All this had been done by his idol Ibsen:

We must consider for a moment the question—if question it can be called—of the soliloquy and the aside. The example of Ibsen has gone far towards the expelling of these slovenlinesses from the work of self-respecting playwrights.[1]

Nevertheless, soliloquy in England died hard, in spite of the cold blast of naturalism from the North. The naturalistic, pre-Ibsen, social-problem-play *Caste* (1867) could find a cosy kind of use for it; Robertson opened his third act with a busy little monologue by his heroine, Polly, uttering a pitter-patter of colloquial thought to herself; but had she spoken in blank verse, Archer would have no less condemned her:

The approach of mental disease is often marked by a tendency to un-restrained loquacity, which goes on even when the sufferer is alone; and this distressing symptom may, on rare occasions, be put to artistic use.[2]

This severe rule awed but did not quell the art entirely, for hardly did it seem to have been abandoned before it was revived. No less a naturalist than George Bernard Shaw, for instance, presented his opinions in a long address, directly delivered to the audience by an actor personating the god Ra, in the 1912 *Preface* to *Caesar and Cleopatra*; Flecker's *Hassan* made use of soliloquy in 1922, and so, in 1936, did *The Ascent of F 6*, by the then avant-gardist writers Wystan Auden and Christopher Isherwood. It was used by Eugene O'Neill (*The Emperor Jones*), Thornton Wilder (*Our Town*), Tennessee Williams (*Glass Menagerie*) and others. More recently the power of the device has been felt in a play of an apparently total naturalism, Harold Pinter's *The Caretaker*, the most moving passage in which is that which closes the second act with Aston's account of the shock-treatment to which he has been subjected in a mental hospital. This is virtually a soliloquy, though technically not, since the reprobate tramp, Davies, is also on stage, in bed, feigning sleep; but in the excitement of the speech that ugly fact is forgotten and Aston claims and gets the same kind of attention, the same private communion, that an audience has with Hamlet, save that he is not out on the apron.

Nothing is more certain than that soliloquy is the most intimate and potent of all the instruments of discourse in theatre; it is of perennial power in a medium that has ranged from heaven to hell and can explore the internal as well as the external world; unless we confine the art of theatre inside Archer's trap, we shall need it.

II

One way of classifying soliloquies is by taking note of those to whom they are addressed; Dr Joseph, following M. L. Arnold, divides them thus:

Dialogue is addressed to one or more of the persons in the drama. 'Mental soliloquy' is not addressed to anyone else, and whoever is present with the speaker makes no sign of having heard the speech. 'Verbal soliloquy' is not addressed to anybody, but can be heard by whoever is present. 'Direct address' is spoken to the audience.[1]

This classification will serve certain purposes; but not ours, because there are too many cases when it is a matter of private opinion into which category a given speech should fall, and even more a matter of opinion into which it fell in Elizabethan and Jacobean times. It would seem that a great deal more was given directly to the audience then than now, if we may trust the character of *A Common Player*, described in *Essayes and Characters, Ironical and Instructive* (1615):

When he doth hold conference upon the stage; and should looke directly in his fellows face; hee turnes about his voice into the assembly for applause-sake, like a Trumpeter in the fields, that shifts place to get an eccho.[2]

For our purposes it is more useful to classify them by function, even though it makes for more sub-divisions; for the greater poets among Elizabethan writers for the stage developed between them many ways of using soliloquy. Lyly, for instance, characteristically uses it for rhetorical prose-poems, especially such as express the joys and griefs of falling in love; there are three such arias, one after another, in *Gallathea*; if Dresden china could speak, it would speak Lyly.

Enter Telusa *alone.*

Tel. Howe nowe? what newe conceits, what strange contraries breede
in thy minde? is thy *Diana* become a *Venus,* thy chast thoughts turnd to
wanton lookes, thy conquering modestie to a captiue imagination?
Beginnest thou with Piralis to die in the ayre and liue in the fire, to
leaue the sweete delight of hunting, and follow the hote desire of loue?

(III, i)

This has no function but to elaborate a luxury of antithesis for the
pleasure of the audience and perhaps for the education in rhetoric
of the boy-actor playing Telusa. Immediately before this, Phillida
has spoken, also in soliloquy and to the same tune:

... Art thou no sooner in the habite of a boy, but thou must be enamored
of a boy? what shalt thou doe when what best lyketh thee, most dis-
contenteth thee?   (II, v)

Immediately before that there is another cadenza of the same kind,
this time by Gallathea. Don Adriano de Armado in *Love's Labour's
Lost* carried on this tradition of soliloquy, though in his case the
tradition is augmented by a sense of its affectation:

And how can that be true loue, which is falsely attempted? Loue is a
familiar, Loue is a Diuell. There is no euill Angell but Loue, yet *Sampson*
was so tempted, and he had an excellent strength: Yet was *Salomon* so
seduced, and hee had a very good witte...   (I, ii, 120)

Shakespeare's dramaturgy continually evolves new ideas out of
old traditions; one has only to remember the diversity of effects he
has elicited from the simple tradition that female parts were played
by young men to see how little he relies on formula and how much
on the possibilities of the acting medium. A boy can present a girl;
a boy can present a girl presenting a boy; a boy can present a girl
presenting a boy presenting a girl: the Pirandellian whimsicalities
of *As You Like It* show the new invention out of the old material.

In the same way, from the simpler tradition of soliloquy found
in his predecessors, Shakespeare evolved an instrument of many
purposes and much delicacy, and a skill in preparing for and placing
a soliloquy, so as to knit it into the necessary structure of a play and

its themes. Yet, although he came to use a self-discipline in this matter, he was not so absolute as never to relax it; so it would be hard to say whether soliloquy was a tenth muse to him, or a maid-of-all-work. Two reasons can be suggested for this, the first a familiar one, the apron stage, which invites an actor to address his audience as a bull-ring invites a matador to show his paces. A second reason, more personal to Shakespeare, arises from that habit we have already noted in him of basing his plays on stories in which the individual scenes jump from strong-point to strong-point. As a consequence of this he often seems to feel the need to consolidate the narrative structure by confirming what has happened and suggesting what is to come. Gower's choric addresses in *Pericles* show this principle in its extreme form, but it is often to be seen, especially in the early plays where the beginning or end of a scene is often marked by a soliloquy that looks before and after, and links the succession of scenes.

For this reason, soliloquies tend to have a more marked dramatic function than other speeches, for, in Shakespeare, a man who addresses the audience directly when he is alone is not embellishing the casual pattern of dialogue, as so often in Lyly, but directing his hearers' attention to some important matter in the story. He is speaking for a purpose.

Shakespeare began with wild experiments; he had at first no policy in the distribution of soliloquies and allowed any character to utter one whenever convenient. Thus in *1 Henry VI* we have soliloquies from the Bishop of Winchester, the Lord Mayor of London, Talbot, a Common Soldier, Richard Plantagenet, the Duke of Exeter, the Duke of Bedford, Sir William Lacy, Joan la Pucelle, the Earl of Suffolk, Margaret: eleven in all. In Part II, the Duke of York, the Duchess of Gloucester, Sir John Hume, First Gentleman, Queen Margaret, Jack Cade, Alexander Iden, Young Clifford and Richard of Gloucester, a total of nine. The only one of these to say anything memorable is Richard; he is the first soliloquist in Shakespeare to offer us a two-line epiphany of his character.

Sword, hold thy temper; Heart, be wrathful still:
Priests pray for enemies, but Princes kill.   (v, ii, 70–1)

After a lavish use of soliloquy in these and other early plays,
Shakespeare began to retrench on them. *Richard III* has a total of
just over two hundred lines of soliloquy, of which Richard himself
speaks nearly a hundred and fifty; he is Shakespeare's first great
achievement in this art; but there are six others, who include such
small fry as a Scrivener and a First Murderer, that are allowed a solo
too. But in the *Comedy of Errors* the total is only some sixty-five
lines, of which over forty go to Antipholus of Syracuse, and the rest
to his Dromio and the Courtesan.

Obviously the nature of the story must determine the amount of
soliloquy to some extent, but between *Richard III* and *Coriolanus*
the average number of soliloquists to a play is just under four and
the casuals among them tend to be fewer and fewer; in *Henry IV*,
Part I, for instance, there are only three: Hal, Hotspur and Falstaff,
the protagonists. *Hamlet* has the expected four, Hamlet, Claudius,
Gertrude and Ophelia; *Othello* (if we exclude the Herald) has two,
Iago and Othello.

But when we enter what is known as 'the last phase', the pattern
changes again. *Pericles* has six (if we include Gower), *Cymbeline* has
ten, *Winter's Tale* has seven and *Tempest* five. The movement towards naturalism recedes.

When is a soliloquy not a soliloquy? This is a riddle that has to
be faced. It cannot be distinguished in every case from an *aside*, and
the distinction in any case is not important to the present argument;
this is inevitable because of the hugeness of the Elizabethan stage.
When Shylock makes the comment on Antonio that we have
already discussed:

How like a fawning publican he lookes
(*Merchant of Venice*, I, iii, 36)

it is virtually a soliloquy, for he is out, alone, on the apron. Bassanio has gone far up-stage to greet Antonio, and is out of earshot.
Shylock is addressing the audience precisely as if he were alone
with them. But soliloquies can be overheard and still be soliloquies.

Malvolio is overheard talking to himself in the Countess's garden
by Sir Toby, Sir Andrew and Fabian (*Twelfth Night*, II, v): yet he is
supposed not to hear what they are saying. This is a further exploit-
ation of the size of the stage; a few well-placed box-hedges on the
Swan apron would make it easy to dispose the three eavesdroppers
in such ways that they always seemed closer to some part of the
audience than Malvolio, and so the absurdities we suffer from seeing
this scene played behind a proscenium arch would disappear. It
may be that we are more sensitive to this kind of anomaly than
Shakespeare was; certainly, in his early days, he permitted himself
violently non-natural effects: we even hear a soliloquy-in-duet performed in stichomythia in the First Part of *Henry VI*, between
Suffolk and Margaret at their first meeting; Margaret partly over-
hears Suffolk, but Suffolk, though on fire with love for her, seems
not to hear a word she says:

> *M.*Why speaks't thou not? What ransom must I pay?
> *Suf.* She's beautifull; and therefore to be Wooed:
>   She is a Woman; therefore to be Wonne.
> *Mar.* Wilt thou accept of ransome, yea or no?
> *Suf.* Fond man, remember that thou hast a wife,
>   Then how can *Margaret* be thy Paramour?
> *Mar.* I were best to leaue him, for he will not heare.
> *Suf.* There all is marr'd: there lies a cooling card.
> *Mar.* He talkes at randon: sure the man is mad.
> *Suf.* And yet a dispensation may bee had.
> *Mar.* And yet I would that you would answer me:
> *Suf.* Ile win this Lady *Margaret*. For whom?
>   Why for my King: Tush, that's a woodden thing.
> *Mar.* He talkes of wood: it is some Carpenter.   (v, iii, 77–90)

This is the work of a confident beginner, trying out a trick, for fun.
A more serious, more complex experiment followed in *Henry VI*,
Part III, in the famous scene of the Father who has killed his Son,
and the Son who has killed his Father. They lament their woes in
soliloquy, each unconscious of the other, yet echoing him in phrase
and verse-form: into their duo is blended a third voice—the King's
—who hears them both, though they do not hear him. This formal-

ism suits with the symbolic cast of the scene, so well discussed in Dr Joseph's book:

> *Son.* How will my Mother, for a Fathers death
> Take on with me, and ne're be satisfi'd?
> *Fa.* How will my Wife, for slaughter of my Sonne,
> Shed seas of Teares, and ne're be satisfi'd?
> *King.* How will the Country, for these woful chances,
> Mis-thinke the King, and not be satisfied? (II, v, 103–8)

Something may have been gained from these early experiments with double and triple streams of speech. Shakespeare did not use them often, but when he did, in later life, it was for great effect. There is a hilarious moment when Parolles is soliloquising on how to get himself out of the situation his rash boast has landed him in; he has undertaken to recover a drum from the enemy. Unknown to him, his fellow soldiers, who have planned this trap for him, are listening and commenting derisively; the two streams of speech interlock at one point, with marvellously comic effect:

> *Par.* .... Or to drowne my cloathes, and say I was stript.
> *Lo. E.* Hardly serue.
> *Par.* Though I swore I leapt from the window of the Citadell.
> *Lo. E.* How deepe?
> *Par.* Thirty fadome. (*All's Well*, IV, i, 48–54)

In completing his sentence he unconsciously answers the question of his unheard tormentor.

A three-stream scene of climactic importance shows us Troilus and Ulysses watching and hearing the dialogue of Diomede and Cressida that proclaims her wanton falsity; the third voice, heard by neither group, is the voice of Thersites soliloquising on them both, in gutter language. Only the audience hears him (*Troilus and Cressida*, v, ii).

The most remarkable of all uses of this device is in the scene when Hamlet comes upon King Claudius at his prayers. It is clear that on a stage like that in the Swan drawing, Hamlet must be up-stage of his uncle and that his words must pass over his head on their way to the audience, though unheard by him. The necessity for this situation is so strong (as we shall see later) that the fiction had to be risked; but little risks must be taken for great gains. In this case the whole structure of the play is involved and depends upon it.

Apart from freak uses of soliloquy, I think it is possible to distinguish seven major uses Shakespeare made of it. It is true that they overlap and merge, and many soliloquies embody several of these uses in a single speech. It may be that by closer scrutiny, more and different categories could be discriminated, but, for the purposes of a general survey, 'better than that would be useless', as the Irish saying has it. Let me make it absolutely clear that I am not suggesting Shakespeare thought in terms of these seven deadly categories. I have sorted them out under headings only to show by a light analysis the extension and flexibility of his use of this instrument of discourse. I doubt if it can be matched in any other writer for the stage.

The seven functions I seem to find are: Comedy, Exposition, Comment, Prediction, Meditation, Prayer and Personal Epiphany.

Comic soliloquy is derived mainly from the Clown-act, a piece of primordial prose buffoonery, a vaudeville turn, a late example of which is found in this stage-direction from Thomas Heywood's *Second Part of King Edward the Fourth* (1599):

Jockie is led to whipping over the stage, speaking some words, but of no importance.

Shakespeare, however, was careful to write their brief solos and to insist that he who played the Clown should say no more than was set down for him. Exponents of the genre are Dromio of Syracuse, Grumio, Launce, Costard, Gobbo, Pompey Bum, the Porter in Macbeth, Autolycus and Trinculo. They run the whole length of the canon. What they say has no more than a minimal connection with the structure of their plays, generally speaking, and is offered as a gratuitous laugh; the best in this kind is the little comic cadenza offered by Launce to begin the third scene of Act II of *Two Gentlemen of Verona*; it is enlivened by the presence of his dog, Crab, who is its principal theme. At the other extreme is the Porter's speech in *Macbeth*, sardonic rather than hilarious, and profoundly structural.

Exposition includes letter-reading, proclamations and the kind of précis of events, common in early Shakespeare, but rare later:

> The Army of the Queene hath got the field:
> My Vnckles both are slaine, in rescuing me . . . (*etc.*)
>
> > (*3 Henry VI*, I, iv)

This function melts into that of *Comment*, which discourses on events in a quasi-choric manner and may be political, moral, social, or personal in tone; its chief use is to tell the audience what to think. Notable examples are the Bastard Falconbridge's soliloquy on Commodity (*King John*, II, i, 561 *et seq.*) or Petruchio's on wife-taming (*Taming of the Shrew*, IV i, 172), or, in tragic vein, Edgar's comment on the miseries of his condition that opens the fourth act of *King Lear*, only to be instantly contradicted by his meeting with his blinded father:

> Yet better thus, and knowne to be contemn'd,
> Then still contemn'd and flatter'd, to be worst:
> The lowest, and most deiected thing of Fortune
> Stands still in esperance. . . (IV, i, 1–4)

(However, he has still to learn that 'there is no worst'.[1])

Melting out of this category there comes what may be called the *predictive*, or *signpost* soliloquy, in which the course to be taken by the action is prophesied, so as to prepare the audience for it. Very frequently the speaker describes his own intentions, to make his hearers privy to them. The last four soliloquies of Iago are of this kind, though there is some admixture of comment in them (II, iii, 371–6, III, iii, 325–7, IV, i, 94–103, V, i, 11–22). But examples abound; of particular interest are those of Enobarbus in Act III of *Antony and Cleopatra*. Enobarbus has a choric function throughout, namely to tutor the audience into a right estimate of Antony's chances against Caesar; if his speeches are singled out and taken in succession they show a steady decline in his confidence; at first he is filled by an assured hope and tells Lepidus

> if *Caesar* moue him,
> Let *Anthony* looke ouer *Caesars* head,
> And speake as lowd as Mars. (II, ii, 4–6)

but this note, by gradual declensions, fades out of his speeches and is replaced by anxieties for his master. When, in the third act, the audience is likely to be twice misled by Antony's false shows of strength, on each occasion Enobarbus pricks the bubble for them, telling them what they should really think. On the first occasion Antony rouses himself to send Caesar a challenge to single combat; lest anyone should be taken in by this absurdity, Enobarbus is given an aside-soliloquy to pour contempt upon it:

> *Caesar* thou hast subdu'de
> His iudgement too. (III, xiii, 36–7)

The second lift of hope for Antony is given to the less discerning among the audience by the whipping of Thyreus, for his presumption in kissing Cleopatra's hand; 'at last (they think) the lion is roused and Antony is himself again'! for they hear him roar 'I am *Anthony* yet'. At the end of the scene, Enobarbus is the last to leave the stage and his comment shatters any impression Antony's anger may have made; at the same time it is a signpost to his own intentions. He sees it is time for him to desert his master:

> Now hee'l out-stare the Lightning, to be furious
> Is to be frighted out of feare, and in that moode
> The Doue will pecke the Estridge . . .
> > . . . I will seeke
> Some way to leaue him. (III, xiii, 195–201)

There is hardly a play without some signposting, and often the purpose of the signpost is to reassure the audience rather than to warn it. A famous example is Hal's soliloquy that promises his reform and the throwing off of his low company:

> I know you all, and will a-while vphold
> The unyoak'd humor of your idlenesse. . .
> > (*1 Henry IV*, I, ii, 187)

he also tells us of a future intended to reassure us:

> My reformation glittering o're my fault. . . (*etc.*)

By an interesting reversal of sensibility this speech tends, in our times, to have an opposite effect and set us against Hal; we think of the death of Falstaff and how 'his heart is fracted and corroborate' because of his treatment by the Prince, now King; so that in this soliloquy we revolt against a doubleness in Hal that brings on the old man's melancholy end. But we have two advantages over the Elizabethan audiences that heard *Henry IV* for the first time; we have undergone the change of values brought about by the Romantic movement; the *res privata* touches us more nearly than the *res publica*. Besides, we have read *King Henry V*.

Another soliloquy that was intended to reassure, but now creates mistrust in many hearts, is one which is given to the Duke in *Measure for Measure*, to explain why he does not relieve Isabella of her anxiety about her brother under sentence of death; his intentions are all for her good:

> She's come to know,
> If yet her brothers pardon be come hither:
> But I will keepe her ignorant of her good,
> To make her heauenly comforts of dispaire,
> When it is least expected. (IV, iii, 103–7)

To some this now seems a cat-and-mouse consolation.

A rarer yet most powerful use of soliloquy is that of pure *Meditation*; we hear it first in the mouth of the saintly King Henry VI: like some other meditative soliloquies it has become a set-piece:

> Oh God! me thinkes it were a happy life,
> To be no better then a homely Swaine...
> (*3 Henry VI*, II, v, 21–2)

The most famous of this kind of soliloquy is the most famous soliloquy in the world

> To be, or not to be, that is the Question.

These meditations are often the theme-bearers of the plays in which they occur, as this one is. It is easy to think of other examples, such as the many meditations in soliloquy that speak of the responsibilities of rulership. One of these moves towards a religious sense of obligation; it is the Duke's sermon to the audience that ends the third act of *Measure for Measure*; its gnomic sayings are marked by the emphasis of rhyme, rare in soliloquy:

He who the sword of Heauen will beare,
Should be as holy, as seueare. . .

Prayer is an extension of the range of soliloquy that has almost as
great an importance; those, for instance, of Angelo gain for him the
sympathy he needs so much when he reaches the watershed of
decision in respect of Isabella; they admit the audience to the
anguish of his mind, but do not save him from the sins that he will
commit. Richmond prays before Bosworth and Henry prays before Agincourt. The curses of Timon may be included in this soliloquy of invocation, and the conjuration of Prospero to the elves of
hills. Marlowe's *Faustus* may have pointed him the way to this
magical use.

Of all types, however, that of *Personal Epiphany* is the most frequent and necessary, and it springs from the special power of the
medium of theatre to present human character. Lovers declare
their love, villains their villainy, and every man and woman their
special passions, thoughts, moods, wishes and feelings in this way.
Whoever has an inner life may be allowed a solo hearing, especially
in a star-part, on a central theme.

This character-building by soliloquy is so frequent in Shakespeare that it scarcely needs illustration; the pattern for this art also
came from Marlowe and his great star-parts, Tamburlane, the Jew,
Faustus, Gaveston and others. They tell us who they are and what
they seek. Very early in his career Shakespeare saw the virtue of
this self-portraiture in a play; he took the idea up and gave it serial
extension; the first character he built up in this way, through successive plays, was that of Richard of Gloucester, whose gradual self-
revelation begins in ferocity on the battlefield and rises by a sardonic
cunning to self-sufficient kingship and tyranny, to end in night-
mare and defeat and the awareness that he needed love, like other
people. To read his soliloquies one after the other is to watch the
growth in self-hood of an antichrist, and see it reach the knowledge
of its despair.

III

The many ways in which Shakespeare used soliloquy are matched by a skill I cannot find in his contemporaries in spacing and bonding them in with the unfolding plot. In the works of his maturity, soliloquies are only placed at points of structural necessity, and are carefully prepared for, often several scenes in advance. The soliloquies in *Hamlet* are of this kind, but let us first look at an earlier example, which has an additional feature that I believe to be unique, in that this soliloquy is four times deliberately interrupted by Shakespeare, to achieve a particular effect. It is the soliloquy of Brutus in his orchard, that begins:

> It must be by his death: (*Julius Caesar*, II, i, 10)

It is mainly a meditation to reveal his character in the anguish of his situation, and to draw sympathy for him; it is broken in upon, three times by Lucius and once by the conspirators. Lucius was invented for this very purpose; he does not appear in Plutarch, Shakespeare's source. It is a source that makes strange reading. Not only is there nothing in it about Lucius; there is nothing in it about an orchard; there is virtually nothing in it about the reluctance of Brutus to join the conspiracy; yet the play makes a great point of this, showing him as one who listens with uncommitted gravity to the soundings and provocations of Cassius and intends to think them over before deciding. In reply he promises no more than

> What you haue said,
> I will consider: what you haue to say
> I will with patience heare...   (I, ii, 167–9)

And so he leaves both him and the audience in suspense; everything will turn on his decision; but it has not yet been made.

In immediately juxtaposed contrast to the guardedness of Brutus we are shown the impulsiveness of Casca. Terrified by the portents he has seen, his superstition and the persuasions of Cassius win him over to join the conspiracy in a moment. There is nothing about this in the source, it is Shakespeare's invention. In view of these

things, it becomes clearer how Shakespeare was plotting his play;
he was preparing the audience for the grave meditation he had in
view for Brutus in the quiet of his orchard; he had already supplied
them with two minor topics, by mentioning them in dialogue (the
Ides of March and the letters to be thrown in at Brutus' window),
which he would use in this meditation.

The orchard is specified in a stage-direction that can only have
come from Shakespeare's hand:

Enter Brutus in his Orchard.

As the orchard is nowhere mentioned in the dialogue, no book-
keeper could have known about it except from Shakespeare. We
are therefore to imagine a stage pleasantly set with trees, to give the
audience a sense of withdrawal from the city to a place of quiet
meditation. There is no reason to think Elizabethans were less able
to make stage trees than we are; it is a superstition to think they
used no scenery. The words of the stage-direction were not written
for fun; Chambers thinks *As You Like It* may reasonably have been
performed in 1599; *Julius Caesar* was certainly performed on
21 September 1599; perhaps *As You Like It* came first, and Shakespeare planned this soliloquy knowing he could use the *As You
Like It* trees.[1]

Lucius appears four times in this scene: first he is sent to fetch a
taper: next he reappears with the forged letters thrown through the
window, which we have been half-consciously expecting; later he
comes again to tell us that 'March is wasted fifteene dayes'; lastly
he comes to announce the conspirators.

It is obvious at once that only the last of these entries is strictly
necessary; Shakespeare could easily have brought Brutus in at the
start of the scene with a taper in one hand and the letters in the
other; his soliloquy could have started with a recollection of the
Soothsayer, whose boding words about the Ides of March Brutus
had himself repeated earlier, for the benefit of deaf Caesar. There
was indeed no reason why he should have been uncertain about
such a date; but Shakespeare chose to make him so, in order to give
Lucius another entry.

Why is Lucius so important? A child on the stage is like a dog, stealing all eyes and begetting sympathy for a loving master. Lucius is there to create compassion for Brutus, to whom he lends his innocence as he gives his obedience; he transforms his stern master into an image of fatherly love and points the contrast between the simplicity of childhood and the cares of grown men. His four entries are four fresh impulses, four shots in the arm of the soliloquy, their greatest sweetness being kept for its conclusion:

> Boy: *Lucius*: Fast asleepe? It is no matter,
> Enioy the hony-heauy-Dew of Slumber:
> Thou hast no Figures, nor no Fantasies,
> Which busie care drawes, in the braines of men. . .
>
> (II, i, 229–33)

For the soliloquy itself, almost at once the long-awaited decision is announced, the difficult argument is over:

> It must be by his death.   (II, i, 10)

To begin a soliloquy in mid-meditation is a skill that Shakespeare may have learnt from Marlowe, for that is how the *Jew of Malta* begins.[1] Here it saves Shakespeare from having to supply Brutus with real reasons (which are hard to find) in defence of preventive murder. The argument has already happened off-stage. It is like Brutus' love for Caesar; we are told about it but we are not allowed to see it; to see it would be too dangerous to Brutus.

We hear a kind of poetic summing-up, however, and are told of the anguish it had cost him to reach it:

> Betweene the acting of a dreadfull thing,
> And the first motion, all the *Interim* is
> Like a *Phantasma*, or a hideous Dreame. . .   (II, 1, 63)

Now that the decision has been taken and announced, Brutus is free to show his virtues; the first is generosity. He admits he knows no personal cause against Caesar. Next, candour; he has never known Caesar to allow his passion to oversway his reason. Then come the images that sum his argument so graphically: the bright day that brings forth the adder that should be killed in the shell. It makes it easier to kill a man if we see him as a snake.

Lucius at his second entry brings the letters he has found thrown in at the window; the fact that we know them to be forged and Brutus does not makes him seem a man deceived by those he trusts. We hear him read them and speak of his ancestor who drove out Tarquin for being called a king; hereditary duty seems to add its justifications.

Then Lucius enters a third time with the reminder of the Ides of March. Fate itself seems to be driving Brutus on to an act predetermined by greater powers than his.

The fourth entry of Lucius announces the conspirators and before they come in Brutus has time to speak of the shame and repugnance that fill him:

> O Conspiracie,
> Sham'st thou to shew thy dang'rous Brow by Night,
> When euills are most free? O then, by day
> Where wilt thou finde a Cauerne darke enough,
> To maske thy monstrous Visage? (ii, i, 77–81)

The meeting with the conspirators is the last interruption to his meditation, which closes, as we have seen, with a final touch of tenderness in Brutus which Lucius was created by Shakespeare to invoke. Never again is Brutus so close to his audience.

In *Othello* there are two soliloquists, Iago and Othello. Iago has eight soliloquies, Othello three. Iago needs this number to reveal, first, the quality of his own tortuous nature and, secondly, the detail of his intentions. Broadly speaking, his first three soliloquies are epiphanies, the last five, signposts.

The three in which he reveals his nature are unique in Shakespeare. Professor Spivak asks: 'Is it not an undeviating practice of the Elizabethan dramaturgy that the soliloquy is an instrument of direct revelation, providing information that the audience need to have and would not otherwise clearly get at all?'[1] The information Iago gives is indeed necessary; but it is information about himself, not about any objective world. When he tells us of Othello that

> it is thought abroad, that 'twixt my sheetes
> Ha's done my office; I know not, if't be true— (Q, I, iii, 381-2)

this is not to be taken as evidence that there was a rumour of this kind going about. If Shakespeare had meant us to believe this, nothing would have been easier for him than to make Roderigo or Montano, or even the Clown, blurt it out. But we never hear the slightest hint of it; it is one of Iago's inventions, and gives us clear information about his state of mind; he is not under hallucination, as Macbeth is in his 'dagger-speech'; he is in the subtler, but very common condition, which almost everyone experiences in some degree, of one who is entertaining a fantasy in order to feed a passion.[1]

Psychologically, Iago is a slighted man, powerfully possessed by hatred against a master who (as he thinks) has kept him down, and by envy for a man he despises who has been promoted over him. All this comes out in the first fifty lines of the play. Such a man will naturally have a fantasy life in which he can hate these enemies the more, that he may revenge himself upon them the more. The fantasy that comes most easily to him is that of crude copulation; it is his theme-song. In the opening scene his language to Brabantio is all stallion, and now his first thought is

> to abuse *Othello's* eares,
> That he is too familiar with his wife.　　(F, I, iii, 389-90)

His next idea is to diet his revenge on Desdemona himself, 'not out of absolute lust', as he says; but in order to spite Othello, whom (of course) he now fancies to have 'leap't into his seat' and debauched Emilia. So strong with him is this vulgar fantasy that he extends it to Cassio as well

> (For I feare *Cassio* with my Night-Cape* too)　　(F, II, i, 301)
> 　　　* [*read* night-cap]

He indulges these imaginings as a sadist will conjure up whole histories of imaginary crimes committed by the victim he is about to chain up and whip, so that he may 'punish' them. He may not exactly 'believe' in the imputed guilt, but he pretends to because it gives relish to his performance.

But these elementary things in psychology are not the most important things in Iago's soliloquies. It does not matter very much whether an audience believes that he has really heard the rumours he speaks of, or whether they have fabricated themselves within him to sharpen his pleasure in revenge.

What is more important (as our analysis will show) is that his first three soliloquies are *graded in order of heinousness*, the foulest last. Their function is not to bring him closer to and create sympathy for him in the audience (as in the case of Brutus) but to distance him from them, to create hatred for him. This is what is unique in them. The soliloquies of Richard III, a very different kind of villain and self-revealer, actually win his hearers over to him: just as he wins Anne to be his wife over the dead body of her father-in-law, so he wins the audience (over many other dead bodies) by his fellow-conspirator wit in soliloquy; but Iago's soliloquies are designed to make him progressively more repellent. They are the hairpin bends by which we descend into the abysses of his nature.

Yet there is a third purpose to be discerned in these speeches. They are there to offer the living image of a man who is the opposite of what he appears to be. He is a walking illustration of the theme with which he opens the play:

I am not what I am. (F, I, i, 66)

Just as in the depths of the sea there have been charted great rivers (that make a trickle of the Amazon) which flow in a constant direction in perpetual spate, so in Shakespeare's mind may be tracked certain powerful and constant currents of thought, that flow through many plays; and this is one of them. It breaks surface from time to time among many other themes, and especially perhaps at this period in his life as a writer (between *Hamlet* and *Macbeth*). In no one is it more sharply presented than in Iago, in whom there is no twilight in the night-and-day of his behaviour: the moment we are alone with him, or when he is alone with his dupe Roderigo, his night falls: but when he is seen in any other company he is bright with good fellowship and honest concern for others, as I shall show. By the peculiar use of soliloquy allotted to Iago, Shakespeare sought to give definition to this embodiment of an obsessive theme of his: we see and hear alternately what Iago is and seems.

He begins with no clear plan at all. We are shown him trying treacherously to embroil his master with a senator. It is never told us what he hopes to gain by this, except the satisfaction of a revenge on the Moor for Cassio's promotion. But, for this opportunist, spite is satisfaction enough. Seeing, however, that his own fortunes are dependent upon Othello's, it does not appear that to rouse a senator against the Moor will advance his personal position. He tells Roderigo that he has a 'peculiar end' for his behaviour (I, i, 61), but this is a fantasy too; his plot against Othello does not become clear to him until much later, when it comes in a flash, in all its monstrous logic, in the third of his graded soliloquies. Let us take them in order.

The first is placed at the end of Act I. The care of Desdemona has just been entrusted to him and he is left with Roderigo, whom he immediately instructs in the means of seducing her. Roderigo, gulled by his hopes and lusts, goes out obediently to sell all his land. It is time for Iago to explain himself a little to the audience. Once again he asserts the basic fact:

> I hate the Moore   (F, I, iii, 380)

and gives us a first pointer to the plot that is forming in his mind:

> Let me see now,
> To get his Place, and to plume vp my will
> In double Knauery. How? How? Let's see.
> After some time, to abuse *Othello*'s eares,
> That he is too familiar with his wife. . .   (F, I, iii, 386–90)

and he finishes this aspect of the soliloquy with

> I haue't: it is engendred: Hell, and Night,
> Must bring this monstrous Birth, to the world's light.
>
> (F, I, iii, 397–8)

In his second soliloquy, he brings his plot into slightly sharper focus; he will abuse Cassio to the Moor and make the Moor thank him and reward him for 'making him egregiously an Asse': but still the line of action is a little blurred:

148

'Tis heere: but yet confus'd,
Knaueries plaine face, is neuer seene, till vs'd. (F, II, i, 305–6)

The complete, explicit plot is reserved for the third soliloquy:

For whiles this honest Foole
Plies *Desdemona* to repair his Fortune,
And she for him, pleades strongly to the Moore,
Ile powre this pestilence into his eare:
That she repeales him, for her bodies Lust. (F, II, iii, 342–6)

His five other soliloquies are direct signposts about the working
of his plots, and their function is to give a practical shape to his
thoughts, rather than a psychological. The three soliloquies we
have discussed offer us a progressive clarification of his schemes;
they also offer a progressive exhibition of the evil in him. Brutus
shows us his soul, Iago his brains, a fresh step down at each epiphany. His first motive is factual: he tells Roderigo that he has been
passed over for promotion; but his first soliloquy already passes
over into the fantasy we have discussed, the inventive mania of a
sense of injury, in a man obsessed by sex:

I hate the Moore,
And it is thought abroad, that twixt my sheetes
Ha's done my office: I know not, if't be true—
Yet I, for mere suspition in that kind,
Will doe, as if for surety... (Q, I, iii, 380–4)

In his first soliloquy he descends from professional jealousy to
sexual jealousy; in his second, the sexual fantasies begin to pro-
liferate and the sharp pleasure of a revenging copulation begins to
rouse in him a kind of lust, leading to the neat, exciting cruelty of

And nothing can, or shall content my Soule
Till I am eeuen'd with him, wife, for wift*. (F, II, i, 292–3)
* [*read* wife]

But there is worse to come. It is not enough for him to use Desdemona's body against Othello, he means to use her soul. We hear no
more about his wanting to enjoy her; that fantasy gives way to the
foulest he can think of, with a diabolical theology of its own, which
he calls 'Divinity of Hell'.

And by how much she striues to do him good,
She shall vndo her Credite with the Moore.
So will I turne her vertue into pitch,
And out of her owne goodnesse make the Net,
That shall en-mesh them all.   (F, II, iii, 347–51)

These three speeches, then, go steadily deeper into a repulsive evil, sauced by a sneering contempt for all that may be thought holy and good. 'Contempt', said Coleridge, 'is never attributed in Shakespeare, but to characters deep in villainy, as Edmund, Iago, Antonio, and Sebastian.'[1]

But Shakespeare is just as careful to show Iago fair in public as he is to show him foul in private. It is this that makes him so detestable, so atrocious in his evil. It is the major strategy of the play, not only that every other character should think him 'honest' but that the audience should see why they do so. Two scenes in particular are planned so as to bring this about. The first is the scene of Desdemona's arrival in Cyprus, and the second is that of the drunken brawl that brings disgrace on Cassio.

Desdemona arrives in the midst of a violent storm; it has separated her from Othello. But why did Shakespeare choose to place them in different ships to begin with, and then invent a storm to part them? Was it to symbolise the inward storm about to break over and separate them till death? Possibly. But there was also a more practical reason. By telling his story in this way he was able to show what a delightful fellow in company Iago was, and how natural it would be to like and trust him.

The audience has so far only seen him as a secret trouble-maker and may well be thinking 'why does Othello have such a man for his Ensign?' The scene in Cyprus gives a part of the answer.

He had been put in charge of Desdemona by Othello before they left Venice (I, iii, 285) and now, when she arrives with him in the midst of a tempest that has sunk the Turkish fleet, she is in deep anxiety for Othello's safety, which is still in doubt. It is Iago who rises to the occasion and steps forward to cheer and entertain her by the improvisation of a set of verses, tossed off on the spur of the moment, and as elegant as anything in *The Rape of the Lock*. It

succeeds completely in taking Desdemona's mind off her worries
and shows Iago's amusing social gifts, and care of a mistress entrusted to him. This is the reason for the little scene and therefore
for the storm and the separation of man and wife. It has the further
usefulness of leaving the audience in doubt whether or not the
marriage of Othello and Desdemona has been consummated; for
this will add sharpness to the second scene that demonstrates the
kindly virtues of Iago.

Delightfulness is one thing, but honest-to-God good comrade-
ship is another, and that is what we are next shown in him. That we
may be certain it is sham, we first hear him priming Roderigo to
stir up trouble against Cassio:

Cassio knowes you not: Ile not be farre from you. Do you finde some
occasion to anger *Cassio* . . . he's rash, and very sodaine in Choller: and
happely may strike at you, prouoke him that he may; for euen out of
that will I cause these of Cyprus to Mutiny. . .   (F, II, i, 262–70)

We then see Iago, in all good fellowship, plying Cassio with drink,
singing a rollicking song or two, with every appearance of high
spirits and honest affection.

Roderigo plays his part; the pre-arranged fight takes place with
a perfect spontaneity, nothing could seem more natural; uproar
ensues, at the height of which Iago, decent fellow that he is, inter-
venes to prevent bloodshed:

> (*Iago*) Nay good Lieutenant. Alas Gentlemen:
>   Helpe hoa. Lieutenant. Sir *Montano*:
>   Helpe Masters. Here's a goodly Watch indeed.
>   (F, II, iii, 150–2)

and keeps it up until Othello, dragged by the riot from his wedding-
bed, enters and demands the reason for it.

Nobody will tell him. At long last, and very reluctantly, Iago
begins:

> I had rather haue this tongue cut from my mouth,
> Then it should do offence to *Michaell Cassio*.
> Yet I perswade my selfe, to speake the truth
> Shall nothing wrong him. . .   (F, II, iii, 213–16)

What could be fairer, more honest, more convincingly friendly, more reliable and soldierly than Iago's behaviour, so far as Othello, Montano and even Cassio can think? And presently, after Othello has gone back to bed, it is Iago who consoles the stricken Cassio and advises him kindly and intelligently for his good. He only has to importune Desdemona to be reinstated, he tells him.

These two incidents—the storm and the brawl—establish Iago's honesty and kindness, and are the Siamese twins of his soliloquies, opposites that cannot be separated; there are other passages that show his manly delicacy, good faith and zeal:

> I do beseech you,
> Though I perchance am vicious in my guesse
> (As I confesse it is my Natures plague
> To spy into Abuses, and of* my iealousie
> Shapes faults that are not) that your wisedome
> From one, that so imperfectly conceits,
> Would take no notice. . .   (F, III, iii, 148–54)
>   * [read oft]

Such delicacy, such self-doubt, such eagerness for the peace of his master's mind, must convince anyone (who had not heard him in soliloquy) of Iago's honesty. In public he is as amiable and virtuous as Dr Jekyll; in soliloquy he shows us Mr Hyde.

Othello has one soliloquy that specially concerns us here; he needs it badly. He has to recreate the sympathy he has forfeited by striking his wife in public and by calling her 'that cunning whore of Venice' to her face. It would have been easy to have started the last scene—the scene of her murder—without a soliloquy. Desdemona need not have been asleep or even in bed, if Shakespeare had chosen to tell his story so. But the need for Othello to right himself with the audience before his murder of her, the need to show that he thought of it not as murder but as justice, was paramount; only by soliloquy could this be achieved.

Once again, as in the case of Brutus, the argument is over before the soliloquy begins; he has decided upon what to do, and what he says is the embroidery on that decision, not the argument that led him to it.

It is the Cause, it is the Cause (my Soule)
Let me not name it to you, you chaste Starres,
It is the Cause.   (F, v, ii, 1–3)

Underlying the soliloquy of Brutus is the axiom that to seek a crown deserves death. Underlying that of Othello is the axiom that to commit adultery deserves death. Many men have held or acted on these axioms, and, in the theatre, we must accept them while we watch these plays; they are matters in which our disbelief must be suspended, for the sake of the other experiences we can derive from seeing them. Othello never questions the axiom that governs his action; his fault is folly, gullibility.

O Foole, foole, foole!   (v, ii, 326)

If the seeming-honesty of Iago, which we have discussed, is given full value in performance, Othello may still seem 'an honourable murderer'. The structure of the last scene is designed to help in this; it is symmetrically planned. It begins and ends in an attempt at an act of justice, on a kiss; and there is visual repetition too, for these acts are both placed on the wedding-death-bed of Desdemona and Othello. What more can be done by Othello to even out his fault than by paying for it in the same coin as he had made her pay? This is what the eye brings home to confirm what the ear hears in the opening soliloquy:

Oh Balmy breath, that dost almost perswade
Iustice to breake her Sword. One more, one more:
Be thus when thou art dead, and I will kill thee,
And loue thee after. One more, and that's the last.
                                        (*He kisses her.* Q)
So sweet, was ne're so fatall.   (F, v, ii, 16–20)

On the same gesture the play finds its close:

I kist thee, ere I kill'd thee: No way but this,
Killing my selfe, to dye vpon a kisse.   (F, v, ii, 361–2)

IV

I come at last to the soliloquies of Hamlet. Out of a total of some two hundred and eighty lines of soliloquy spoken in the play, over two hundred are spoken by him. No one else in all Shakespeare is allowed so close to the audience: it is his soliloquies that have made him the most celebrated, as he is the most enigmatic, figure in the drama of the world.

Suppose all his soliloquies were cut out. The action would hardly suffer at all; a little cobbling and it would still present an intelligible story of an admirable if crafty prince, playing a lone hand against wickedness in high places and succeeding in the purgation of his country at the cost of his life. It would still be the best Revenge Play ever written, crammed with breathless action. But no one would ever have supposed there had been a moment of delay on Hamlet's part; no one would ever have imagined that he had a smack of Hamlet himself.[1] For these speeches that he makes in soliloquy create a relationship between Hamlet and his audience that no one other character in drama enjoys. Because they are many and seem scattered through the play with no more plan behind them than the whim to speak, they may give the impression that there is something careless in its construction. This impression, however, is not supported by an analysis of them.

Hamlet's first soliloquy is simply but carefully prepared for, yet when it comes it is something of a surprise. The appearance of the Ghost in the previous scene, and Horatio's closing lines

> Let vs impart what we haue seene tonight
> Vnto yong *Hamlet*. For vpon my life,
> This Spirit dumbe to vs, will speake to him:
>
> (F, I, i, 169–71)

create a natural presumption that when at last we are alone with young Hamlet, it will be of his dead father that he will speak. His mourning wear singles him out for such a purpose, as do the remonstrances he receives so publicly for his obstinate grief. Thus isolated from the court and left alone when it sweeps out, he seems groomed for a soliloquy of exposition that will throw light on the mysterious apparition of his father in the first scene. But instead, by a dramatic surprise, he speaks of his mother, as if the soloist in a concerto, at his first entry, were to ignore the first subject just announced by the orchestra and go on to the second. This is a fair analogy for the way in which Shakespeare has apportioned his themes. To old Hamlet is given the theme of murder, to young Hamlet, the theme of incest. Together they make the crimes that mark the rottenness of Denmark. By the time the exposition is complete, at the end of the first act, it will be seen that these two themes make a counterpoint, one with the other; both are aspects of the same thing, but must first be sounded separately. A theme-bearer is chosen for each. The murder-theme is the more important of the two, because it is the motive of the main action; the murder, not the incest, is what demands revenge, and must lead straight into the second act. So Shakespeare reserved the secret of it for the end of his first act and gave young Hamlet a soliloquy, not about his father but about his mother.

As he reaches its climax in a wish for death, Horatio enters with Marcellus and Barnardo and their news. Hamlet has spoken the second theme, they bring back the first in a new key. In this way his soliloquy dovetails perfectly with the action as well as with the thematic exposition.

Hamlet's next soliloquy comes after the revelations made to him by the Ghost. It is natural and necessary. Natural because the Ghost would not speak except when they were alone together and the Ghost has now departed; Hamlet is therefore alone and whatever he says will be in soliloquy, just as in the previous case when he is left alone after the court has withdrawn. Necessary because he must show how the two themes of murder and incest combine and sound the major theme of Denmark; his soliloquy is like the kind of cadenza in which the soloist unites the first and second subjects:

> O most pernicious woman!
> Oh Villaine, Villaine, smiling damned Villaine!
> My Tables, My Tables; meet it is I set it downe,
> That one may smile, and smile and be a Villaine;
> At least I'm sure it may be so in Denmarke...
>
> (F, I, V, 105–9)

His third soliloquy needs more examination, to discover why it comes where it does. It ends Act II, coming immediately after the exit of Rosencrantz, Guildenstern, Polonius and the Players. We need to go back to the beginning of the act to understand this. In its first scene, Ophelia tells her father of Hamlet's extraordinary behaviour in her closet; Polonius makes a wild guess:

> *Polon.* Mad for thy Loue?
> *Ophe.* My Lord, I doe not know: but truly I do feare it.
>
> (F, ii, i, 85-6)

In the next scene we hear the King and Queen briefing Rosencrantz and Guildenstern. The politic King tells them of Hamlet's 'transformation', a delicate periphrasis; the Queen talks of her 'too much changed Sonne'.

In due course Polonius arrives; disdaining to be mealy-mouthed, he says straight out that he has found the cause of Hamlet's *lunacy* (ii, ii, 49). When he comes to speak of this, he makes no bones about it.

> Your Noble Sonne is mad. (F, ii, ii, 92)

All these are reminders to the audience of what, at the end of Act I, Hamlet has told Horatio and the others about 'putting on an Antic disposition', warning them to expect great changes in Hamlet's style of behaviour when next they see him.

Presently he enters reading; Polonius takes over from the King and Queen and tries to engage him in conversation. Hamlet's answers are highly eccentric; Polonius thinks he is 'far gone', though he is later forced to admit that there is method in his madness. There are, of course, no stage-directions to tell the actor how to play this scene, other than those that we have noted in the dialogue (the proper place to look for them in Shakespeare). We must therefore imagine Hamlet in very disordered dress and clowning his remarks, to bear up the impression of madness he has created in the Court, so heavily underlined in this and the previous scene.

Polonius departs, giving place to Rosencrantz and Guildenstern; to them Hamlet behaves quite rationally, but confesses to a total lethargy; he has forgone all mirth, lost all custom of exercise. The world seems to him a sterile promontory and man the quintessence of dust. This is not the language of a man of action capable of the revenge he had so solemnly undertaken in sight of the audience at his last appearance. But worse is to follow. The arrival of a visiting company of tragedians is suddenly announced, and Hamlet with a burst of energy and excitement throws himself into the relatively trivial thrill of it; his welcome to the actors is more than friendly, it is almost fulsome for a man in sables. He demands a passionate speech on the spot; what is more, he tries his own hand at reciting one.

The dramatic purpose of this is twofold; first, to emphasise the unaccountable but whole-hearted self-immersion of Hamlet at this moment in a thing so trifling as Court theatricals; secondly to show the enormous difference between the ineffectiveness of an amateur like Hamlet doing a piece of reciting, and the virtuosity of the professional Player who takes the speech over from him. It is a speech of magnificent power, that surges up out of its surrounding prose dialogue like a spouting whale. The tragedian, trained in the matching of gesture to rhetoric, makes so exciting a thing of it that when, after some twenty-eight lines of it, he is interrupted by Polonius, he is made to continue for another fifteen or so by Hamlet. Two whole minutes in a long play, given to a piece of play-acting about Hecuba, needs some justification; but we are not yet told what it is. We are only told that the actor's performance is so vivid that he pales and has tears in his eyes at its conclusion. It would need to be vivid if it is to move a Claudius.

But what is an audience, that does not know the story, to make of this? Their hero, whom they have last seen on his knees, dedicating himself to the revenge of his father's murder, has reappeared first as a clown, next as a man without a purpose, scornful of all values, and lastly as a man fired to enthusiasm by a pack of strolling players. This is no behaviour for a Prince-Revenger.

Hamlet is given his longest soliloquy to explain it. He dismisses Polonius; he dismisses the actors; he dismisses Rosencrantz and Guildenstern, and he turns at last to the audience, with a sudden relaxing and relief, as to old friends, and says: 'Now I am alone'.

This phrase is not so banal as it seems: it marks his first chance to take them back into his secrets. He begins with violent self-reproach for inaction and even for cowardice, though guilty of neither: he has 'delayed' no longer than was needed to convince the court that his mask of madness showed his true face, as we have seen. This kind of self-reproach becomes obsessive and recurs (less violently) in two later soliloquies (III, i, 83–8 and IV, iv, 32–66). But it is purely soliloquial: it never occurs to him to talk like this to Horatio, his close confidant. Why is this?

I suggest that Shakespeare knew he could command the patience of Horatio for his hero but was less certain of commanding that of an audience which expected violence and cunning in a 'revenger' and had seen neither in Hamlet during this long second act. So in this soliloquy he gave them both, beginning with a violence of self-reproach for 'delay' that anticipates and prevents what any audience might feel towards him. It is a superb piece of audience-craft.

This analysis (of course) does not 'explain away' the strange trait in Hamlet's character that compels him to torture himself for a supposed procrastination. On the contrary, it explains why it was necessary for Shakespeare to discover this obsession in him which, psychologically considered, starts a thousand exciting suggestions. It is another example of what we have seen in the case of Cressida— the solution of a technical theatre problem calling forth a unique stroke of creative genius.

Of his next soliloquy ('To be, or not to be') I have already said why I think it to be placed where it is, at the heart of the play. It is a meditation on the central theme of the duties and temptations of a noble mind in an evil world, and creates the stillness and intimacy that are needed to prelude his only scene with a girl he once loved, and still loves well enough to wish to keep her unspotted from it.

There remain three soliloquies to be considered:

(1) *'Tis now the verie witching time of night* (III, ii, 378–89)

(2) *Now might I do it pat, now he is praying* (III, iii, 73–96)

(3) *How all occasions doe informe against me* (IV, iv, 32–66).

The functions of the first and last of these are not difficult to see. The first comes after the success of the Mousetrap has convinced Hamlet of the guilt of Claudius, and of Gertrude, in the murder of his father. At the height of this new certainty he receives a summons to his mother's closet. Revenge must therefore be the uppermost thought in his mind, as it is in the minds of the audience; yet he must pause to consider how such thoughts should govern his behaviour to his mother; this is so important that he quite naturally dismisses his company to consider how he should act towards her:

Leaue me Friends   (III, ii, 377)

He begins in revenger-language; it reminds us that ghosts may walk at night and bring with them airs from hell, such as the audience has already heard breathed in the word '*Swear!*' from under the stage.

> 'Tis now the verie witching time of night,
> When Churchyards yawne, and Hell it selfe breaths out
> Contagion to this world. Now could I drink hot blood... (F)

But to this reminder of his duty as a revenger must be added a reassurance of his humanity as a son:

> O Heart, loose not thy Nature; let not euer
> The Soule of *Nero*, enter this firme bosome:
> Let me be cruell, not vnnaturall... (F)

His last soliloquy (the third of those listed above) is even simpler in function; it is to reassert his dedication to the task of revenge 'from this time forth', and to point the contrast between his own scruples and the uninhibited confidence of a Fortinbras. The audience might be thought to need this reassurance that his thoughts are still bent on his terrible task, for it will be some time before they see him again; the story has to turn to the madness of Ophelia and the rebellion of Laertes. In practice, it seems, this retainer on the minds of the audience was found unnecessary, for the speech is not in Folio and may be presumed to have been usually cut in performance.

I come to the second of the last three soliloquies of Hamlet, the soliloquy he makes when he comes upon the King at his prayers. Prayer is an unusual activity for incestuous fratricides. But so necessary was it (for the structure of the play) that Claudius should be found by Hamlet in an attitude of prayer, that Shakespeare took the risk of its unlikeliness, and prepared us for it as well as he could by suggesting that even so great a villain as the King could suffer the twinges of conscience. In an earlier scene when Polonius is encouraging him to conceal himself so as to overhear Hamlet's meeting with Ophelia, and instructing his daughter in hypocrisy, he jauntily remarks:

> *Ophelia*, walke you heere. Gracious so please ye
> We will bestow our selues: Reade on this booke,
> That shew of such an exercise may colour
> Your lonelinesse. We are oft too blame in this,
> 'Tis too much prou'd, that with Deuotions visage,
> And pious Action, we do surge o're*
> The diuell himselfe. (F, III, i, 43–9)
>
> * [*read* sugar o're]

This, strangely, touches Claudius to the quick, and, in a soliloquy given aside, he says

> How smart a lash that speech doth giue my Conscience?
> The Harlots Cheeke beautied with plaist'ring Art
> Is not more vgly to the thing that helpes it,
> Then is my deede, to my most painted word.
> O heauie burden! (F, III, i, 50–4)

This intimation that Claudius has a conscience comes so unexpectedly and so seriously in the context as to be striking and memorable. It rounds him out suddenly into a wretched creature, miserable in his triumphs of power and lust. It seems as if this is to prepare us for the success of the Mousetrap, which entirely depends on his ability to feel remorse: we have already heard Hamlet say

> The Play's the thing,
> Wherein Ile catch the Conscience of the King. (F, II, ii, 600–1)

but both these passages look ahead, even further than the play-within-the-play, to the moment when the King's conscience brings him to his knees:

Bow stubborne knees, and heart with strings of Steele,
Be soft as sinewes of the new-borne Babe,
All may be well.

Enter Hamlet   (F, III, iii, 70–3)

The situation that follows sets all naturalism at defiance: it is a *tableau*, a *coup de théâtre* of sensational force. It was Shakespeare's invention (as far as we can tell from his surviving sources, which have no such scene) and, like that other astonishing scene of the ghost-under-the-stage, it is one of an absolute structural necessity, deeply concerned with the central themes of the play. All Hamlet's soliloquies are great arches that bridge the inner world of the play, across which the themes pass from action to action in its outer world; but this one is the most ingenious of them all, and has to bear the greatest weight. Whether Shakespeare hit on it by inspiration or by taking thought, we can come to see its necessity by the following pedestrian argument.

The purpose of the 'antic disposition' has been achieved, in that it leads directly to the play-within-the-play. The purpose of the play-within-the-play has been achieved by giving a violent certainty to Hamlet (and the audience) of the King's guilt. Its effect cannot be allowed to cool or evaporate. But the story (in the source) brings Hamlet to the Queen's chamber and so to the murder of Polonius; and that murder can only be followed by the instant arrest and banishment of Hamlet. If Hamlet is to have a chance of confronting the King alone, in the white heat of certainty of his guilt after the play-scene, it must happen before he is sent to England, and therefore before he visits his mother. But just as it is essential for the story that he should be given this chance of taking his revenge, so it is equally essential that it should be impossible for him to take it. The King must be preserved for the end of the play.

This being so, the only thing on earth that could save Claudius from death at Hamlet's hands would be some situation that gave him sanctuary. So the only safe place for him (though he does not know this), is on his knees. Hamlet must be ready to strike, but Claudius must be in baulk.

To kill a man at prayer would be a sacrilege that no audience could forgive, the action of a scoundrel. Shakespeare makes this perfectly clear by giving the idea to Laertes later in the play:

> (*King*) ... *Hamlet* comes backe: what would you vndertake,
> To show your selfe your Fathers sonne indeed,
> More then in words?
> *Laer.* To cut his throat i' th' Church.   (IV, vii, 124–6)

Yet although it is a relief to the audience that Hamlet does not kill the 'praying' king, it is also a disappointment; for audiences are ambivalent in their desire for revenge and in their reprobation of it. They want the horror, but it horrifies them.

So Shakespeare gave them what they wanted, took it from them, and then restored it to them in another form. The revenge is postponed, but a later one is promised, far worse, one of a diabolical malignity. But a promise, in theatre, does not have the force of a visible action, and much can happen before it is carried out. This is how the promise, or threat, is phrased:

> Vp Sword, and know thou a more horrid hent
> When he is drunke asleepe: or in his Rage,
> Or in th'incestuous pleasure of his bed,
> At gaming, swearing, or about some acte
> That ha's no relish of Saluation in't,
> Then trip him, that his heeles may kicke at Heauen,
> And that his Soule may be as damn'd and blacke
> As Hell, whereto it goes.   (F, III, iii, 87–95)

It is a threat of a revenge not unlike that actually performed by Cutwolf, the dwarfish cobbler in *The Unfortunate Traveller*, printed by Thomas Nashe in 1594. Cutwolf forces his enemy, Esdras, at pistol-point, to blaspheme away his soul, and then shoots him instantly in the throat 'that he might neuer speake after and repent him'. For this appalling vengeance, we are told, Cutwolf was broken on the wheel, and the people

(outragiously incensed) with one conioyned outcrie, yelled mainely, Awaie with him, away with him, Executioner torture him, teare him, or we will teare thee in peeces if thou spare him.

162

The executioner needed no exhortation herevnto, for of his owne nature was he hackster good inough: olde excellent was he at a bone-ach.[1]

In like manner the audience thrills to the horror that Hamlet proposes for Claudius, and which, indeed, ultimately comes to him; for Providence arranges that Hamlet shall kill him at a moment when three fresh murders are on his soul (Gertrude's, Laertes' and Hamlet's). So, in a sense, the audience gets all the horror it hankers for in the end, but by the act of God; for in the interim Hamlet has abdicated from his revenge, as such, after resting his case before the jury in his speech to Horatio:

> Does it not, thinkst thee, stand me now vpon
> He that hath kil'd my King, and whor'd my Mother,
> Popt in betweene th'election and my hopes,
> Throwne out his Angle for my proper life,
> And with such coozenage; it's not perfect conscience,
> To quit him with this arme?   (v, ii, 63–8)

For when it comes to the point, Hamlet leaves the issue in the hands of higher powers:

there is speciall prouidence in the fall of a Sparrowe . . . the readinesse is all, . . . let be.   (v, ii, 211–17) (Q, 1604)

He is no Laertes, no Cutwolf. He is a just man, and that is what all audiences, without expressly knowing it, wish him ultimately to be shown. But more consciously, incited by the story, they long for that 'wild justice' which Bacon called revenge. The delay theme, borne by these soliloquies, was Shakespeare's means to satisfy the contrary appetites of his audience.

CHAPTER VII

REVISION AFTER PERFORMANCE

Entia non multiplicanda praeter necessitatem

(Old saw, known as Occam's razor)[1]

*This chapter will offer a dramaturgical analysis of certain passages in the
1623 Folio text of Othello which diverge from the 1622 Quarto text, and
will show that these divergences can only be explained on the supposition
that, in this play at least, Folio embodies a Shakespearean revision of the
play that appears in Quarto. As this conclusion is directly contrary to the
most recent findings of textual criticism, the chapter will begin with a
study of received opinions.*

I

What seems to have happened to Shakespeare's plays in the
printing-house can sometimes be tested by what seems to have
happened in them on the stage. *Othello* is a play which, when discussed in terms of the former, has been judged to have been cut for
acting purposes; the cut version is believed to be represented by the
1622 Quarto text. When, however, it is discussed in terms of the
latter, this will be seen to be impossible; it must therefore follow
that the supposed cuts in Quarto were in fact not cuts but additions,
included in Folio, and that we are in the unsuspected possession of
evidence as to how Shakespeare, on this occasion at least, set about
the revision of a play that, in performance, had seemed not wholly
satisfactory to him.

Great authority has warned us more than once against the notion
that Shakespeare could ever have revised his plays. Sir Edmund
Chambers stated that he felt little doubt 'that, broadly speaking,
when he had once written them, he left them alone',[2] and Sir
Walter Greg, concurring with Miss Alice Walker, expressed contempt for the 'supposition that, after a play had been written and
performed, its author continued to tinker with the dialogue'.[3]

Why Shakespeare should, in this respect, have differed from other playwrights working in the theatre is not too clear; but the way to meet an *a priori* objection is not to counter it with another, but to show it breaking down in particular examples. Yet it may be pointed out that telling a story in terms of the stage is an art in which first thoughts, so easily replaced by second thoughts, may disappear and leave no trace; it was a mere textual accident that betrayed Shakespeare's second thoughts in the case of the double dismissal of Pandarus, already discussed in Chapter IV. The fact that we have two early texts of *Othello* turns out, I think, to be another such accident.

The two texts differ from each other in several ways, and for several reasons, in upwards of a thousand passages; the kinds of difference that concern us may be listed as follows:

(1) Quarto has over fifty oaths;[1] Folio has none.

(2) There are about a thousand minor variations in phrasing pepper-potted through the text—every scene has some—that make no important modifications in meaning, either to the passages in which they occur, or to the play as a whole.

(3) Stage-directions are more numerous and elaborate in Quarto than in Folio.

(4) There are about a hundred and fifty lines, undoubtedly Shakespeare's, that appear in Folio but not in Quarto.

It is agreed by most authorities that, generally speaking, Folio readings are more reliable than those in Quarto,[2] but this judgment, in passages which cannot be shown to have been misprinted, is based upon personal taste. I hope to show that there is better reason for trusting the Folio text.

The explanations offered to account for differences between the two texts also diverge, in some cases into a frightening complexity. After long and complex argument, Greg sardonically remarks:

It will have become evident whither all this is tending. . . we get a picture of two different scribes struggling with, and at times variously interpreting, much and carelessly altered foul papers. . . That one scribe was the book-keeper and that he was preparing the prompt-copy there seems no reason to doubt; but that the two scribes were the same is unlikely, nor indeed is there anything to suggest that the Q transcriber was the book-keeper, once we realize that there is no need to credit him with an intimate knowledge of the play. . .[1]

Miss Walker, *per contra*, thinks the Q transcriber possibly was the book-keeper, one who knew the play well: '. . . the 1622 quarto was a memorially contaminated text, printed from a manuscript for which a book-keeper was possibly responsible and based on the play as acted.'[2] It is clear that she regards this book-keeper as imbued with a theatrical knowledge of the play, for she says of him elsewhere that he was 'one who relied on his knowledge of the play as acted and on his invention where memory failed'.[3] Greg, on the other hand, thought 'he was occasionally high-handed and indulged in a certain amount of editing in a literary rather than a theatrical direction.'[4]

Greg's scribe is literary rather than theatrical, Miss Walker's theatrical rather than literary; both critics, however, tend to agree as to the interpretation of Miss Walker's discovery that there are certain passages strangely identical in Folio and Quarto: Miss Walker explains the matter thus:

> It is, in fact, only possible to reconcile the evidence of the verbal variants between the printed texts with their close orthographical connexion, common errors and common typographical features by supposing that the Folio text was printed (with correction and amplification) from a copy of Quarto.[5]

There remain, however, two unspoken questions raised by these conjectures that are far more searching than those they seem to answer. What possible reason could there be for causing, or even allowing a transcript of *Othello* to be made in about 1620, when, as Greg himself has shown, preparations for printing the Folio were already in progress? And what possible authority could such a transcript have in the eyes of the editors of Folio? Why should they have made it the basis of their forthcoming text?

Not to tease my readers by plunging into a close argument that leads in a concealed direction, I shall briefly state at once the conclusions I am led to about what happened to produce these two texts, deferring the evidence and the argument supporting my conjectures until Miss Walker's views have been considered in greater detail, for they seem to bar my way with formidable authority.[1]

II

I imagine, then, Quarto to have been printed in 1622 (with the usual mistakes) from the first prompt copy of the play made (with the usual mistakes) from Shakespeare's 'foul papers' by the book-keeper in, or shortly before, 1604, and that Folio was printed from a second prompt copy, made (also with the usual mistakes) from a revised set of foul papers, in or not long after 1606; the immediate occasion that prompted Shakespeare to revise the play was perhaps the Act of that year against profanity and swearing in stage-plays,[2] but the real motive can, I think, be shown to have been Shakespeare's dissatisfaction with certain features in the play as it was first written.

In making the second prompt copy, it seems possible that the book-keeper found certain passages in Shakespeare's notoriously difficult handwriting indecipherable, and that when in doubt he helped himself to the earlier prompt copy, to seek clarification; embedded, therefore, in both manuscripts might be certain spellings and phrases specially recognisable by their oddity, and this idea may help, together with Miss Walker's theory already quoted, to explain the curious phenomenon that she was the first to observe. If the view I am putting forward is true, it would mean that the text of Quarto was substantially Shakespeare's, but suffered from such bruises as playhouse transcription (to make a prompt-book) and type-setting (to make Quarto) may be seen to have inflicted. Miss Walker thinks that Quarto does indeed represent a prompt-copy version, but she feels haunted by 'an uneasy suspicion that the mind behind the quarto text had not quite grasped its sense'.[3] She believes it to contain memorial perversions that 'lose the appropriateness of Shakespeare's art in approximations'.[4] As my view is that the text of Quarto represents a prompt-book made from Shakespeare's autograph not later than 1604, there would have been no time for memorial perversions to accrue and be recorded in it, and I must therefore meet Miss Walker's objections in detail.

I do not doubt that there were some passages in the 'foul papers' before him that the book-keeper did not well understand and may have perverted; for instance the famous lines of Othello's disclaimer, in asking to be allowed to have the company of Desdemona in Cyprus (I, iii, 261 *et seq.*)

> I therefore beg it not
> To please the pallat of my appetite,
> Nor to comply with heate, the young affects
> In my defunct, and proper satisfaction   (Q)

These lines reappear with equal obscurity in Folio; a fact I would account for by supposing that the book-keeper, in making a second prompt-book from Shakespeare's revised foul papers, found the passage difficult to read and supplied it with a shrug from the earlier prompt-book already in his keeping; meaningless it may have been, but he was accustomed to hearing it. Actors frequently speak lines they cannot understand, and sometimes lines that nobody can understand.

But Miss Walker senses a more general perversion than can be proved from the ten cases—this is one of them—she cites of agreement between Folio and Quarto which, she rightly says, 'seem pretty certainly wrong'.[1] She believes there is a persistent vulgarisation throughout the Quarto; and this is a serious charge. As it is one which contains an element of the subjective it is not easy to refute convincingly.

The evidence she offers for her view deserves thought. There are three occasions upon which (as she points out) Othello is stung, in Quarto, into an ugly oath, which (in common with all other Quarto oaths) Folio removes. The first passage is when Iago is beginning to tighten the rack by refusing to disclose his 'uncleanly apprehensions' about Cassio's relations with Desdemona; Quarto reads:

> It were not for your quiet, nor your good,
> Nor for my manhood, honesty, or wisedome,
> To let you know my thoughts,

Oth. Zouns.
Iag. Good name in man and woman's deere my Lord;
  Is the immediate Iewell of our soules.   (Q)

(Q, III, iii, 156-60)

Instead of Zouns and what follows, Folio reads:

Oth. What dost thou meane?
Iag. Good name in Man, & woman (deere my Lord)
  Is the immediate Iewell of their Soules;   (F)

Miss Walker regards restraint as the dominant trait in Othello's character; and so it is. The destruction of that restraint, so that he not only falls in a fit, but strikes his wife in public, after calling her a devil, is the work of Iago, begun in this scene with 'Hah? I like not that' a hundred and fifteen lines before: and certainly this *Zouns* comes something too soon in the process of his destruction. This process is marked not only in the action but in the progressive use of foul imagery, uttered from Othello's infected mind, as other critics have noticed:[1] it is consistent with the view I have proposed that Shakespeare thought better of having a *Zouns* at this early point in Othello's moral disintegration, and later amended it to *What dost thou meane*, to keep Othello's violences in reserve a little longer. It may also be noticed that the Folio readings in the lines that follow seem to show an authoritative re-touching in their new form, and above all in the repunctuation of Iago's lines: if, as we are assured, this was the work of Compositor B,[2] he was showing genius for the dramatic pointing of a line; the comma and the bracket indicate precisely how this line should be spoken, for the comma adroitly turns a generalisation made on Cassio's account into something that sticks a barb in Desdemona too. One has only to say it to be aware of this:

  Good name in Man—and *woman*—(dear my lord). . .

Who is to say that, on this occasion at least, Compositor B did not find in the copy before him a revised punctuation from Shakespeare's 'foul papers' that anticipated his own mannerisms? That Shakespeare sometimes cared about commas is certain from Peter Quince's Prologue to *Pyramus and Thisbe*.

Another 'Zouns' given in Quarto to Othello is in the scene that follows (III, iv, 95), where Othello is demanding his handkerchief of Desdemona, and she, ignoring his demands, presses for the re-instatement of Cassio. The readings are these:

(Quarto) *Oth.* The handkercher.
        Des. I pray talke me of *Cassio*.
        Oth. The handkercher.
        Des. A man that all his time,
          Hath founded his good fortunes on your loue,
          Shar'd dangers with you.
        Oth. The handkercher.
        Des. Ifaith you are too blame.
        Oth. Zouns.   (*Exit*)   (III, iii, 93–9)

(Folio) (for the last three lines above)

        Oth. The Handkerchiefe.
        Des. Insooth, you are too blame,
        Oth. Away.   *Exit Othello.*

Folio's elimination of *Zouns* seems differently motivated here, and may be thought due to the Act against profanity in stage-plays, of 1606: for the oath is not only in keeping with the mounting fury of Othello, but also, considered as his *exit-line*, makes good effect: whereas Folio's *Away* is a word demanding or designating a move-ment of retreat by Desdemona, rather than by Othello.

Othello's third oath is in the last scene of the play, when he can-not bring himself to say to Desdemona what it is that he believes Cassio to have done to her:

(Quarto) *Oth.* He has confest.
        Des. What, my Lord?
        Oth. That he hath—vds death.
        Des. How, vnlawfully?
        Oth. I.   (v, ii, 71–4)

For the third line above, Folio has

        Oth. That he hath vs'd thee.

It is hard to determine if *vds death* is a swear-word or an acci-dental metathesis of the letters in *vsde the* (as M. R. Ridley has suggested):[1] but if it was one of Quarto's oaths and the line originally read

> That he hath—vds death—vs'd thee

as Professor Alexander conjectures,[2] there seems nothing vulgarly inappropriate in it. This, however, must remain a matter of private feeling.

Two other examples of the persistent vulgarisation, claimed as characteristic of Quarto, are offered by Miss Walker. They both come in a single speech of Desdemona's (I, iii, 247–59) when she is pleading to be allowed to go with her husband to Cyprus. Quarto reads:

> *Des.* That I did loue the Moore, to liue with him,
> My downe right violence, and scorne of Fortunes,
> May trumpet to the world: my hearts subdued,
> Euen to the vtmost pleasure of my Lord:
> I saw *Othelloes* vissage in his minde. . .
> So that deere Lords, if I be left behinde,
> A Mothe of peace, and he goe to the warre,
> The rites for which I loue him, are bereft me. . .
>
> (Q, I, iii, 247–57)

For the fourth line above, Folio reads

> Euen to the very quality of my Lord;

which I think to be Shakespeare's own revision of his earlier line. But though most readers will think Folio here 'improves on' Quarto, it does not follow that there is anything vulgar in the idea that Desdemona's heart is subdued to Othello's pleasure: it does not even need to have—if that be vulgar—a sexual connotation. It simply means that she is glad to do whatever pleases her husband, however great the demand upon her. But the revised line, concerning quality, leads in more skilfully to the next thought, namely her understanding of Othello's mind.

The second example for Miss Walker's thesis, offered in this speech, is in the last line quoted above, which in Folio reads:

> The Rites for why I loue him, are bereft me:

Miss Walker thinks that Shakespeare meant *rights* (privileges of sharing the hazards of war) not *rites* (love's rites) and that both texts here misrepresent Desdemona's point of view in a vulgar way. Yet I must oppose the opposite, though equally subjective, opinion that there is nothing degrading in the thought that Desdemona should love to be with Othello for the great reason that makes all lovers love to be with one another, their nuptial rites.

These, I believe, are all the passages adduced by Miss Walker in confirmation of her impression that Quarto is a vulgarised text: I have tried to show that they involve no vulgarisation and that if, on one occasion, Shakespeare used the too violent *Zouns*, it was not out of keeping (though coming a shade too soon) with his presentation of the destruction of Othello's restraint, a restraint which it is his glory to have recovered once more in the measured opening of the final scene.

III

Having done what I can to clear Quarto of the implication that it is a vulgarised text, I can pass to a consideration of the two kinds of difference to be found between Quarto and Folio that should be of special interest to anyone attempting to stage the play, namely the differences in the matter of stage-directions, and those occasioned by the Folio-only lines. First, for the stage-directions.

Although the stage-directions cannot absolutely be left out of account in considering the relationship between the two texts, it must be said at once that, as so often in Shakespeare, they are virtually useless to anybody, whether directors, actors, book-keepers or critics. The reason is that almost all the instructions they give can be inferred from the dialogue and their inclusion in the early texts is so absolutely haphazard (except on the whole for entrances and exits) that many a necessary and major move or gesture is passed over in silence, as will be presently shown; more than this, they tell us very little about the texts in which they appear, as Greg has remarked: 'the great mass of stage directions are of very little assistance in distinguishing between foul papers and prompt copy.'[1] There are one or two stage-directions in the Quarto of *Othello* that have the vague, tentative quality of an author's imagining, but would never suit a prompter; these may be regarded as survivals copied into the text from Shakespeare's foul papers; so we find:

Enter Desdemona, Iago, *and the rest.* (Q, at I, iii, 171)

It is equally vague in Folio:

Enter Desdemona, Iago, Attendants.

Many crucial stage-directions can only be inferred from what is said. In *Othello*, for instance, the two absolutely climactic stage-directions one would expect to find would surely be

She drops her handkerchief

at III, iii, 292, and

He strikes her

at IV, i, 236. But neither Quarto nor Folio give any directions at these points; both gestures must be inferred from the dialogue. This, however, is no argument against supposing the two texts to have both been printed from prompt copies; the moves and pro-perties needed in *Othello* are few and obvious; most of them can be safely left to the stage-gumption of the actors and would be easily remembered, once the play had been worked on the stage. In matters of doubt they had the author present among them to direct them if necessary. But even if they had not, in the case of the first missing stage-direction noted above, the boy playing Emilia had only to tell the boy playing Desdemona to drop his handker-chief just before he made his exit, for Emilia would know from his lines that he was about to need it:

> *Oth.* Your napkin is too little:
>   Let it alone, come I'le goe in with you.
> *Des.* I am very sorry that you are not well.
> *Em.* I am glad I haue found this napkin,   *Ex.* Oth. *and* Desd.
>   (Q, III, iii, 291–4)

Lastly, and perhaps too obviously, many actions implicit in the dialogue can appear in one text and not in the other, without mak-ing a rap of difference to an actor: for instance, when Othello re-joins Desdemona in Cyprus at the beginning of the second Act, Quarto reads:

Oth. Amen to that sweete power,
   I cannot speake enough of this content,
   It stops me heere, it is too much of ioy:
   And this, and this, the greatest discord be,   *they kisse.*
   That ere our hearts shall make.   (II, i, 193–7)

Folio has the same lines, but leaves out '*they kisse*'. But what of that? These are lines that could not possibly be said without kisses.

Let us note, however, that Quarto is more copious than Folio in explicit directions of this kind: here is a more complex example of this fact, which shows, first, how Quarto notes actions that Folio does not bother to mention and secondly how neither text notes some necessary moves of minor importance (including an *exit*) because they could safely be left to the stage-sense of the actors concerned. The passage comes in the third scene of the second act. Iago's plot to make Cassio drunk enough for him to start 'some action that may offend the isle' has already been revealed to the audience in a soliloquy of his (II, iii, 44–57). The plot has been successfully launched and Cassio has just tottered off the stage after demonstrating his drunkenness by trying to prove his sobriety. The audience is waiting expectantly for the 'action that may offend the isle'. At this point Roderigo enters and Iago sends him off after the drunken Cassio and this, as the audience knows, is the moment for setting fire to the fuse, for we have heard Iago coaching Roderigo in a previous scene for this precise occasion (II, ii, 260–70). Roderigo's entry and Iago's instant sending of him off to provoke Cassio is given thus in Quarto (II, iii, 128):

Iag. How now *Roderigo*,   *Enter* Roderigo.
   I pray you after the Leiutenant, goe.   *Exit Rod.*
Mon. And tis great pitty that the noble Moore
   Should hazard such a place, as his owne second,
   With one of an ingraft infirmity:
   It were an honest action to say so to the Moore.
Iag. Nor* I, for this faire Island:
   I doe loue *Cassio* well, and would doe much
                Helpe, helpe, within

           *[read Not]

To cure him of this euill: but harke, what noyse.
> *Enter* Cassio, *driuing in* Roderigo

Cas. Zouns, you rogue, you rascall.

Mon. What's the matter Lieutenant?

Cas. A knaue, teach mee my duty: but I'le beate the knaue
into a wicker bottle.

Rod. Beate me?

Cas. Doest thou prate rogue?

Mon. Good Lieutenant; pray sir hold your hand.

Cas. Let me goe sir, or ile knocke you ore the mazzard.

Mon, Come, come, you are drunke.

Cas. Drunke? *they fight.*

Iag. Away I say, goe out and cry a muteny. *A Bell rung.*
Nay good Lieutenant: godswill Gentlemen,
Helpe ho, Lieutenant: Sir *Montanio*, sir,
Helpe maisters, here's a goodly watch indeed,
Who's that that rings the bell? Diabolo—ho,
The Towne will rise, godswill Lieutenant, hold,
You will be sham'd for euer.

The directions *Helpe, helpe, within* | *they fight* | and *A Bell rung*
do not appear in Folio: nevertheless, with a little patience, all of
them can be inferred from the dialogue, for, later, Iago tells
Othello 'There comes a Fellow crying out for helpe' (II, iii, 218),
and '... I heard the clinke and fall of Swords' (II, iii, 226). Othello
himself, with 'Silence that dreadfull Bell' (II, iii, 167) makes it clear
that this noise-off is needed.

As to those other directions that can only be inferred from what
is said, it is clear that Montano must start struggling with Cassio
when he says 'pray sir hold your hand' or else it will make nonsense of Cassio's retort 'Let me goe sir': and this, in turn, shows that
the explicit direction *they fight* must mean that *they draw their swords
and fight*: for they are at grips already. So too when Iago says 'Away
I say, goe out and cry a muteny' it is clear that he must be addressing
some particular soldier, who thereupon makes his *exit* at a run, and,
once off-stage, either must ring a bell himself or else sign to the
noises-off man to do so.

Lastly let us look at those stage-directions in Quarto and Folio that contain some instructions that cannot be illated with certainty from the dialogue: I believe the following to be a complete list:

	QUARTO	FOLIO
I, i, 81	Brabantio *at a window.*	*Bra. Aboue.*
I, i, 160	*Enter* Barbantio *in his night gowne, and seruants with Torches.*	*Enter Brabantio, with Seruants and Torches.*
I, ii	*Enter Othello, Iago, and attendants with Torches*	*Enter Othello, Iago, Attendants, with Torches.*
I, iii	*Enter Duke and Senators, set at a Table with lights and Attendants.*	*Enter Duke, Senators, and Officers.*

QUARTO

v, ii, 83   *Oth.* Tis too late. *he stifles her.*
          Des. O Lord, Lord, Lord. Emilia *calls within.*
          Em. My Lord, my lord, what ho, my Lord, my Lord.

FOLIO

          Oth. It is too late. *Smothers her.*
                    Aemilia at the doore.
          Aemil. My Lord, my Lord? What hoa? My Lord, my Lord.

	QUARTO	FOLIO
v, ii, 201	*Oth. fals on the bed.*	(no direction here)
v, ii, 236	*The Moore runnes at* Iago. Iago *kils his wife.*	(no direction here)
v, ii, 285	*Enter* Lodouico, Montano, Iago, *and Officers,* Cassio *in a Chaire.*	*Enter Lodouico, Cassio, Montano, and Iago, with Officers.*

This is no great haul to have made from a whole play: all that we have gleaned from these directions that we could not know without them are a few rather obvious touches of detail: torches upon two occasions (to show the audience that the action must be imagined to be taking place at night): the precise moment for the stifling of Desdemona, together with Emilia's position at that point (these are in both texts). Quarto adds Brabantio's window and his night-gown, the Duke's table with Cassio's chair: it also makes clear that when Emilia says 'Nay, lay thee downe and rore', Othello has fallen on to the bed and not on to the floor; and it gives the necessary detail of the movements of Othello and Iago when the latter 'kils his wife'. This last is the only important contribution made by the stage-directions to our understanding of how to present the play.

What can be argued from this evidence? First, that much could safely be left to the Company to interpret, improvise and remember; stage-business was their business. Yet in the early stages of rehearsal it saves time if explicit directions are written into the prompt-book, even if incompletely: but after the early stages the actors know their moves and no great harm would come from leaving them out, were a second prompt-book to be made while they still remembered them. The greater copiousness of Quarto in this respect, then, is consistent with the view that it is based on an earlier text than Folio, though of course it does not prove this: but it certainly contains a few practical directions that would be useful in the early stages of first production, such as those requiring torches and a table for the scene at the Sagittary, and the details of the death-blow given by Iago to Emilia.

IV

The lines that appear in Folio but not in Quarto may now claim our attention. Of these Miss Walker says: 'The bulk of the omitted matter, however, fairly certainly represented cuts for performance, motivated . . . by practical rather than artistic considerations.'[1] In discussing these lines it is certainly well to be as practical as we can, though it is not always easy, in analysing the medium of an art, to distinguish between a practical and an artistic consideration: theatrical effect, however practical in its contrivance, is usually there to create an artistic effect of some sort. There are, however, some almost purely practical motives that might be suggested and may be worth getting out of the way. It is, for instance, a practical rather than an artistic thing to save running-time in a production, but that motive can never have affected the texts of *Othello*: we may strengthen Greg's remark that 'obviously the omission of 160 lines out of 3,300 does nothing appreciable to shorten the play'[2] by calculation: if we reckon on a speed of about twenty lines a minute (the majestic pace of Home Service Shakespeare),[1] eight minutes in two hours and three quarters would be saved. It seems ludicrous to suppose that so inconsiderable a saving of time could have been a motive in Elizabethan days. We may also notice that the lines in question are scattered through many scenes and shared by many speakers: therefore there can have been no intention to eliminate a particular actor, or group of actors, and so effect an economy: if that had been an object, the first scene to cut would have been that which opens Act III, since it does nothing to advance the action and involves unnecessary musicians and a Clown. Nor is any economy in costume effected by these supposed cuts. The omission of the *Willow Song* (IV, iii) from Quarto has often been accounted for by the conjecture that, at the crucial moment of some production of the play, Desdemona's voice, 'like a piece of uncurrent gold', was 'cracked within the ring' and that there consequently was no boy who could both sing and act to take his place: this is an attractive supposition and would provide a practical motive for this cut (if it be a cut): but, as we shall see, there are reasons for doubting this explanation.

I am unable to think of any other practical reasons for cuts that could apply in the problems before us: let us then turn to the lines themselves in their 'immediate context', as Greg suggests we should,[2] and see, if we can, how they *work*. Many of the passages will resist enquiry, giving us no certain information why they are there except that the first editors of Folio possessed a fuller text than Quarto and thought fit to use it. But there are some which I believe can be shown to have a practical function in the working of the play—that is, that they are not mere discourse, but examples of a deft stage-craft at work.

If this can be proved, we shall be in a position to say that not only would there be no good reason imaginable for cutting them, but very good reason for adding them (if they were lacking before). I shall try to avoid putting any 'aesthetic' pressure into what I aim to make a purely functional argument: but, as I have said, the two kinds of consideration are hard to keep separate in considering great art. Without the counter-thrusts of pinnacles and flying buttresses, many a cathedral would fall down. Yet while we compute their usefulness, we feel their beauty to the point at which feeling seems to condition argument.

Returning to the lines in Folio, if we can think of no good reason why they should be cut from their context, and see clearly why they are a necessary strength to it, nothing entitles us to assume stupid cutting, still less destructive cutting, except a blind reliance on the supposed axiom that Shakespeare never revised his work; but no such axiom should be allowed to become a trip-wire to truth and we must be prepared to have the courage of our reasoning (if we feel it to be firm) and believe that, axiom or no, in certain instances cutting will not explain the facts and that a revision must therefore have taken place. For if the lines were not cut, but added, they were added by Shakespeare. Rather than think he permitted his play to be maimed by senseless mutilations, one must think that in the course of rehearsal and performance he noted certain passages that had seemed to him viable in the study when he wrote them, but which, he found, needed strengthening when he brought them to the stage. If this can be made clear, then the text of Folio (apart from the normal errors of transmission from manuscript to print wherever these can with certainty be detected) has a final authority, except, perhaps, in the matter of swear-words and oaths: for an editor must no doubt consider whether, in this small matter, Shakespeare was acting under *force majeure* or not, when they were eliminated.

With these provisos in mind, let us move steadily through the play and analyse all those passages that occur in Folio only, for which some purpose in stage-craft can be demonstrated to account for their presence in the text. I shall reserve the use of italics for Folio-only lines, so that their contextual place and function and the way in which the Folio passage is dovetailed into the Quarto text may leap to the eye.

QUARTO

i, i, 121   *Rod.* Sir, I will answer anything: But I beseech you,
         If she be in her chamber, or your house,

Let loose on me the Iustice of the state,
For this delusion.

FOLIO

Rod. Sir, I will answere any thing. But I beseech you
Ift be your pleasure, and most wise consent,
(As partly I find it is) that your faire Daughter,
At this odde Euen and dull watch o' th' night
Transported with no worse nor better guard,
But with a knaue of common hire, a Gundelier,
To the grosse claspes of a Lasciuious Moore:
If thus be knowne to you, and your Allowance,
We then haue done you bold, and saucie wrongs.
But if you know not this, my Manners tell me,
We haue your wrong rebuke. Do not beleeue
That from the sence of all Ciuilitie,
I thus would play and trifle with your Reuerence.
Your Daughter (if you haue not giuen her leaue)
I say againe, hath made a grosse reuolt,
Tying her Dutie, Beautie, Wit and Fortunes
In an extrauagant, and wheeling Stranger,
Of here, and euerywhere: straight satisfie your selfe.
If she be in her Chamber, or your house,
Let loose on me the Iustice of the State
For thus deluding you.

The function of these seventeen and a half lines could hardly be
clearer: it is to state exactly what is happening between some Moor
and Brabantio's daughter: they state it twice over, a fact to which
Roderigo himself draws our attention by his phrase '*I say againe*'.
It is the purest, most lucid piece of exposition in the scene and gives
us the reason for 'this terrible summons' that has brought Brabantio
out of bed.

Let us remember that in 1603 nobody knew the story of *Othello*.
The name that has become a world-symbol for tragic jealousy had
then never been heard of, for Shakespeare invented it. A beholder
of the first performance would have had absolutely no idea what he
was going to see and hear; it is hard for us to imagine this, but it
would be a fact that he had never so much as heard of Iago, or

speculated upon motiveless malignity. For this was not a play about Yorkists and Lancastrians, of whom everyone knew something, but a completely new invention: if one could suppose that anyone in the audience had read its source in Cinthio, he would still have been none the wiser for it during that opening scene, which is also Shakespeare's invention.

I have laboured this point, so obvious, yet so easily forgotten, so that we may the better imagine an intelligent spectator in 1604 trying to pick up his bearings in those first moments of the play, before Roderigo's explanatory speech. He would have gathered that a disgruntled soldier called Iago had been passed over for promotion and that his master, a Moor, had promoted 'one Michael Cassio, a Florentine' in his stead; in spite of which, this Iago intended still to remain in the Moor's service, though hating him, for reasons of self-interest. Then, suddenly, the following:

> *Rod.* What a full fortune does the thicklips owe,
> If he can carry 'et* thus? (Q, I, i, 67–8)
>   * [*read* carry it]

Thicklips is a strange word, not too easy instantly to identify with the Moor, who has not yet been *seen*; yet straight on top of this 'thicklips' comes a reference to some woman and her father of whom we have heard nothing, and we are plunged into uproar, still ignorant of what Brabantio and his daughter have to do with the Moor, with Michael Cassio, or with the speakers.

> *Ia.* Call vp her father,
> Rowse him, make after him, poyson his delight. (I, i, 68–9)

And this they do together 'with timerous accent and dire yell'.

Brabantio appears above and they tell him of *thieves*: he is robbed: an old black ram is tupping his white ewe, the Devil will make a grandsire of him: his daughter will be covered with a Barbary horse: his nephews will neigh to him, he'll have coursers for cousins and jennets for germans; his daughter and the Moor are making the beast with two backs.

All this is being shouted up in an altercation the excitement of which tends to gain more attention than the meaning of these lewd crossword-puzzle riddles of Iago's. Perhaps our intelligent auditor, who no doubt has read Rabelais[1] and knows what is meant by the beast with two backs, may take in the situation. But how many others will? Folio brings Roderigo to their assistance.

His lines are the most purely informative lines in the scene, and to cut them would be to remove a structural feature: it would be like eliminating a flying buttress built in later to hold a powerful, unanticipated thrust: without it the building may not fall, but it is endangered. In like manner, without these lines the scene may not be wrecked, but it will not tell its story clearly to meaner capacities. If we suppose the lines to have been originally present but cut, we have to suppose a cutter who could not recognise plot-lines when he saw them; he might without danger to the scene have cut some other dozen lines (for instance lines 45–56 'Many a duteous and knee-crooking knave . . . as you are Roderigo') but instead he chose to cut these lines of functional exposition: he was a fool, in fact. And yet not such a fool that he could not show adroitness; for he was clever enough to see that *But I beseech you* could be divorced from the lines

If it be your pleasure, and most wise consent, etc.

and the thought they contain, and harnessed to

If she be in her Chamber, or your house

which is an opposite thought. I do not find it easy to believe in such a clever fool; we have no right to postulate him. Cuts are not made by prompters or book-keepers, but by a person in authority. Perhaps by Shakespeare.

Let us see what we are being asked to believe if we take the view that Roderigo's lines were added, not cut. It is no more than this; that it was found in performance that the play opened too confusedly: someone may have expressed himself bewildered: Shakespeare may have been persuaded it needed a strengthening of information: so he built one in, turning the thought after *But I beseech you* to suit this purpose: or, even without prompting, he may have made a mental note that if ever occasion should arise for another production of the play, here was a passage which needed revision.

Not all the passages that appear in Folio but not in Quarto yield
so firm an answer to the question what their function is. I shall deal
only with those that can lead us to something better than guess-
work. The passages from which a firm argument can be drawn
revealed themselves (to my surprise) in many cases to be *serially
connected*; the connections are in fact *thematic*, and this is a fact that
must affect our judgment in the matter of whether or not they are
revisions. The first group of these thematically connected lines is
made up as follows: I, ii, 65, I, ii, 72–8—I, iii, 63: I have italicised
Folio-only lines.

I, ii, 62–78 (*Bra.*) Oh thou foule Theefe,
       Where hast thou stow'd my Daughter?
       Damn'd as thou art, thou hast enchaunted her
       For Ile referre me to all things of sense,
I, ii, 65   *(If she in Chaines of Magick were not bound)*
       Whether a Maid, so tender, Faire, and Happie,
       So opposite to Marriage, that she shun'd
       The wealthy curled Deareling of our Nation,
       Would ever haue (t'encurre a generall mocke)
       Run from her Guardage to the sootie bosome,
       Of such a thing as thou: to feare, not to delight?
I, ii, 72   *Iudge me the world, if 'tis not grosse in sense,*
       That thou hast practis'd on her with foule Charmes,
       Abus'd her delicate Youth, with Drugs or Minerals,
       That weakens Motion. Ile haue't disputed on,
       'Tis probable, and palpable to thinking;
       I therefore apprehend and do attach thee,
       For an abuser of the World, a practiser
       Of Arts inhibited, and out of warrant;
(Quarto: 'to fear, not to delight,
       Such an abuser of the world, a practiser, etc.)
I, iii, 59–64 (Folio)
       Bra. I, to me.
       She is abus'd, stolne from me, and corrupted
       By Spels, and Medicines, bought of Mountebanks;
       For Nature, so prepostrously to erre,
I, iii, 63   *(Being not deficient, blind, or lame of sense,)*
       Sans witch-craft could not.

If we now consider the function of these italicised lines, it is apparent that scattered as they are, they all insist upon a single idea. This rules out the possibility that the two singletons could have fallen out of Quarto's text by accident: the coincidence would be too great. Their single idea is the unnaturalness of Desdemona's choice, which is only to be explained by supposing that Othello has made use of magic. This is Brabantio's obsession: he first utters it on meeting with Othello in I, ii. It is in his first words:

> Damn'd as thou art, thou hast enchaunted her

and he carries his one idea before the Duke, with reiteration:

> Judge me the world, if 'tis not grosse in sense, *etc.*　　(I, ii, 72)

This at once recalls Quarto's (and Folio's) line

> For Ile referre me to all thing(s) of sense　　(I, ii, 64)

and is again recalled by the Folio-only line

> Being not deficient, blind, or lame of sense　　(I, iii, 63)

These ideas of magic and the unnatural are importantly developed later in the play, when Iago recalls Brabantio's words in order to raise suspicions of Desdemona's honesty:

> She that so young could giue out such a Seeming
> To seele her Fathers eyes vp, close as Oake,
> He thought 'twas Witchcraft.
> 　　(III, iii, 213–15) (F and Q, except for differences in spelling)

and again:

> (*Oth*.) I do not thinke but *Desdemona*'s honest
> *Iago*. Long liue she so;
> 　And long liue you to thinke so.
> *Oth*. And yet how Nature erring from it selfe.
> *Iago*. I, there's the point:
> 　As (to be bold with you)
> 　Not to affect many proposed Matches
> 　Of her own Clime, Complexion, and Degree
> 　Whereto we see in all things, Nature tends:
> 　Foh, one may smel in such, a will most ranke,
> 　Foule disproportions, Thoughts vnnaturall. (F, III, iii, 229–37)

The lines we are considering that appear, in Folio only, in the mouth of Brabantio, are thus not only linked to each other, but also to a crucial argument in the central scene of the play, and help to force entry into Othello's mind for the idea of Desdemona's falsity, and oblige him to judge between her honesty and Iago's. This scene is the crux of the play, the watershed: after that decision has been taken, there is no going back.

It would not, I think, be unduly speculative to suggest that Shakespeare was fully conscious of the importance and intricacy of this scene, for it is managed with an extreme economy, in a series of complex moves, each one of which achieves its own climax, yet leads in to the next in obedience to a whole strategy that is to bring Othello to his knees in a great oath of vengeance on Desdemona, the top and final climax of the scene. The essential action is the making of the decision by Othello to trust Iago rather than Desdemona, and this is what kindles the demand for proof, first uttered almost lightly by Othello, secure in his belief in Desdemona's love:

> For she had eyes, and chose me. No *Iago*,
> Ile see before I doubt; when I doubt, proue;
> And on the proofe, there is no more but this,
> Away at once with Loue, or Iealousie. (F, III, iii, 193–6)

The demand for proof is first answered by Iago's reminders of the Brabantio themes of magic and unnaturalness, as we have seen; after the injection of this poison, Iago makes his exit, leaving Othello to comment:

> This Fellow's of exceeding honesty (F, III, iii, 262)

but he has no sooner uttered this opinion and meditated a little on what Iago has put into his mind, than Desdemona appears, and the sight of her at first dispels all doubts, though only for the moment:

> If she be false, heauen mock'd it selfe:
> I'le not beleeue't. (F, III, iii, 282–3)

This is the point chosen for Desdemona to drop her handkerchief, as if in answer to the demand for 'proof'. Emilia picks it up and Iago is brought in to snatch it from her. The audience now

knows him armed with the makings of an ocular demonstration
when he feels the time is ripe for it: this makes more ominous the
scene which follows between him and Othello during which he
refrains from using it: but the audience can feel the handkerchief
burning in his pocket, so to speak. He is holding it in reserve.

Othello returns, heavy with the workings of the poison which
'not poppy nor mandragora' can mitigate: his first speeches are
about lust in Desdemona: the see-saw of his doubt has once more
come down against her and the demand for proof returns with a
new force:

> Villaine, be sure thou proue my Loue a Whore;
> Be sure of it: Giue me the Occular proofe . . .
>
> (F, III, iii, 363–4)

But his rage is also against Iago; he slams the see-saw back once
more:

> If thou dost slander her, and torture me,
> Neuer pray more . . .   (F, III, iii, 372–3)

Iago meets this passion with the hypocritical simulation of passion,
on *his* side:

> God buy you: take mine Office. Oh wretched Foole,
> That lou'st to make thine Honesty, a Vice!
> Oh monstrous world! Take note, take note, (O World)
> To be direct and honest, is not safe. . .   (F, III, iii, 379–82)

This outburst gives Othello pause

> Nay stay: thou should'st be honest.   (F, III, iii, 385)

To which Iago replies

> I should be wise; for Honestie's a Foole,
> And looses that it workes for.

It is here that Folio has a speech of seven and a half lines which
exactly epitomise the situation and which are not in Quarto:

> *Iago.* I should be wise: for Honestie's a Foole
> And looses what it workes for.
> *Oth. By the World,*
> *I thinke my Wife be honest, and thinke she is not:*

186

I thinke that thou art iust, and thinke thou are not:
Ile haue some proofe. My name that was as fresh
As Dian's visage, is now begrim'd and blacke
As mine owne face. If there be Cords, or Kniues,
Poyson, or Fire, or suffocating streames
Ile not indure it. Would I were satisfied.
Iago. I see you are eaten vp with Passion:
  I do repent me, that I put it to you.
  You would be satisfied?
Oth. Would? Nay, and I will.   (F, III, iii, 386–97)

The speech contains the ideas of having to judge between Desdemona and Iago, of Othello's insistence on proof, of his black face, and of vengeance: it sums up Othello's dilemma, with a backward hint at the unnaturalness of loving one like him, and points forward to a revenge with the swearing of which the scene is to end: every word has its function too in the texture of the whole play. We may pause here to consider whether these interlocking ideas could possibly have been selected for elimination by a cutter. Why should a director of the play, with so obviously intimate a knowledge of it, eliminate passages of such structural strength? Can he have been so intelligent and yet so foolish? If anyone is willing to think so, he can feed his credulity further, for we now come to this cutter's masterpiece of folly-in-discernment: once more we are faced with interlocking passages.

We have already, in an earlier chapter,[1] noted the importance of the gesture of kneeling. The climax of Act III, Scene iii, in *Othello* is the visual image of Othello kneeling before Iago: it is in both texts; in every sense of the words, Iago has brought Othello to his knees. The texts are as follows:

QUARTO

Oth. O that the slaue had forty thousand liues,
  One is too poore, too weake for my reuenge:
  Now doe I see tis time, looke here *Iago*,
  All my fond loue, thus doe I blow to heauen,—tis gone.
  Arise blacke vengeance, from thy hollow Cell,
  Yeeld vp O loue thy crowne, and harted Throne,

> To tirranous hate, swell bosome with thy fraught,
> For tis of Aspecks tongues.
>
> *Iago.* Pray be content.   *he kneeles.*
>
> *Oth.* O blood, *Iago*, blood.
>
> *Iago.* Patience I say, your mind perhaps may change.
>
> *Oth.* Neuer:
>
> In the due reuerence of a sacred vow,
> I here ingage my words.
>
> *Iago.* Doe not rise yet:
>
> Witnesse you euer-burning lights aboue,
> You Elements that clip vs round about,   *Iago kneeles*
> Witnesse that here, *Iago* doth giue vp
> The excellency of his wit, hand, heart,
> To wrong'd *Othello's* seruice. . .   (III, iii, 446–71)

In Folio there are no explicit stage-directions, but the kneel is certainly there and delayed by an even more powerfully conceived rhetoric, to give it a still greater prominence: it looks as if Othello should sink to his knees on the line *Now by yond Marble Heauen.*

FOLIO

> Yeeld vp (O Loue) thy Crowne, and hearted Throne
> To tyrannous Hate. Swell bosome with thy fraught,
> For 'tis of Aspickes tongues.
>
> *Iago.* Yet be content.
>
> *Oth.* Oh blood, blood, blood.
>
> *Iago.* Patience I say: your minde may change.
>
> *Oth.* Neuer Iago. *Like to the Ponticke Sea,*
> *Whose icie Current, and compulsiue course,*
> *Neu'r keepes retyring ebbe, but keepes due on*
> *To the Proponticke, and the Hellespont:*
> *Euen so my bloody thoughts, with violent pace*
> *Shall neu'r looke backe, neu'r ebbe to humble Loue,*
> *Till that a capeable, and wide Reuenge*
> *Swallow them vp. Now by yond Marble Heauen,*
> In the due reuerence of a Sacred vow,
> I heere engage my words,
>
> *Iago.* Do not rise yet:
>
> Witnesse you euer-burning Lights above,
> You Elements, that clip vs round about,

Witnesse that heere Iago doth giue vp
The execution of his wit, hands, heart,
To wrong'd Othello's Seruice. . .

This greater build-up for the climax of the scene is not the only
purpose of these lines: they are also there to herald, by the importance given to Othello's kneel, a still more important kneel that is
to come in the next act, and appears in Folio, but not in Quarto: it
comes in the colloquy of Iago, Emilia and Desdemona, in Act IV,
Scene ii; Emilia has just given it as her opinion that

The Moore's abus'd by some most villanous Knaue,
Some base notorious Knaue, some scuruy Fellow.

(F, IV, ii, 140–1)

Iago tries to prevent her from pursuing this thought: and Desdemona turns to him, in pure trust, for advice:

Des. Alas Iago,
What shall I do to win my Lord againe?
Good Friend, go to him: for by this light of Heauen,
I know not how I lost him. *Heere I kneele:*
If ere my will did trespasse 'gainst his Loue,
Either in discourse of thought, or actuall deed,
Or that mine Eyes, mine Eares, or any Sence
Delighted them: or* any other Forme.
Or that I do not yet, and euer did,
And euer will, (though he do shake me off
To beggerly diuorcement) Loue him deerely,
Comfort forsweare me. Vnkindnesse may do much,
And his vnkindnesse may defeat my life,
But neuer taynt my Loue. I cannot say Whore,
It do's abhorre me now I speake the word,
To do the Act, that might the addition earne,
Not the Worlds Masse of vanitie could make me.
Iago. I pray you be content: 'tis but his humour. . .

* [*read on*]   (F, IV, ii, 149–66)

The first part of this passage (until '*Comfort forsweare me*') is there
for this kneel, echoing Othello's. That she, as well as he, should be
brought to her knees before their trusted tormentor is a stroke of

stage-craft of great visual force and point, a double demonstration of Iago's triumph and at the same time an image the eye will retain for her utter innocence, as it retains that of Othello kneeling as the image of his resolved vengeance.

After thus vowing her innocence, Desdemona rises to add two important but simple thoughts. The first is that the *unkindness* of her husband may kill her but never taint her love: the second is that she would not commit adultery *for the whole world*. These two thoughts are the entire argument of the second-half of the next scene—as it appears in Folio. Once again we meet with an element of consequential alteration in the Folio-only passages we are considering.

> And his vnkindnesse may defeate my life,
> But neuer taynt my Loue.

This notion is taken up later by Emilia in a long passage that also appears only in Folio, which we must now consider.

It is a counterbalancing passage, working in three ways. First it counterbalances the effect given by Emilia's earlier grossness of attitude when she seems frivolously to condone adultery: thus it helps to put her right with the audience. Secondly it counterbalances Desdemona's extreme of constancy (that has the absoluteness of a Griselda) by the worldly-wise view that an unkind husband must take a large measure of the blame if his wife falls: thirdly it counterbalances without destroying the sentiment in the Willow Song (also in Folio only) by the cool commonsense of humane sympathy; it makes a unity with it, of complementary meditation on the same central theme. It is perhaps impossible to speak of these elements in the structure of the speech without seeming to rouse something subjective in the course of what is meant as mere analysis: but perhaps the passage will speak to the same purpose for itself. It may be noted that it swings gravely but unexpectedly into verse from a prose beginning, a small but certain fact, that gives the air of afterthought:

> *Des.* I do not thinke there is any such woman.
> *Aemil.* Yes, a dozen: and as many to' th' vantage, as would store the world they plaid for.

But I do thinke it is their Husbands faults
If Wiues do fall: (Say, that they slacke their duties,
And powre our Treasures into forraigne laps;
Or else breake out in peeuish Iealousies,
Throwing restraint vpon us: Or say they strike vs,
Or scant our former hauing in despight)
Why we haue galles: and though we haue some Grace,
Yet we haue some Reuenge. Let Husbands know,
Their wiues haue sense like them: They see, and smell,
And haue their Palats both for sweet, and sowre,
As Husbands haue. What is it that they do,
When they change vs for others? Is it Sport?
I thinke it is: and doth Affection breed it?
I thinke it doth. Is't Frailty that thus erres?
It is so too. And haue not we Affections?
Desires for Sport? and Frailty, as men haue?
Then let them vse vs well: else let them know,
The illes we do, their illes instruct vs so.
  Des. Good night, good night:
  Heauen me such vses send,
  Not to picke bad, from bad: but by bad, mend.   *Exeunt*

                         (F, IV, iii, 81–103)

The argument, on both sides, is complete.

It remains to consider the Willow Song in the structure of this scene. The view suggested by many critics is that it was cut in Quarto because the boy-actor's voice broke inconveniently, or that for some other reason he could not sing and so the song was cut. This at first sight is by no means implausible, but those who accept it as the right explanation point to a later passage, in Folio only, when Emilia, as she dies, refers back to the Willow Song: as this reference is not in Quarto and as those who think in this way believe Quarto to have been cut, its omission in Quarto is held to prove that the Willow Song itself was deliberately cut. But the supposed cutting of the song cannot be 'proved intentional by the omission of a reference to it in v, ii, 246^b-8', as Greg declares,[1] unless it proves that a room has had a fireplace removed because there is no sign of a chimney. Once again the axiom that Shakespeare never revised has made it impossible for Greg to think in terms of additions. Let us begin by looking at Emilia's dying speech, with its Folio-only lines:

> *Aemil. What did thy Song boad Lady?*
> *Hearke, canst thou heare me? I will play the Swan,*
> *And dye in Musicke: Willough, Willough, Willough.*
> Moore, she was chaste: She lou'd thee, cruell Moore,
> So come my Soule to blisse, as I speake true. . .
>
> (F, v, ii, 249-53)

As the Willow Song gave something more to Desdemona, so this echo of it gives something more to Emilia, and unites them both in a harmony that recalls the scene of their elaborated difference of opinion about chastity in marriage; this admirably links with the line in both Quarto and Folio.

> Moore, she was chaste: She lou'd thee, cruell Moore. . .

For all Emilia's worldliness, of which the song reminds us, she could value chastity in love, and so seem to be atoned with her mistress in death.

Those who think these lines were cut regard it as evidence of the cutter's intelligence that, when he cut the Willow Song, he remembered to cut its echo in Emilia's mouth; but once again this intelligent cutter dissolves on closer scrutiny into the clever-moron, for in this passage too we find care and carelessness, knowledge and ignorance, in an impossible mixture. We have only to turn to the Willow Song and its context to see at a glance that if this supposed cutter had cut from the beginning of Desdemona's speech, that is, from the line

> My Mother had a Maid call'd *Barbarie*   (F, IV, iii, 25)

he would successfully have ousted *all* reference to the Willow Song whatever, without losing anything necessary to the flow of the dialogue: clever enough to remember Emilia's echo some four hundred and fifty lines later, he did not think of looking to the start of the speech he was mainly concerned to cut, only five lines up. Surely the facts of the text must be open to a more consistent explanation: let us look at them in Folio:

Aemil. Come, come: you talke.

Des. My Mother had a Maid call'd *Barbarie*,
 She was in loue: and he she lou'd prou'd mad,
 And did forsake her. She had a Song of Willough,
 An old thing 'twas: but it express'd her Fortune,
 And she dy'd singing it. That Song tonight,
 Will not go from my mind: *I haue much to do,*
 But to go hang my head all at one side
 And sing it like poore Brabarie; prythee dispatch.

Aemi. Shall I go fetch your Night-gowne?

Des. No, *vn-pin me here,*
 This Lodouico is a proper man.

Aemil. A very handsome man.

Des. He speakes well.

Aemil. I know a Lady in Venice would haue walk'd
 barefoot to Palestine for a touch of his nether lip.

Des. The poore Soule sat singing, by a Sicamour tree.
 Sing all a greene Willough;
 Her hand on her bosome her head on her knee,
 Sing Willough, Willough, Willough.
 The fresh Streames ran by her, and murmur'd her moanes
 Sing Willough, &c.
 Her salt teares fell from her, and softened the stones,
 Sing Willough, &c. (Lay by these)
 Willough, Willough. (Prythee high thee: he'le come anon)
 Sing all a greene Willough must be my Garland.
 Let no body blame him, his scorne I approue.
 Nay that's not next. Harke, who is't that knocks?

Aemil. It's the wind.

Des. *I call'd my Loue false Loue; but what said he then?*
 Sing Willough, &c.
 If I court mo women, you'le couch with mo men.
 So get thee gone, good night: mine eyes do itch:
 Doth that boade weeping?

Aemil. 'Tis neyther here, nor there.   (F, IV, iii, 25–57)

How should we imagine this song in its performance? The kind
of singing required for it surely does not call for a fine voice: it is not
intended to be sung as a formal solo, but as a sort of *fredonnement* or

singing-to-one-self. In this respect it differs from another song of the same date, if we may trust to well-established chronology, namely the song in *Measure for Measure*, 'Take, oh take those lips away', for which, presumably, Shakespeare had a boy with voice enough. Let us also note that the skill in intercalating the lines of the Willow Song with the rest of the dialogue—

> (*Nay that's not next.* Harke, who is't that knocks?
> *Aemil.* It's the wind
> *Des. I call'd my Loue false Loue;* (etc.)

and making the smoother junction that appears in

> *Des.* I haue heard it said so. *O these Men, these men!*
> *Do'st thou in conscience thinke (tell me Aemilia)*
> *That there be women do abuse their husbands*
> *In such grosse kinde?*
> *Aemil. There be some such, no question*
> *Des.* Would'st thou do such a deed for all the world?

—is all of a piece with the skill we noted in the dovetailing of Roderigo's Folio-only lines in the opening scene, and in other intercalations we have looked at. A like hand, with a like purpose of improvement seems to be at work, to expand and add power to the scene as a whole, by developing implications it already contained. The notion, for instance, of pitting the whole world against the deed of adultery is thrice reiterated in this scene by Desdemona, in both texts:

> IV, iii, 62   Would'st thou do such a deed for all the world?
> 66   Would'st thou do such a deed for al the world?
> 76   Beshrew me, if I would do such a wrong
> For the whole world.

It is a notion prepared for in the Folio-only lines she speaks when kneeling to Iago (IV, ii, 164–5):

> To do the Act, that might the addition earne,
> Not the worlds Masse of vanitie could make me.

These lines link her kneel with what is to come in the Willow scene just as her kneel itself links with Othello's in the Propontic passage.

Is it possible to think that such thematic linkages could have so ingeniously been cut out? For what purpose? But if they were not cut, they were added. And one can see why.

There remain two passages in the Folio version of the last scene of the play that are even better witnesses for the view I have put forward: Emilia figures prominently in both. The first of them comes as climax to her personal discovery, and the second as climax to her public discovery, of Desdemona's murder. A rather full context is necessary to show how these climaxes occur: here is the first of them:

> *Oth.* Cassio did top her: Ask thy husband else.
> O, I were damn'd beneath all depth in hell:
> But that I did proceed vpon iust grounds
> To this extremity. Thy Husband knew it all.
> *Aemil.* My Husband?
> *Oth.* Thy Husband.
> *Aemil.* That she was false to Wedlocke?
> *Oth.* I, with Cassio: had she bin true,
> If Heauen would make me such another world,
> Of one entyre and perfect Chrysolite,
> I'ld not haue sold her for it.
> *Aemil.* My Husband?
> *Oth.* I, 'twas he that told me on her first,
> An honest man he is, and hates the slime
> That stickes on filthy deeds.
> *Aemil.* My Husband?
> *Oth.* What needs this itterance, Woman?
> I say, thy Husband.
> *Aemil. Oh Mistris,*
> *Villany hath made mockes with loue:*
> *My Husband say she was false?*
> *Oth. He, Woman;*
> *I say thy Husband: Do'st vnderstand the word?*
> *My Friend, thy Husband; honest, honest Iago.*
> *Aemil.* If he say so, may his pernicious Soule
> Rot halfe a graine a day: he lyes to'th'heart,
> She was too fond of her most filthy Bargaine.
>
> (F, v, ii, 139–60)

Greg believes the italicised lines to have been cut in the copy for Quarto, lest one too many of Emilia's reiterations should raise a laugh.[1] Her repetitions are, of course, deliberate, to show the slow dawn of her amazement into horror: it seems likely the editors of Folio who were Shakespeare's fellow-actors, would have known, if anyone knew, that these lines had given rise to laughter (if they did) and would have eliminated them rather than let them stand, as they prepared their text from their superior manuscript with the help of Quarto. But this is to argue *a priori*. If we look at this Folio-only passage from the point of view of dramatic analysis, we shall see that even more important than Emilia's repetitions are Othello's repetitions: the passage leads to the summit line

> *My Friend, thy Husband: honest, honest Iago.*

Iago's seeming honesty is the foundation-stone on which the imaginative structure of the entire play is built: it is laid in the opening lines of the play

> For when my outward Action doth demonstrate
> The natiue act, and figure of my heart
> In Complement externe, 'tis not long after
> But I will weare my heart vpon my sleeue
> For Dawes to pecke at: I am not what I am.   (F, I, i, 62–6)

To cut the line that reiterates Iago's 'honesty' at the moment when it is most needed would rise above folly into malice. If it had been true that Emilia's dumbfounded repetitions raised a laugh, it would have been easy to cut the preceding repetition. But there is no reason whatever to suppose the lines seemed funny at such a moment: Emilia's slowness to understand and believe that her husband could have acted as Othello asserts he has, is as much an extenuation for her part in the murder of Desdemona as Othello's belief in Iago's honesty in an extenuation for his. These Folio-only lines pin-point this aspect of the situation—the hypocrisy of Iago, the denseness of Emilia, the trustfulness of Othello, are brought to their sharpest moment of focus in the whole play.

This Folio passage, then, gives prominence, through the mouth of Othello, to Iago's '*honesty*': the second Folio-only passage we are

to consider in this scene gives prominence, through the mouth of
Emilia, to his *villainy*; it is indeed the only word she can think of:

> *Aemil.* But did you euer tell him,
>   She was false?
> *Iago.* I did.
> *Aemil.* You told a Lye an odious damned Lye:
>   Vpon my Soule, a Lye: a wicked Lye.
>   Shee false with Cassio?
>   Did you say with Cassio?
> *Iago.* With Cassio, Mistris?
>   Go too, charme your tongue.
> *Emil.* I will not charme my Tongue;
>   I am bound to speake,
>   *My Mistris heere lyes murthered in her bed.*
> *All.* O Heauens, forefend.
> *Emil.* And your reports haue set the Murder on.
> *Othello.* Nay stare not Masters,
>   It is true indeede.
> *Gra.* 'Tis a strange Truth.
> *Mont.* O monstrous Acte.
> *Emil.* Villany, villany, villany:
>   I thinke vpon't, I thinke: I smel't: O Villany:
>   I thoght so then; Ile kill my selfe for greefe.
> *Iago.* What, are you mad?
>   I charge you get you home.   (F, v, ii, 181-97)

But in addition to bringing her speech to a climax by reiterating
'villainy' as she had previously reiterated 'husband' and 'lie', the
Folio version has a further function, not supplied in Quarto, yet
very necessary to the situation—the public announcement of the
murder to the newly entered Montano, Gratiano, Iago and those
in attendance on them, given in Emilia's line

> *My mistris heere lys murthered in her bed.*

As well as strengthening Emilia's part, her public declaration gives
an opening to the other characters on stage for their public reaction
of horror, of which they give no sign in Quarto and the situation
almost misses fire.

It seems a parallel case with Roderigo's Folio-only speech in the first scene; all the necessary information is there, but it has not been made enough of, it needs to be brought into greater prominence. So, at Emilia's first awareness that a murder has taken place, she is alone on stage; her cries bring the others in, ignorant and bewildered, and they are left in this condition while Emilia welcomes Iago, not yet quite believing in his guilt:

> (*Emilia*) . . . helpe, helpe, O helpe;
> The Moore has kild my Mistresse, murder, murder.
> *Enter* Montano, Gratiano, Iago, *and others.*
> *Mon.* What is the matter? How now Generall?
> *Em.* O, are you come *Iago*? you haue done well
> That men must lay their murder on your neck.
>
> (Q, v, ii, 169–73)

The dialogue continues in Quarto without thought for the feelings of 'Montano, Gratiano and others', and this is a thing that might well happen in a play that had not been worked on the stage; it is a weakness, however, that would soon become apparent in performance. There is no such weakness in Folio, for it supplies the deficiency.

If we now look at the Folio version of the last two acts as a whole, we will see that, in every case, it is the character of Emilia that receives the fullest benefit, though others profit as well. It is as if Shakespeare had set himself methodically to strengthen her part at the four key-points we have considered; his purpose seems to have been to *endear* it to the audience: it is as if he had sensed that Emilia's guilt in the matter of the handkerchief had been insufficiently wiped out in the eyes of her critics: she is 'coarse clay' no doubt (as Granville Barker has well said)[1] but to be coarse is one thing, to be an accessory to a murder—even though without full consciousness of what she was doing—is another, and the Quarto text does very little to reinstate her: now this is precisely what all the relevant Folio-only passages do for her: first, the intimacy between her and Desdemona is much increased by the Willow Song itself, for while her mistress is singing it, Emilia is busying herself with those close personal attentions, as unpinning Desdemona's dress and combing her hair ('Lay by these—Prithee hie thee') which visually create affection *between*, and therefore *for* them both. (To show love between two characters is one of Shakespeare's commonest ways of creating it between them and the audience.) Secondly her long speech at the end of the Willow scene is an effort at moral self-justification which softens her earlier and somewhat frivolous attitude towards adultery: it shows she has her philosophy, her sense of what is fair in marriage. These things endear her even if they do not wholly excuse her to us for her theft of the handkerchief; this, however, is further absolved by her inability to credit her husband's wickedness when Othello tells her that it was from him he had learnt of Desdemona's adultery. Her reiteration of '*My Husband!*' and later of '*Villainy!*' do much to reinstate her with an audience: but it is that last touch of the Willow Song at her death that finally gives her her place beside her mistress. These differences between Emilia as she appears in Quarto and as she appears in Folio, viewed in this way, cannot but seem part of *a strategy of revision*: for, as they cannot be accidental, and as it is impossible to imagine a director who set himself to undermine her character by these omissions, they can only be accounted for by purposeful revision. It is unfortunate that *force majeure* seems to have robbed Emilia of the one touch by which Quarto shows her anguish (on realising her part in the crime) better than Folio. Quarto gives her the sublime exclamation 'O God, O heauenly God.' This is watered away by Folio to 'Oh Heauen! Oh heauenly Powres!' But perhaps the lines that Folio adds to her part may be thought sufficient compensation for this loss, which, after all, the twentieth century can restore without fear of prosecution by the crown.

V

So far we have argued, and I think shown, the following things: (1) The explicit stage-directions in this play, whichever version we choose, are no more than a rough guide here and there to actors and directors, but this in no way prevents us from supposing either text could have been used to rehearse and prompt the play from, since all the directions that matter are contained in the dialogue, except for the few supplied by Quarto that we have considered—torches, a table, a chair and the business when Iago knifes Emilia in the last act. If the Company had first presented the play from the version underlying Quarto these things would have been known and remembered well enough for them to present the version underlying Folio without missing any basic point in production.

(2) No practical reason for cutting any of the Folio-only passages has been found in the context, or can be plausibly imagined, in any instance; on the contrary, the passages we have studied have all shown themselves to be severely structural and thematic, the expressions of a practical stage-craft and dramaturgy. For these reasons we are forced out of the supposition that they were cut; and since they seem to be interconnected by a chain of thematic consequences, they cannot have been dropped by accident. They can only, therefore, have been additions made by some process of revision, and this, as we have already observed, means revision by Shakespeare.

The reader is now possessed of such evidence and argument as I am able to offer in the confusing problems of the texts of *Othello*, and it remains for me to form a picture of what I think happened, on this showing, to bring them both into being.

To do so I must of course step off into pure conjecture, the only checks on which are that it must account for all the known facts, and use no gratuitous fancy. In obedience to this, following Chambers, I suppose the play to have been composed, at latest, in 1604, and certainly performed at Court on the first of November in that year; I believe the text used on this occasion was that of Quarto, oaths included. During rehearsal, or at that performance, or possibly in retrospect, Shakespeare noted certain confusions and weaknesses in the play and began to think of ways in which they could be eliminated—by giving a new speech to Roderigo here and another to Emilia there, a kneel and a song to Desdemona, and so on. But he did nothing about it, having no compelling occasion to undertake a revision. After all, he had *King Lear* and *Macbeth* coming over his horizon. Nevertheless, somewhere at the back of his mind lay a certain dissatisfaction with *Othello*, and perhaps some notions how to improve it.

Then came the Act against profanity of 1606 and, perhaps, not long after it, a revival of *Othello*, by the Company; there is no record of one until 30 April 1610, but as the records are incomplete, we need not expect one. If the play was to be revived, it had to be purged of its fifty-two profanities, some of which would leave gaps in the dialogue that an underling could not be trusted to fill in. So Shakespeare sat down to purge and improve the play in ways he had for some time occasionally meditated. In doing so we may presume he had access to the playhouse copy and to his own original foul papers. With characteristic rapidity he set to work, relying partly on a fluent memory and making many light and cursive alterations as he went along, as well as the more radical ones we have noted. This would explain many of the thousand minor variations that are admitted generally to give better readings without altering the gist; it cannot, of course, explain them all, for some are manifestly due to mistakes in transcription.

When Shakespeare had completed his revision he gave his manuscript to the book-keeper to copy, returning at the same time the earlier version; in this way a second playhouse copy came into being. In ten or a dozen passages it may have retained some queer spellings from the first, at points where the transcriber found Shakespeare's new manuscript indecipherable and turned to the old one for help. There may have been more such passages than those we know of that were smoothed out later by the printers.

The playhouse now possessed two texts of *Othello*, the text we know from Quarto (but still of course in manuscript and put away), and the text we know from Folio, also in manuscript and in use. It was performed at Court in 1610. Some ten years later, Thomas Walkley, the bookseller, approached the Company to purchase the text of a play if he could, and was offered the earlier of the two *Othello* texts. No doubt he had to pay well for it, since the project to publish all Shakespeare's plays in Folio was already under discussion, and to let slip an important play could damage the sales; perhaps he was not told that the Company had a fuller, better version than the one he was buying. In selling it to him the editors of Folio may well have stipulated that he should allow them to use his text, if and when they should set up their collected edition, of which they may have told him. This would have the double advantage of reassuring Walkley as to the excellence of his text and of allowing the editors of Folio to collate the earlier text with their better one, just in case there might be some points at which it could be helpful. In this way the 'great Variety of Readers' could be truthfully assured of the superiority of the Folio text over all other publications; meanwhile the inferior version might be allowed to escape, at a price. Posterity would know how to judge between them...

POSTSCRIPT

Partial and miscellaneous as these studies must seem in their approach to a subject almost infinite and largely unknowable—the workings of Shakespeare's dramatic imagination—they have this in common, that they have been governed by a kind of discipline created by the medium in which that imagination was working.

But now comes an objection that may be made to all that I have written, and it must be faced. All Shakespeare criticism, from that of Dr Johnson onward, has displayed progressive subtleties of interpretation, and even now continual discoveries are being made of minute points in Shakespeare's texts that can be shown to have some overwhelming significance, hitherto unsuspected.

Yet the records of performances, whether public or private, given in Shakespeare's lifetime, give little support to our faith in these subtleties which too often seem like things imposed on his plays by a later sensibility, rather than things which he and his contemporaries (whatever their genius) could have realised in Elizabethan theatre conditions.

First to consider is the fantastic speed at which Shakespeare is known to have written; he wrote, or had a major hand in, at least thirty-eight plays between 1590 and 1613 (I am including *Henry VIII* and *Two Noble Kinsmen*); that is, he wrote nearly two plays a year, of a magnitude and complexity that have no equal; it is thought that in some years he wrote three. How then could he have had the elaborate care for detailed subtleties of effect that has been claimed for him, by implication if not directly?

Next, due allowance must be given to what we can glean of the conditions of rehearsal and performance; the evidence is far from direct, yet we get a certain picture from the receipts recorded, over several years, in Henslowe's diary.[1] Let us, for instance, consider the entries that run from 27 October 1596 to the end of October in the following year, that Henslowe headed:

In the name of god Amen
begynynge one simone & Jewde*s* daye
my lord admeralles men as ffoloweth

In the course of this year there are no entries for August or September; there are also other gaps in the continuity of week-day performances; these together amount to over fifteen weeks during which no plays, apparently, were given. In the thirty-seven weeks left of the working year, thirty-three different plays were given in repertory. There is no pattern of repetition; only twice is the same play given on two consecutive nights: *Vortigern* was performed on 4 and 8 December, with no other performance in between, and *Alexander and Lodowick* was performed on 11 and 12 February. The number of performances of any given play varies from a maximum of fifteen (*Alexander and Lodowick*) to a single performance; eight plays had over ten performances each, at irregular intervals.

If Henslowe had a system behind his programme-building, I do not discern it; but it is at least certain that plays were being put on at the rate of nearly one a week, dispersedly yet with enough unsystematic repetitions to lay a big load on the memories of actors. It is simply impossible to rehearse and retain the style and detail of fine performance in such circumstances; in twentieth-century weekly repertory, where a play may hope to gain style during its week of performance, and may be forgotten by the actors once that week is over, attention to detail is not beyond hope; nevertheless it leaves little time for the rehearsal of next week's play, and a fortnightly rather than a weekly change of play is generally preferred, in the interests of quality.

Shakespeare's Company, one would like to think, was more carefully coached and under less pressure; but I know of no evidence that it was. Let us glance at the record of some Court performances, on a spectacular occasion, such as should call forth a fastidious care in rehearsal and distinction of style on the night. If we look into the *Chamber Account* quoted by Sir Edmund Chambers,[1] we find the following:

Item paid to John Heminges upon Cowncells warrant dated att Whitehall xx° die Maij 1613, for presentinge before the Princes Highnes the Lady Elizabeth and the Prince Pallatyne Elector fowerteene several playes, viz: one play called Filaster, One other called the Knott of Fooles, One other Much Adoe abowte Nothinge, The Mayeds Tragedy, The Merye Dyvell of Edmonton, The Tempest, A Kynge and no Kynge, The Twins Tragedie, The Winters Tale, Sir John Falstaffe, The Moore of Venice, The Nobleman, Caesar's Tragedye, And one other called Love lyes a bleedinge, All which Playes weare played with-in the tyme of this Accompte. . .

Even if *Philaster* and *Love Lies Bleeding* are one and the same, it is a formidable list; we have thirteen plays to present in succession for a particular betrothal; what polish can have been put upon so many clapped together? For so many actors to carry in their heads the niceties of production for so many plays in succession is a task beyond any *expertise* imaginable.

And what of the quality of the audiences? What *nuances* can they be supposed to have grasped? We have little to reassure us on this point either. The two best witnesses however may be brought forward. The first is John Manningham of the Middle Temple, an educated man. On 2 February 1602 he saw a performance of *Twelfth Night*:[1]

At our feast wee had a play called 'Twelue Night, or What You Will', much like the Commedy of Errores. . . A good practise in it to make the Steward beleeve his Lady Widdowe was in love with him, by counter-feyting a letter as from his Lady in generall termes, telling him what shee liked best in him, and prescribing his gesture in smiling, his apparaile, &c., and then when he came to practise making him beleeve they took him to be mad.

'*his Lady Widdoe*'! Manningham had completely missed the point of Olivia's mourning weeds; they were for a brother, not a husband. As for their being a means of keeping Orsino at arms' length, as I have supposed, there is no sign of corroboration in Manningham's account.

But even Manningham was a sensitive playgoer compared with

simple Simon Forman. He has left us his impressions of *Macbeth* and *The Winter's Tale* at the Globe and of *Cymbeline* at some unspecified theatre.[1] He gives a sort of brute synopsis in each case easily recognisable by anyone who has read the plays, and it is interesting to note that he says Macbeth and Banquo came 'Ridinge thorowe a wod', which suggests trees (as in Brutus' orchard) and the skilled use of hobby-horses; Forman clearly has not enough imagination to invent the idea of their riding through a wood if Macbeth and Banquo had been on foot, and there was no scenery. He is somewhat at a loss to describe the witches, whom he calls '3 women feiries or Nimphes' (can nymphs be thought to have beards and choppy fingers?) but he gets the main point of the sleep-walking scene:

Obserue Also how Mackbetes quen did Rise in the night in her slepe, & walke and talked and confessed all, & the docter noted her wordes.

He has previously, in this account, told us that 'when Mack Beth had murdred the kinge, the blod on his handes could not be washed by Any meanes, nor from his wiues handes'; but he shows no perception of the ironies that hang about these actions and are so obvious and important to us.

His account of *The Winter's Tale* is no better; he does not so much as mention the return of Hermione in the statue scene at the conclusion of his synopsis, and reserves his final remark for Autolycus, of whom he says:

Remember also the Rog that cam in all tottered ... and how he feyned him sicke & to haue bin Robbed of all that he had and howe he cosened the por man of all his money... Beware of trustinge feined beggars or fawninge fellouss.

And that is the moral of *The Winter's Tale*. From no side do we get support for the belief that the subtleties we discern in Shakespeare's plays were presented, or appreciated, in his own times.

It is undeniable too that there are signs of carelessness here and there in them. I do not speak of those which can be dismissed as a matter of opinion, but of examples that cannot be denied. I have, for instance, noted the subtle gradations in grief that open *Twelfth*

Night, and these seem to suggest a certain care in balancing and pointing these scenes; yet Viola tells us, at her first appearance, that she can sing:

> Thou shalt present me as an Eunuch to him,
> It may be worth thy paines: for I can sing. . .

But never do we hear her do so; all the songs go to Feste. Some say that this is due to the sudden breaking of some boy's voice; I rather think it may have been the sudden discovery by Shakespeare that Robert Armin could sing (for Touchstone, who came before Feste, has no songs, but every Jester from Feste onwards, has). Be that as it may, neither explanation excuses the carelessness of not eliminating the lines written for the Viola-boy.

The best way with an unanswerable difficulty is to look it squarely in the face and pass on. It may be that Shakespeare was often careless, it may be that his best audiences were crude enough, it may be that his plays were rapidly written, seldom corrected and often under-rehearsed. But for all that, the subtleties we have studied are not fictions, they are there in the text. They cannot be a flock of flukes.

We remain confronted by a strategic intelligence working within an inexhaustible poetic power. There are those who can make lightning calculations in mathematics, not knowing how they reach their results, which nevertheless are right. It may be that Shakespeare had some such faculty in respect of the organic interconnections of story, theme, character, discourse, imagery and the physical *media* of theatre; it is possible that he wrote better than he knew, better than his actors or his contemporaries knew; but the weight of evidence suggests to me that the disposition of much of his imaginative material implies a willed and conscious craft, co-operatively exercised at every stage of the act of creation. The native woodnotes of poetic inspiration, prodigal as they were, will not, by themselves, account for the facts.

Let us take one last, quick example of this incredible craft. It is shown in his conception and use of the Soothsayer in *Antony and Cleopatra,* who is one of those 'minor characters' that nevertheless have power enough in their lines to steal the play. In the second scene of the first act, there is a riotously naughty dialogue between Charmian, Iras and this Soothsayer. They are consulting him about their fortunes. The incident is not in Plutarch; Shakespeare invented it.

It is a gay conversation on the girls' part, but it is clear that the Soothsayer, as he pores over their hands, one after the other, has a growing fore-knowledge of the impending doom. First he looks at Charmian's hand:

Sooth. You shall out-liue the Lady whom you serue.
Char. O excellent, I loue long life better then Figs.
Sooth. You haue seene and proued a fairer former fortune, then that which is to approach.

Then he takes the hand of Iras and the shapeless misfortune he foresees becomes clearer to him; six light speeches go by while he gazes at it. At last he says: 'Your Fortunes are alike.' Iras clamours for particulars, but he simply answers: 'I haue said.' Here is a gift to an actor and an intimation to an audience set in a soap-bubble. But I have seen it performed in such a way that when the Soothsayer rises and leaves them, the fate of Egypt is in his eyes and bearing, and the catastrophe is adumbrated in the protasis.[1]

I had thought this little incident was self-contained, a little vignette that reached no further than this adumbration, which is subtle enough. I had not noticed the detail of Charmian's light-hearted exclamation

O excellent, *I loue long life better then Figs.*

Mr H. V. Dyson has pointed me to the scene of her death, in the last moments of the play. A Guardsman enters to tell her and her mistress of the countryman who brings them the asp:

Heere is a rurall Fellow,
That will not be deny'de your Highnesse presence,
He brings you Figges.

NOTES

Quotations from Shakespeare have been taken from the First Folio of 1623, or from earlier Quartos. I have here and there used italics for emphasis.

In the numbering of acts, scenes and lines, I have followed Professor Peter Alexander's edition of *The Complete Works of William Shakespeare* (Collins, London and Glasgow, 1951).

PAGE xiii
[1] M. C. Linthicum, *Costume in the Drama of Shakespeare and his Contemporaries* (Clarendon Press, Oxford, 1936), p. 25.

PAGE 2
[1] The relevance of 'fawning' has been discussed, but not in connection with its obvious function as a direction to Antonio. See J. M. Brown, note in Arden Ed. (1953), p. 20.

PAGE 4
[1] *Folk-Tales of Mallorca, from L'Aplec de Rondaies Mallorquines de Mossen Antoni M. Alcover*, translated by David Huelin (Buenos Ayres, 1945), p. 40.

PAGE 5
[1] Thomas Dekker, *The Guls Horne-Booke*, ed. R. B. McKerrow (London, 1904), ch. VI.
[2] Martin Holmes, *A New Theory about the Swan Drawing* in *Theatre Notebook*, vol. 10, no. iii. See also A. M. Nagler, *Shakespeare's Stage* (Yale University Press, 1958), p. 10, and (for a contrary opinion) the review of this book by R. Horsley in *Comparative Literature*, vol. XII, no. 1. For a yet more contrary opinion see Leslie Hotson, *Shakespeare's Wooden O* (London, 1959), p. 91.

PAGE 8
[1] 'The frame of the said howse to be sett square . . . And the said fframe to conteine three Stories in heighth. . .', see E. K. Chambers, *The Elizabethan Stage* (Clarendon Press, 1923), vol. II, p. 436.

PAGE 10
[1] See Glynne Wickham, *Early English Stages* (London, 1959), vol. I, p. 89.

PAGE 11
[1] John Dover Wilson, ed., *Hamlet* (Cambridge, 1934), p. 164, note to l. 149, Act I, Sc. v.
[2] *Jack Juggler* (Third Edition), ed. Malone Society by Ifor B. Evans and W. W. Greg, 1936 (1937).

PAGE 14
[1] John Dover Wilson, *What Happens in Hamlet* (Cambridge, 1937), p. 84.
[2] Malone Society Reprints, ed. W. W. Greg, 1921.
[3] See also Anthony Caputi, *John Marston Satirist* (Cornell University Press, 1961), p. 147.

PAGE 16
[1] See Nevill Coghill, *Six Points of Stage-craft in The Winter's Tale* in *Shakespeare Survey*, no. 11, 1958.

P

PAGE 17

[1] W. W. Greg, *The Shakespeare First Folio* (Clarendon Press, 1955), p. 301.

PAGE 19

[1] Richard Flatter, *Hamlet's Father* (London, 1949), p. 95.

PAGE 20

[1] *What Happens in Hamlet*, p. 106.
[2] *Ibid.*, p. 128.

PAGE 21

[1] See John Bartlett, *Complete Concordance to the dramatic Works and poems of Shakespeare* (London, 1957).

PAGE 22

[1] *Op. cit.*, p. 134.
[2] See O.E.D., which gives three examples, one from 1593, one from 1617 and one from the eighteenth century.
[3] *Measure for Measure*, III, ii, 187.
[4] *Pericles*, IV, ii, 15.

PAGE 26

[1] See ch. VII, pp. 187–90.

PAGE 28

[1] Quotations from Shakespeare's sources are taken from Professor Geoffrey Bullough's edition of them, in five volumes, entitled *Narrative and Dramatic Sources of Shakespeare* (London and New York, 1957), unless otherwise stated.

PAGE 32

[1] S. T. Coleridge, *Biographia Literaria*, ch. 13.

PAGE 33

[1] See Geoffrey Bullough, *op. cit.*, and Kenneth Muir, *Shakespeare's Sources* (London, 1957), vol. I.
[2] See T. W. Baldwin, *William Shakespeare's Five-Act Structure* (University of Illinois Press, 1947).
[3] Book VIII, lines 271–2008.

PAGE 34

[1] *The Minor Poems of John Lydgate*, ed. H. N. MacCracken, E.E.T.S. Original Series, 192 (1934), vol. II, pp. 675–82.
[2] Both are reproduced (in monochrome) in Allardyce Nicoll, *Masks, Mimes and Miracles* (London, 1931) and closely described, pp. 153–4.

PAGE 35

[1] *Lydgate's Troy Book*, ed. H. Bergen, E.E.T.S. Extra Series, xcvii (1906).
[2] *Isidori Hispalensis Episcopi Etymologiarum sive Originum Libri XX, recognovit*, W. M. Lindsay (Clarendon Press, 1911). I am indebted for this reference to Professor C. S. Lewis.

PAGE 36

[1] W. W. Greg, *Dramatic Documents from the Elizabethan Playhouse* (Clarendon Press, undated). Professor F. D. Hoeniger, in his Arden edition of *Pericles* (1963), suggests Barnabe Barnes's *The Divil's Charter* and *The Travailes of the Three English Brothers*, by John Day, William Rowley and George Wilkins, as possible models for Shakespeare in the matter of a choric compère. He dates these plays early in 1607 (p. xxi) and *Pericles* 'some time between 1606 and 1608' (p. lxiv). It does not seem clear who had the priority:

there was a great deal of free fishing in the common pool of theatrical devices, as we have seen in our glance at *Antonio and Mellida* (see pp. 14–15), and as we shall presently see, in the case of *John a Kent and John a Cumber*, when Shakespeare was the fisher. But it seems certain that Shakespeare knew Lydgate's *Troy Book*, and that his use of Gower was a great hit. I think it more likely that Barnes, Day, Rowley and Williams copied him than he them.

² See also *Shakespeare's Stage*, by A. M. Nagler (Yale University Press, 1958), p. 26.

³ See Introduction, Cambridge ed. by J. C. Maxwell (London, 1956), p. xxvii.

PAGE 37

¹ W. H. Auden, *The Dyer's Hand* (New York, 1962), p. xii.

PAGE 39

¹ *Biographia Literaria*, ch. XIV.

² Cf. Michael Polanyi, *Science and Religion: Separate Dimensions or Common Ground?* (*Philosophy To-day*, vol. VII, Spring 1963), pp. 7–8:

... Thus we recognize that when we attend from a set of particulars to the whole which they form, we establish a logical relation between the particulars and the whole, similar to that which exists between our body and the things outside it... We may describe this relation by saying that the act of comprehending a whole *is an interiorisation of its parts, which makes us dwell in them* in a way that is logically similar to the way we dwell in our body... It is not by attending to the particulars of the whole, but by dwelling in them that we comprehend their joint meaning.

PAGE 40

¹ W. H. Auden, *op. cit.*, p. 8.

PAGE 41

¹ Ed. Malone Society, by Muriel St Clare Byrne, 1923.

² See *Shakespeare Survey*, No. 8, 1955, pp. 100–5.

PAGE 42

¹ Quoted by Shapiro, *op. cit.* See also H. Harvey Wood, *The Plays of John Marston* (London, 1939), vol. III, p. 321.

PAGE 45

¹ See *Jacobean Studies*, presented to Frank Percy Wilson (Oxford, 1959), pp. 98–9.

PAGE 46

¹ Cf. 2 *Tamburlane*, IV, iii, 119:

> Like to an almond-tree y-mounted high
> Vpon the lofty and celestial mount
> Of ever-green Selinus...

and *Faerie Queene*, Bk I, Canto VII, stanza 32:

> Like to an Almond tree ymounted hye
> On top of greene *Selinis* all alone...

These passages, coming as they did upon the public between 1587 and 1590, would give a topical touch to Turnop's 'roration', if Mr Shapiro is right, as I believe, about the date of *John a Kent*. Miss St Clare Byrne has told me that in preparing her edition she had also read the date as 1590, but the General Editor differed from her on this point.

PAGE 52

¹ See a presentation and applications of this concept, in reference to pictorial art, in E. H. Gombrich, *Art and Illusion* (London, 1960), a work which has many ideas equally applicable to literature.

PAGE 54

[1] Geoffrey Bullough, *Narrative and Dramatic Sources of Shakespeare*, vol. I, pp. 388–9.
[2] *Ibid.*, p. 385.

PAGE 55

[1] *Ibid.*, pp. 390–1.

PAGE 56

[1] See Dorothy Bethurum, *Shakespeare's Comment on Mediaeval Romance in A Midsummer Night's Dream*, Mod. Lang. Notes, LX, 1945.

PAGE 60

[1] It is true, as Professor F. P. Wilson has pointed out to me, that Theseus' speech shows him to be a disbeliever in the Fairy World that the audience has been allowed to see, as well as a supporter of the 'harsh Athenian law' and of a tyrannical parent. Yet when he speaks of the nature of poetry, one asks who has spoken better. And he overbears the will of Egeus.
[2] *Troilus and Criseyde*, III, 1261.

PAGE 61

[1] These traditional categories are convenient for analysis; in the synthesis of the play they are, of course, inseparable.

PAGE 65

[1] The analysis here offered of *1 Henry IV* is structural; that is, it gives the general design of scene-alternation in relation to theme. Within this general design, and embellishing it, are many other confrontations, juxtapositions, echoes and ironical devices; they follow the structural line I have analysed. Some of them have been already pointed out; see, for instance, A. R. Humphreys' Introduction to the Arden edition of the play (1960), John Dover Wilson, *The Fortunes of Falstaff* (Cambridge, 1943); W. Empson, 'Falstaff and Mr Dover Wilson', in the *Kenyon Review*, XV, 223 (1953); John Lawlor, *The Tragic Sense in Shakespeare*, ch. I (London, 1960), etc.

PAGE 68

[1] Unferð to Beowulf: Bēot eal wið þē
 sunu Bēanstānes sōðe gelǣste.
(The son of Beanstan truly performed his boast against thee.) *Beowulf*, ed. C. L. Wrenn (London, 1953), p. 108, ll. 523–4.

PAGE 72

[1] *Plutarch's Lives of Coriolanus, Caesar, Brutus and Antonius in North's Translation*, ed. R. H. Carr (Oxford, 1906), pp. 235–7.

PAGE 76

[1] *Ibid.*, p. 213.

PAGE 79

[1] In this discussion I am particularly indebted to the following authorities: Peter Alexander, 'Troilus and Cressida, 1609' (*Library*, IX, 1929); Philip Williams, 'Shakespeare's Troilus and Cressida: the relationship of Quarto and Folio' (*Studies in Bibliography*, University of Virginia, III, 1950–1), and 'The "Second Issue" of Shakespeare's *Troilus and Cressida*, 1609' (*Studies in Bibliography*, II, 1949–50); E. K. Chambers, *William Shakespeare*, vol. I (Clarendon Press, 1930); W. W. Greg, *The Shakespeare First Folio* (Clarendon Press, 1955); and Miss Alice Walker's several works on the subject: viz. *The 1622 Quarto and the First Folio of Othello* (Shakespeare Survey, no. 5), *Textual Problems of the First Folio* (Cambridge, 1953) and her edition of *Troilus and Cressida* (Cambridge, 1957).
[2] Stationers' Register, ed. Edward Arber, 1876 (privately printed, Bodleian copy), vol. III.

PAGE 81
[1] See W. W. Greg, 'The Printing of Shakespeare's Troilus and Cressida in the First Folio' (*Papers of the Bibliographical Society of America*), XLV (1951).

PAGE 82
[1] W. W. Greg, *The Shakespeare First Folio* (Oxford, 1955), p. 340.
[2] *Gesta Grayorum*, ed. W. W. Greg, Malone Society, 1914.
[3] Cambridge ed., p. xxv.
[4] *Ibid.*, p. xxvi.
[5] E. K. Chambers, *William Shakespeare* (Oxford, 1930), vol. I, p. 442.

PAGE 86
[1] See *The Poems and Fables of Robert Henryson*, ed. H. Harvey Wood (London, 1933), p. xxv.
[2] *Twelfth Night*, III, i, 52.
[3] *The Testament and Complaynt of our Sovereign Lordis Papyngo*, l. 390, first published 1538. See *The Poetical Works of Sir David Lyndsay*, ed. David Laing (Edinburgh, 1879), vol. I.
[4] See Gerard Legh, *Accedence of Armorie* (1562, 1568, 1591, 1597, 1612).

PAGE 87
[1] See Baldwin Maxwell, *Studies in the Shakespeare Apocrypha* (New York, 1956), pp. 27–8.

PAGE 88
[1] See *Henslowe's Diary*, ed. R. A. Foakes and R. T. Rickert (Cambridge, 1961), pp. 47–8 and 320 n.
[2] See W. W. Greg, *Dramatic Documents from the Elizabethan Playhouse* (Clarendon Press, undated).
[3] Thomas Dekker, *Troia Nova Triumphans*, Percy Society, vol. X, Part II (London, 1849). A similar pageant, the reference to which I owe to the kindness of Professor Wickham, called *The Triumphes of Re-United Britania*, by Antony Mundy, was given to celebrate the entrance of Sir Leonard Holliday into the office of Lord Mayor on 29 October 1605. In this work, King Brute tells Brytania of the happiness he has won for her by his victory over the giants of Albion, 'Goemagot and his barbarous brood', and instructs her, 'how to raigne as an Imperial Lady, building his *Troya Nova* by the River Thamesis.' See John Nichols, *The Progresses, Processions and magnificent Festivities of King James the First* (London, 1828), vol. I, p. 564.

PAGE 94
[1] The *Gesta Grayorum* (Malone Society, 1914) gives a full account of these festivities.
[2] The name Purpoole was chosen for topographical reasons. See Stow's *Survey of London*, ed. C. L. Kingsford (Oxford, 1908), vol. II, p. 87: '... beyond the which Barres on the same side is *Porte Poole*, or Grayes Inne lane...'

PAGE 95
[1] In her edition of *Troilus and Cressida* (Cambridge, 1957), p. xxv.

PAGE 96
[1] Though the point has no bearing on our argument, it is tempting to think Shakespeare may have played the Prologue himself, because of the sudden and characteristic touch of modesty in the lines, that seems to strike a note of personal disclaimer.
> ... but not in confidence
> Of Author's pen, or Actors voyce...

PAGE 98
[1] *Chapman's Homer*, ed. Allardyce Nicoll (London, 1957), Bk. II.

213

1 The relationship between Patroclus and Achilles calls for further investigation than I have been able to make. In Homer it appears to be a heroic man-to-man friendship without sexual overtones (see Gilbert Murray, *The Rise of the Greek Epic*, Clarendon Press, 1924, p. 125, and A. J. B. Wace and Frank H. Stubbings, *A Companion to Homer*, London, 1962, p. 68). The following note has been supplied to me by the kindness of Professor A. Raubitchek:

... In later literature Achilles and Patroclus soon came to be regarded as a pair of lovers. This begins as early as the fifth century in Aeschylus' *Myrmidons* (fr. 135) and the historian Hellanicus (fr. 145). The idea is often found later, for instance in Plato, *Symposium*, 179 E, Apollodorus III 176, Lucian *Amores* 54, but most strikingly in one of the speeches of the orator Aeschines. His words are (*Contra Timarchum* 142–3) 'Although Homer often speaks of Patroclus and Achilles he conceals their love and avoids giving a name to their friendship: for he thinks that the very great power of their affection is clear to any educated man who hears his poems recited. In fact Achilles says somewhere in the course of his lament for Patroclus (*Iliad* 18, 324–9) that he has unwillingly broken his promise to Menoetius, Patroclus' father, and he recalls this as one of his most bitter sorrows. For he had promised to bring his son safe back to Opus if Menoetius would entrust him to his care and send him off to Troy in his company. From this it is evident that he undertook to take care of him for love.' Unfortunately it is not clear how this tradition could have been known to the Latin middle ages, since none of the above-mentioned authors who record it seems to have been available in translation...

Dares Phrygius seems not to have heard of it, though he tells us that Patroclus had a beautiful body and bluish grey eyes (*De Excidio Troiae Historia* recensuit Ferdinandus Meister, Lipsiae, 1883, p. 16). Dictys Cretensis (lib. III, cap. 12) reports that Diomedea, daughter of King Phorbas, was beloved by him.

Yet, strangely, in the *Roman de Troie* of Benoit de St Maure, the author knows all about the love of Achilles for Patroclus and makes no bones about its nature. Achilles, for instance, in the course of a long lament for the death of his beloved, that ends with his fainting, grieves thus (see *Le Roman de Troie*, ed. Leopold Constans, Société des Anciens Textes Français, Paris, 1904, vol. II):

> Plus m'amiëz que nule rien,
> Qar jo ere vostre, e vos mien.
> O plors, o lermes vos plaindrai
> Toz les jorʒ mais que jo vivrai. (10355–8)

A glowing portrait is painted of him (5171–8). Hector, who also knows of this love, regards it as shameful and accuses Achilles about him:

> Que *tantes feiz** avez sentu
> Entre voz braz tot nu a nu,
> Et *autres gieux vis e hontos,*
> Dont li plusor sont haïnos...† (13183–6)

*(*so many times*)   †(other vile and shameful games, most of which are hateful)

Lydgate does not seem to know of this; to him Patroclus is 'the manful noble Patroclus' (*Troy Book*, III, 577) and he resumes a fully heroic character, lamented in all manly affection by Achilles:

> As he that was with teris al be-reined
> So inwardly he loved hym in his herte (III, 2190–1)

The Laud *Troy Book* says that Patroclus was 'A riche duk and a glorious' and his relation to Achilles (like that of Palamon to Arcite in *The Knight's Tale*) was one of sworn brotherhood:

> For he was his sworen brother,
> So was that on to that other. (4927–8)

Caxton's *Recuyell of the Historyes of Troye* (ed. H. O. Sommer, London, 1894), vol. II, p. 579, sounds the same pure and heroical note:

... this patroclus was a moche noble duc and ryche and louyd so moche Achylles that they were bothe of one Alyance.

Further than this I have not traced their imaginary loves; how Benoit and Shakespeare can have heard of its supposed sexuality I cannot conjecture; but it seems impossible that they could have independently invented what was already a tradition in Greece. In an article '*Greeks*' *and* '*Merry-Greeks*': *A Background to Timon of Athens and Troilus and Cressida*, published in *Essays on Shakespeare and Elizabethan Drama in honour of Hardin Craig* (University of Missouri Press, 1962) Professor T. J. B. Spencer writes: 'The "Greek vice", too, was of course a by-word, and Shakespeare deliberately introduces this Renaissance notion in relation to Achilles and Patroclus.' But I understand he has not come across any specific coupling of these names in this context before Shakespeare.

² *Yvain*, ed. T. B. W. Reid (Manchester University Press, 1942), ll. 31–2.

PAGE 101

¹ The stratagems of Ulysses, like those of Polonius, fail utterly. Eloquence, not wisdom; disingenuousness, not integrity; coldness, not kindness; mappery, not impulse are his nature; nothing he thinks, says or does is to be trusted. All his rhetoric and scheming come to nothing. The story enacts Shakespeare's judgment *of* him and *on* him.

PAGE 102

¹ All earlier versions of the story end with Lear restored to the throne. In due course Cordelia succeeds him.

PAGE 108

¹ *John the Evangelist* (*Tudor Facsimile Texts*, ed. J. S. Farmer, 1907), Sig. B1 recto. I am indebted to Glynne Wickham for this reference. There is also the famous letter of Erasmus, describing the pleasures of a visit to England, where 'sunt hic nymphae divinis vultibus, blandae, faciles. . .' and how 'Sive quo venias, omnium osculis excipieris: sive discedas aliquo, osculis dimitteris. . .' etc. (*Letters of Erasmus*, ed. P. S. Allen, vol. I, p. 239).

PAGE 109

¹ In this discussion I am much indebted to J. Kleinstück, *Ulysses' Speech on Degree*, *Neo-philologus*, 1958, and to an essay by Mrs Winifred Nowottny, '*Opinion*' *and* '*Value*' *in Troilus and Cressida* (*Essays in Criticism*, IV, 1954) where she says:

The contrasts between Ulysses and Troilus [are] contrasts between Policy and the Poetic Imagination . . . whereas to Ulysses and to Achilles, Honour is that which is conferred (and may be withheld), to Troilus it is that which is a man's own. . .

. . . The Cressida betraying him before his eyes *is* Cressida, but *is not* the Value he had taken her to embody. . . This subtly articulated system of contrasts is one of the main features of the design of the play.

PAGE 117

¹ Chrétien de Troyes, *Arthurian Romances*, translated by W. W. Comfort (Everyman ed., 1955), pp. 344–6. The original reads:

. . . et si li dites a consoil
que 'au noauz' que je li mant. (5644–5)

Les Romans de Chrétien de Troyes, Mario Roques (Paris, 1958), vol. III, 'Le Chevalier de la Charette'.

² *The Works of Sir Thomas Malory*, ed. Eugene Vinaver (Oxford, 1947), vol. III, p. 1184.

PAGE 118

¹ 'Damesell,' seyde Bewmaynes, 'a knyght may lytyll do that may nat suffir a jantyll-woman. . . The mysseyng that ye mysseyde me, in my batayle furthered me much and caused me to thynke to shewe and preve myselffe. . .' (*Ibid.*, vol. I, pp. 312–13).

2

Thise vilayns arn withouten pitee,
Frendshipe, love and all bountee.

Roman de la Rose, 2183–4

PAGE 125

[1] *Op. cit.*, vol. I, pp. 119–20.

[2] See Konrad Z. Lorenz, *King Solomon's Ring, New Light on Animal Ways* (New York, 1952), pp. 185–9.

PAGE 126

[1] See, for instance, his fragment of a play, 'King Edward III' (*The Writings of William Blake*, ed. in three volumes by Geoffrey Keynes, London, 1926), vol. I, p. 42.

PAGE 127

[1] See *The Prose Edda* by Snorri Sturluson, translated by A. G. Brodeur (New York, 1929), pp. 77–80.

Then shall happen what seem great tidings: the wolf shall swallow the sun. . . Then the other wolf shall seize the moon, and he shall also work great ruin: the stars shall vanish from the heavens. . . Then shall Fenris-Wolf get loose. . . Fenris-Wolf shall advance with gaping mouth, and his lower jaw shall be against the earth, but the upper against heaven —he would gape yet more if there were room for it: fires blaze from his eyes and nostrils. . . . Then the Ash of Yggdrasill shall tremble, and nothing shall be without fear in heaven or earth. . . Odin rides first with the golden helmet. . . He shall go forth against Fenris-Wolf. . . The Wolf shall swallow Odin: that shall be his ending.

PAGE 129

[1] W. Creizenach, *The English Drama in the Age of Shakespeare* (London, 1916), p. 273.

[2] William Archer, *Playmaking, a Manual of Craftsmanship* (London, 1912), p. 307.

[3] *New Shelley Letters*, ed. W. S. Scott (London, 1948), p. 151.

[4] Archer, *loc. cit.*

PAGE 130

[1] *Ibid.*, p. 305.

[2] *Ibid.*, p. 309.

PAGE 131

[1] B. L. Joseph, *Elizabethan Acting* (Oxford, 1951), pp. 117–18.

[2] See E. K. Chambers, *The Elizabethan Stage*, vol. IV, p. 256.

PAGE 138

[1] See W. Empson, *The Structure of Complex Words* (London, 1952), p. 134.

PAGE 143

[1] For use of trees on the Elizabethan stage, see also E. K. Chambers, *The Elizabethan Stage*, vol. III, pp. 52, 89, 107. For the dates of performance of *As You Like It* and *Julius Caesar*, see E. K. Chambers, *William Shakespeare*, vol. I, pp. 397 and 402.

PAGE 144

[1] See F. P. Wilson, *Marlowe and the Early Shakespeare* (Cambridge, 1953), p. 58.

PAGE 145

[1] Bernard Spivak, *Shakespeare and the Allegory of Evil* (Columbia, 1958), p. 5.

PAGE 146

[1] For a more penetrating and imaginative analysis of Iago's psyche and its eternal relation to society, see W. H. Auden's admirable essay, *The Joker in the Pack*, which appears in *The Dyer's Hand*, published after I had completed this chapter. I am happy to think

there is some measure of agreement between his views and mine, in that we both see Rodorigo and the early soliloquies as Shakespeare's instruments to elicit aspects of Iago's nature that cannot be shown to anyone except the audience. It may be, as Auden suggests, that we have better reason to recognise Iago in ourselves than the early Jacobeans had: if that is so, it may not be so easy to direct our sympathies against him; he will be harder honestly to hate without hating ourselves. That he was designed to be thought odious I do not think anyone will doubt: my attempt is to show how Shakespeare handled his instruments to achieve this design.

PAGE 150

[1] S. T. Coleridge, *Shakespearean Criticism*, ed. T. M. Raysor (*Everyman*, 1960), vol. II, p. 259.

PAGE 154

[1] S. T. Coleridge, *The Table Talk and Omniana* (Oxford, 1917), p. 65.

PAGE 163

[1] Thomas Nashe, *The Unfortunate Traveller*, ed. H. F. Brett-Smith (Oxford, 1927), pp. 121–2.

PAGE 164

[1] I am told that this famous phrase has never yet been found in the works of William of Occam. The first recorded formulation of the idea I have come upon is among the nine Hypotheses in Newton's *System of the World*, Bk II, quoted in *A Program towards Rediscovering the Rational Mechanics of the Age of Reason* (Archive for History of Exact Sciences, Springer-Verlag, Berlin, vol. I, no. I, p. 13) by Professor Clifford Truesdell:
Hypothesis I. We are to admit no more causes of natural things than such as may be both true and sufficient to explain their appearances. Indeed, Nature is simple and affects not the pomp of superfluous causes.

[2] See his *William Shakespeare*, vol. I, p. 235.

[3] W. W. Greg, *The Shakespeare First Folio* (Clarendon Press, 1955), p. 375.

PAGE 165

[1] Miss Walker counts fifty-two in her edition (Cambridge, 1957), p. 132.

[2] See E. K. Chambers, *William Shakespeare*, vol. I, p. 460; W. W. Greg, *op. cit.*, p. 365; Alice Walker, *op. cit.*, p. 135. M. R. Ridley (Arden edn, 1958), p. xliii, is more guarded, but seems in the end to regard Folio as containing some of Shakespeare's second thoughts.

PAGE 166

[1] Greg, *op. cit.*, p. 369.

[2] Alice Walker, *Textual Problems of the First Folio* (Cambridge, 1953), p. 138.

[3] Alice Walker, *The 1622 Quarto and the First Folio Texts of Othello* (*Shakespeare Survey* no. 5, 1952), p. 24.

[4] Greg, *op. cit.*, p. 371.

[5] *Shakespeare Survey*, no. 5, p. 23.

PAGE 167

[1] I would like here to express my gratitude to Miss Walker for her kind help in the struggle with these problems: if I have come to some conclusions different from hers, I have done so with trepidation, and if they are wrong she is in no way to blame for them. Whoever works on the texts of *Othello* is under great obligation to her, not only for her textual inerrancy but also for the good sense of her return to a proper understanding of the moral values in this play and how they are presented by Shakespeare *through the medium of theatre*, in terms of character in speech and action. See particularly her *Introduction* (in her edition), pp. li–liii. I have added (in the Preface) some stage reasons in support of her argument

against Mr Eliot's interesting but unactable fantasy about Othello's last speech, and I warmly concur with her judgment on A. C. Bradley's view which has a feeling for theatre; he was, at least, a man who understood the medium of theatre, and was himself a great theatre-goer during most of his life, as I am assured by Mrs Sarah Davis, who is engaged on research for a study of his life and work. The views of Dr Leavis, in his essay on *The Diabolic Intellect and the Noble Hero*, recently republished, in *The Common Pursuit* (1952), seem to me to lack this grace: he treats *Othello* as if it were a novel and expressions escape him such as the following, which betray this fact (my italics): 'Any *reader* not protected by a very obstinate pre-conception would take this, not for a new development of feeling, but for the fully explicit expression of something he had already, *pages back*, registered as an essential element in Othello's behaviour. . .' This attitude prevents him from perceiving the difference between what the imagination accepts as probable in one medium (the novel) and in another (the theatre), particularly in respect of the *time* at the disposal of a playwright in which to tell his story (two or three hours): consider, for instance, how long (in a novel) it would take to convince another character of the need to do a murder, and compare (for examples) the fifty-five lines it takes King John to persuade Hubert to murder Arthur (III, iii, 19–66) and the ninety lines in which Antonio persuades Sebastian to murder Alonzo (which I believe is the longest persuasion to murder in Shakespeare) in *The Tempest* (II, i, 195–286). This will help in understanding the 'speed' of Othello's collapse, and other like difficulties raised in this essay. Professor Marvin Rosenberg's *The Masks of Othello* (Cambridge, 1963) cannot be neglected in this connection, for it shows us what actors of genius have contributed to the Othello-image, and discusses the relevance of theatre to all Shakespeare criticism.

[2] See E. K. Chambers, *Elizabethan Stage* (Oxford, 1939), vol. IV, pp. 338–9. I quote:

May 27, 1606. *An Acte to Restraine Abuses of Players:*
. . . For the preventing and avoyding of the great Abuse of the Holy Name of God in Stage plays . . . Be it enacted . . . That if . . . any person or persons doe or shall in any Stage play . . . jestingly or prophanely speake or use the holy name of God or of Christ Jesus, or of the Holy Ghoste or of the Trinitie . . . shall forfeite for everie such Offence by him or them committed Tenne Pounds. . .

The First Quarto version of *Othello* would, on this computation, have cost the Company £520, if it had been performed at the time of this Act.

[3] *Textual Problems of the First Folio*, p. 161.

[4] *Ibid.*, p. 139.

PAGE 168
[1] *Shakespeare Survey*, no. 5, p. 19.

PAGE 169
[1] I believe Dr Leavis, in the article already referred to (see note 1 to p. 167 above), was the first to note this trend in the imagery.

[2] Cambridge ed., footnote, p. 123.

PAGE 171
[1] M. R. Ridley, ed., *Othello* (Arden, 1958), note to V, ii, 71.

[2] See *Complete Works of William Shakespeare*, ed. Peter Alexander (Collins, London and Glasgow, 1951), p. 1150.

PAGE 172
[1] *Shakespeare First Folio*, pp. 134–5.

PAGE 177
[1] Cambridge ed., p. 123.

[2] *Shakespeare First Folio*, p. 358.

PAGE 178
¹ I am indebted to Mr Raymond Raikes of the B.B.C. for information from which I have deduced this average statistic. Of course the pace varies from moment to moment.
² *Shakespeare First Folio*, p. 358.

PAGE 182
¹ See François Rabelais, *Gargantua* (Bk I), ch. 3.

PAGE 187
¹ See ch. I, pp. 25–7.

PAGE 191
¹ *Shakespeare First Folio*, p. 358.

PAGE 196
¹ *Ibid.*, p. 372.

PAGE 198
¹ Harley Granville Barker, *Prefaces to Shakespeare*, Fourth Series, *Othello* (London, 1945), p. 191.

PAGE 203
¹ *Henslowe's Diary*, ed. R. A. Foakes and R. T. Rickert (Cambridge, 1961), pp. 54–60.

PAGE 204
¹ E. K. Chambers, *William Shakespeare* (Oxford, 1930), vol. II, p. 343.

PAGE 205
¹ *Ibid.*, pp. 327–8.

PAGE 206
¹ *Ibid.*, pp. 337–41.

PAGE 208
¹ In a production by Mr George Rylands for the Marlowe Society at Cambridge, in March 1946.

INDEX OF NAMES